ENCOUNTER
IN THE DESERT

ENCOUNTER
IN THE DESERT

THE CASE FOR *ALIEN* CONTACT AT *SOCORRO*

KEVIN D. RANDLE

New Page Books
A division of The Career Press, Inc.
Wayne, N.J.

ENCOUNTER IN THE DESERT
EDITED BY JODI BRANDON
TYPESET BY KARA KUMPEL
Cover design by Wes Youssi/M80 Branding
Cars photo by Amy Johansson/shutterstock
Sky photo by MarcelClemens/shutterstock
UFO photo by Alin Popescu/shutterstock
Printed in the U.S.A.

To order this title, please call toll-free 1-800-CAREER-1 (NJ and Canada: 201-848-0310) to order using VISA or MasterCard, or for further information on books from Career Press.

The Career Press, Inc.
12 Parish Drive
Wayne, NJ 07470
www.careerpress.com
www.newpagebooks.com

Library of Congress Cataloging-in-Publication Data

CIP Data Available Upon Request.

Acknowledgments

As I have said before, the problem with acknowledgments is that someone is always left out, but not on purpose. Without Rob McConnell offering me an opportunity to host a radio show, I would have never started my research into the Socorro UFO landing. Ben Moss and Tony Angiola told me things that I hadn't heard and wanted to learn more about. This led to Ray Stanford, who had investigated the case in 1964 and is the only living person who had been on that site within days of the landing, collecting samples and taking pictures. Rob Mercer sparked some of this because he searched Craigslist for UFO-related material and bought a box of documents that came from Project Blue Book. Carmon Marano, whom I had mentioned in another book but who had been one of those anonymous officers who worked on

Project Blue Book, provided insight into that investigation as it wound down. Paul Harden and Rick Baca, of Socorro, provided guidance in my search, and Rick had been the man (kid, then) who drew the craft as described by Lonnie Zamora, which showed us what it looked like. Jerry Clark, as always, provided information and guidance in this search.

There are many others whose names appear in the book who witnessed UFO landings and found burned areas caused, in most cases, by UFOs, including Robert Shaw, who had been an Iowa sheriff, and Howard Grove, who was an Iowa farmer. Pat Barr and her father provided information about her 1969 UFO sighting. Brad Steiger's work is always valuable, and Ralph DeGraw interviewed two men who claimed to have seen the same craft as Lonnie Zamora. I'm not sure that it does any good at this late date, but Coral and Jim Lorenzen of APRO helped, as did several members of the Fund for UFO Research.

There are many more who contributed in some fashion and whose names escape me at the moment. I don't mean to overlook your contribution; it's just that there was so many others who helped in so many ways that it is impossible to produce a proper list. For your help, I thank you, too.

Contents

Introduction

Anyone who has been interested in UFOs for very long is aware of the landing that took place in Socorro, New Mexico, in April 1964. It was national news the day after police officer Lonnie Zamora reported the sighting. He saw the craft on the ground and there were reports that he had witnessed two people, two beings, or small adults standing near the object before it took off moments after he arrived on the scene. Zamora's sighting was one of the best of 1964 and might be considered one of the best ever reported to Project Blue Book. It is one of the few in which the witness claimed to have seen alien creatures that was not immediately written off as a psychological problem, an illusion, or some sort of a hoax.

Those who write UFO books often mention the sighting, providing little in the way of new and additional information or personal analysis of the data. Their research into the case is usually superficial, based almost solely on what other UFO researchers had written before them, and often the Socorro landing is only mentioned in passing rather than described in depth. It is a well-known sighting that suffers from too much rumor and too little fact, but it is one that helps make the case for alien visitation that much more plausible.

I knew of the sighting, and I have been in Socorro a number of times, mostly in my research into the Roswell UFO crash, and I did have occasion to speak to some of the locals about the sighting. Because this was always of secondary importance to me, the conversations were just that: conversations rather than serious research. I never took it much further and made few notes. I was interested in a distracted sort of way.

That changed when Ben Moss and Tony Angiola were guests on my radio show, *A Different Perspective*,[1] which airs on the X-Zone Broadcast Network. They have spent the last couple of years investigating the case, had access to some little-known or unknown documents, and had talked with the only living person who had investigated the case in 1964: Ray Stanford.[2] They mentioned some things that I hadn't heard or read elsewhere, and that was quite intriguing to me. They talked about the symbol that Zamora had seen on the side of the craft, they talked about a picture taken in the months after the landing that might show craft similar to that seen by Zamora in the New Mexico sky, and they said that they had seen the "real" Project Blue Book file on the case—which didn't exactly match what was eventually released to the public after Blue Book operations were suspended in late 1969. All of this was news to me, and I wanted more information about it.

After the show, I emailed Ben to ask for that additional information. He responded with a DVD of the presentation that he and Tony had made to the MUFON Symposium in Orlando during summer 2016. It was an abbreviated version of their longer lecture given at other venues. Though it seemed to answer some of my questions, it opened up others. I asked about that Blue Book file and was told that Rob Mercer of the Miami Valley UFO Society was the one who had found it. They said that he pulled the file from a box that he had bought at a garage sale and those documents were definitely from Blue Book.

I found it difficult to believe that a box of files from Project Blue Book would be sold at a garage sale, but I have learned that you just don't reject data because it seems a little strange or nearly unbelievable. Besides, Ben had given me the contact information for Rob and he responded quickly. Email and the Internet are wonderful ways of investigating a case in the 21st century. Responses come in a matter of hours instead of days or weeks, or at the cost of huge telephone bills.

Rob's tale of how he had found the Blue Book files was even stranger than I had thought. He hadn't found them at a garage sale; he found them for sale on Craigslist because he had been told that UFO-related materials sometimes were put up for sale there.[3] The man who was selling the files hadn't bought them at a garage sale, specifically; he had bought a load of lumber at the garage sale and had found the box hidden, or forgotten, behind the lumber as he cleaned out that part of the garage. After listening to the man's description of what he had found, Rob bought the box and, to his delight, it contained precisely what had been claimed. It held files and other documents that related to UFOs and Project Blue Book. He looked through it to make sure that none of it was classified and none of it was.

In a nice piece of detective work, Rob found the man who had collected the files. He had been a member of the Project Blue Book staff in the late 1960s as Blue Book came to an end. He was First Lieutenant Carmon Marano, and as they were closing the Blue Book offices, he was cleaning out desks and thought that the documents shouldn't be just thrown out. Instead, because they weren't classified, and because they were destined for the garbage heap, he took them home. But that wasn't all. He told Rob he had other boxes of similar material and if Rob wanted them, he could have them as well. Marano said that he hadn't looked at them since he saved them back in 1969 and that he had no real interest in UFOs. He hadn't volunteered for Blue Book, it had just been an Air Force assignment, given to him, I suspect, because of his physics background. In fact, his ignorance about UFOs was so complete, he hadn't actually heard about the Roswell case even at this late date.[4]

Much of that material sent to Mercer, which included movie footage, color slides and photographs, audio tapes of interviews, and many case files from the Blue Book investigations that extended back to its original conception as Project Sign, was in those boxes. Rob could compare much of it to actual Blue Book files and saw that there were some, but mostly minor, differences. There were handwritten notes that didn't seem to have been included in the official files, for example.

Marano said that he had originally collected the material, while assigned to Blue Book, so that he would be able to brief the press or have something to show reporters when they visited the Blue Book office. Other files seemed to be the "working papers" of other officers who had held positions at Blue Book in the past and who might have been thinking along the same lines as Marano. These, then, weren't the official files, but had been created from those official files and had been preserved not in the official file cabinets, but in the desk drawers of the officers who had used them.

The other point about these files is that they hadn't been redacted. When the Project Blue Book files were sent from Maxwell Air Force Base, where they had first been housed after the closure of Blue Book to the National Archives, Air Force officers went through every case file and removed the names of the witnesses. Even the master index, which had contained the names of the witnesses, had been redacted, but the names were intact in the copy of the index Rob had found. The Air Force had removed the names of the witnesses, suggesting that the witnesses had been told their names wouldn't be released publicly so they could speak freely about their sightings without fear of being bombarded by UFO researchers attempting to find out more or ridiculed by their neighbors who thought they were crazy. That seems reasonable to me, though I suspect some will claim cover-up. The mere fact that Rob had a master index of all the files that held the names of all the witnesses was, in and of itself, an important find.

When I talked with Marano, he told me that there had been nothing classified about the Blue Book files he had saved and that almost all of the Blue Book files were unclassified.[5] When I went back and looked at the Socorro case, there was nothing to indicate that any of the statements or other documentation collected by a variety of military investigators and by their chief scientific consultant, Dr. J. Allen Hynek, had ever been classified. The documentation was available for review by reporters; I wondered if someone had shown up at the Project Blue Book office in the late 1960s and asked to see the files if they would have been let in. You couldn't just walk in off the street, but it seemed that if you had attempted to make an appointment, it might just have been granted especially if you could provide some legitimate reason, such as writing a magazine or newspaper article. A few old-time UFO investigators seemed to have been able to get an appointment and had the chance to look at the files before Blue Book closed.

My interest, however, was what was in those files about the Socorro landing. Rob had scanned that entire file and sent me copies of it. When I compared the two, there were some variations between the official files and what Rob had found. They weren't big variations and may not be overly important ones, but there are these discrepancies.

My sources for this book include Ben Moss, Tony Angiola, Rob Mercer, and Carmon Marano. I interviewed them all at the end of 2016, and I exchanged emails and other information with them. I even loaned Ben Moss my copy of the Blue Book microfilm that contained the Socorro case so that he could make his own analysis. I had questions, and they all had some of the answers. But they weren't my only sources. As I had in the past, as I worked on other books and as I wrote my blog postings, I gathered additional information from sources in Socorro and throughout the world. The Internet is a wonderful thing when you are trying to reconstruct an event that is now half a century old.

I have said many times that over the years, I had accumulated a complete set of Project Blue Book files. Once the information left Maxwell AFB, and once the names had been redacted, it was all microfilmed. As I understand this, back in the early 1970s, Jack Webb of *Dragnet* fame was developing a television program he called *Project UFO*. He wanted the Blue Book files to use as the basis of his fictionalized account of the UFO investigation and paid for the microfilming process. Once that was completed, the National Archives sold rolls of the Blue Book microfilms to anyone who wanted them. There were 94 rolls, originally sold for 10 bucks a roll. I didn't buy them all at once—just what I needed for research—until I realized I had most of them. At that point I made arrangements to gather the rest of them. Thus I have a complete set of the Blue Book files and even have a microfilm reader (though it has no capability to make a hard copy).

But even without that, in the world of the 21st century, you can find nearly everything online. Some of it costs money and some of it requires that you sign up, but much of it is free, and the Blue Book files fall into that latter category. Many of the files can be found on the NICAP Website and nearly everything else at Fold3. From my research, it seems that not everything is available at Fold3, but what is left out seems to be rather trivial. I'm not sure why some of it was skipped, but there are a few holes in that information.

I have been able to gather additional information about the Socorro landing through email with some of those who live in Socorro. All of it is relevant to the discussion of the case, but what is truly amazing is that I was able to accomplish this while sitting at home. Sure, you can start to yell about "armchair researchers," but I have no need to visit the archives of newspapers because they are online, I have no need to travel to the National Archives to see the Blue Book files because they are online (and I already have a copy), and I have been able to locate other information about the men involved by searching their names online. I have, on my blog and on my radio program, *A Different Perspective*, discussed some of this, and there are those who have contacted me because they knew of my interest. They have emailed me documents, photographs, and other information about the Socorro landing that in another time would have taken weeks to arrange through telephone calls and snail mail—or that might have just never been found. I have been able to accomplish this because of the Internet, modern communications, and email.

I suppose that I should point out that I have access, in my armchair, to dozens of other relevant sources. Over the years, I have collected a complete set (or nearly so) of *The A.P.R.O. Bulletin*, the NICAP *U.F.O. Investigator*, all of MUFON's *Skylook* (their original publication) and the later *MUFON UFO Journal* through 2009, the *International UFO Reporter*, copies of the magazines that were devoted to UFOs, and, of course, dozens of UFO books (some in foreign languages). I should also mention here that Isaac Koi and others have been putting a great deal of information online as well. There are literally dozens of old UFO periodicals, newsletters, and other materials available through those efforts as well, much of it uploaded with a search engine to help in research. This is not to mention I have met many of the people in the UFO field so that when I have specific questions, I can ask them through email and usually have a response in a matter of hours (and sometimes minutes). In other words, having done the original legwork on the scene, I now can relax at home and pull up the information on my laptop, search through the other material, or call or write a friend.

And, yes, in case you are wondering, I have been able to interview some of these people face-to-face via Skype. But there is one difference, which I mentioned earlier: I have been to Socorro; I have talked to people in Socorro and have been to the scene of the landing. It is just that in the 21st century, the investigation is easier because of the access to so much data on the Internet.

I add one other comment here: As you read the book, you will find some duplication of material. I have done this because I wanted to show that I was aware of what some others have written about the case, and to put the record straight it was necessary to revisit some of that material. There isn't all that much duplication, but there is some. Be aware of it and be aware of the reason for it.

This, then, is a work that was literally years in the making. Some of it was gathered specifically because it related to the Socorro landing, but much of it was collected because of the value it held to UFO research in general. That it also helped in the research into the Socorro case is serendipity. This book exists simply because of all that research that began during my teenage years. The experience I gained has enabled me to put it all into perspective. This is the result of all that and is the best information available at this particular point in time.

Chapter 1:

The Beginning

In April 1964, the U.S. Air Force still investigated UFO sightings as required by regulation and military mission.[1] The command structure—those who worried about such things—weren't happy about the UFO situation, wished that it would just go away, and hoped that civilians would forget about flying saucers as they became bored with the topic.[2] Unfortunately, as had happened several times since 1947, a UFO report would gain national attention, renew interest in flying saucers, and in this case result in a large-scale investigation that would eventually involve an Army captain and others from the U.S. Army, an FBI agent, the Air Force scientific consultant to Project Blue Book and one of the sergeants assigned there, members of the Socorro, New Mexico, police department, and the New Mexico State Police. There would be physical evidence that included landing gear traces and damage done as the craft lifted off, and the description of an insignia on the craft that would become a hot point of debate in the years that followed.

The main player was Socorro police officer Lonnie Zamora, a veteran of the Korean War who would serve for 23 years in the New Mexico National Guard and who remained a police officer for 10 years after the sighting. He would eventually be chased from his job on the police force by the ridicule directed at him after his "flying saucer" sighting became public. He remained in Socorro and took another job with the city as a landfill supervisor until he retired.[3] He was reluctant to speak with anyone about the sighting because of the pressures he felt but seemed to have been a kindly, friendly man with a good reputation in town and who hosted barbeques at his home—with the only requirement that they not talk about UFOs.[4] It could be that he still thought he might have observed a black project from either Holloman Air Force Base or the White Sands Missile Range, but the more likely reason was that he resented the way he had been treated by those who did not know him, by the news media that was too sophisticated to believe in alien visitation in any form, and by many of those who came to investigate the sighting in the weeks, months, and years that followed.[5]

The event began innocently enough late in the day of April 24, while Zamora was on routine patrol.[6] He spotted a new, black Chevrolet driven by a teenager he thought he recognized and who he thought was speeding. He followed that car, keeping his distance and trying to determine the exact speed without being seen by the driver. Before he could close the distance between his patrol car and the speeder, about a minute into the chase, he heard a roar that sounded like an explosion to the southwest. Thinking that noise came from the location of a dynamite shack, Zamora turned away from the chase and drove toward the shack that he knew was on the southside of the town. He thought that it might have blown up.

Zamora then saw what he would later describe as a brilliant blue cone of flame above the horizon to the south-southwest, more or less in a line with the dynamite shack. He couldn't tell how large the flame was and he didn't see any sort of a craft or object above it, but he did note that the top of the flame was flat. He couldn't see the bottom of the flame because it was behind a hill. The sun was in the west and that was obscuring his vision as well. He turned onto a gravel road and could still hear the roar overhead. He had his windows open, and he said that there was a car in front of him but he didn't see any reaction from that driver to the noise. Zamora didn't know if that driver heard the roar or not.

Zamora turned off the road and attempted to drive up one of the hills but the tires dug in and spun, and the car stopped. He backed down, tried again, failed, and then, on his third try, he made it. He turned onto a gravel road heading to the west. From the top of the hill he could no longer see the flame and he could no longer hear the roar.

Zamora stopped and, below him, in an arroyo about 150 to 200 yards away, saw a shiny, metallic object that he thought might be a white car lying upside-down. From his vantage point he saw two figures, two people, dressed in white coveralls—or, as he described them, kids who might have flipped their car. He thought they might be inspecting it as if there had been some kind of trouble. He said, "The only time I saw these two persons was when I had stopped, for possibly two seconds.... I don't recall noting any particular shape or possibly hats, or headgear. These persons appeared normal in shape—but possibly they were small adults or large kids."[7] One of them, the one closest to him and standing near a large creosote bush, turned toward Zamora and seemed surprised to see him. Zamora would say that the figures were about the size of boys and that they looked to be normal.

The object itself, according to what Zamora would later say in his interviews with various authorities, was white "against the mesa background, but not chrome."[8] To him it looked as if it had been made of aluminum. It "seemed like an 'O'" in shape and at first glance took it to be overturned white car. "Car appeared turned up like standing on radiator or trunk."[9]

Zamora now believed that he was seeing people who were in trouble and began to drive toward them with the "idea to help" them.[10] He drove down into a dip and lost sight of the object momentarily. He radioed the dispatcher that he was at the scene of a traffic accident. He stopped his car again and got out, dropping the microphone, which momentarily distracted him. He picked it up, put it back in the slot, and got out of the car so that he could walk down to the object.

Zamora would write in his police report of the incident that he had hardly turned around when he heard a roar. It wasn't a blast but a loud roar. He dove to the ground, his head away from the object in case it blew up. He wrote, "Started low frequency quickly and then rose in frequency and in loudness.... At the same time of the roar [I] saw flame. Flame was under the object. Object was starting to go straight up.... Flame was light blue and at the bottom was sort of orange color.... [I] thought from the roar, it might blow up...."[11]

As soon as he saw the flame and heard the roar, Zamora jumped to his feet and ran from the object. He bumped his leg on the patrol car's rear bumper and lost his glasses. He left them there and ran to the north to put the car between him and the object. As the craft climbed, he got a look at it from another angle. He said, "[The] object was oval in shape. It was smooth—no windows or doors.... Noted red lettering of some type. Insignia was about 2½' high and about 2' wide I guess. [It] was in middle of object."[12]

The Socorro landing site within days of Lonnie Zamora's observation. Photo courtesy of the U.S. Air Force.

Zamora climbed to his feet, and dodged around the car for the protection it would offer. In one of the official reports, he said:

After [I] fell by [the] car and glasses fell off [I] kept running to north, with car between me and object. Glanced back a couple of times. Noted object to rise about level of car, about 20 to 25 feet [I] guess—took, I guess about six seconds when object started to rise and I glanced back. I guess I ran about halfway to where I ducked down, just over the edge of the hill. I guess I had run about 25 feet when I glanced back and saw the object about level with the car and it appeared directly over the place it rose from.

I was still running and I jumped just over the hill—I stopped because I did not hear the roar. I was scared of the roar, and I had planned to continue running down the hill. I turned around toward the object and at the same time put my head toward the ground, covering my face and arms. Being that there was no roar, I looked up, and I saw the object going away from me, in a southwest direction. When the roar stopped, heard a sharp tone whine from high tone to low tone. At the end of roar was this whine and the whine lasted maybe a second. Then there was complete silence about the object. That's when I lifted up my head and saw object going away from me. It did not come any closer to me. It appeared to go straight line and at same height—possibly 10 to 15 feet from the ground, and it cleared the dynamite shack by about 3 feet. Shack about 8 feet high. Object was travelling very fast. It seemed to rise up, and take off immediately cross country. I ran back to my car and as I ran back I kept an eye on the object. I picked up my glasses...and [got] into the car and radioed Nep Lopez, radio operator, to "look out of the window, to see if you can see an object." He asked, "What is it?" I answered, "It looks like a balloon." I don't know if he saw it. If Nep looked out his window, which faces north, he couldn't have seen it. I did not tell him at the moment which window to look out of.

As I was calling Nep, I could still see the object. The object seemed to lift up slowly, and to "get small" in the distance very fast. It seemed to just clear Box Canyon or Six Mile Canyon mountain. It disappeared as it went over the mountains. It had no flame whatsoever as it was traveling over the ground and made no smoke or noise....

Noted no odors. Noted no sound other than the described. Gave directions to Nep Lopez at radio and to Sgt. M.S. Chavez to get there. Went down to where the object was (had been), and I noted the bush was burning in several places. At that time, I heard Sgt. Chavez calling me on radio for my location, and I returned to my car, told him he was looking at me. Then Sgt. Chavez came up and asked me what the trouble was, because I was sweating and he told me I was white, very pale. I asked the Sergeant to see what I saw, and that was the burning bush. Then Sgt.

Chavez and I went to the spot, and Sgt. Chavez pointed out the tracks.[13]

Sergeant Sam Chavez Arrives

Chavez, according to Coral Lorenzen, was at the police station fingerprinting a prisoner, a point that would later become important. After Zamora called, by radio, Chavez turned the prisoner over to another officer and walked out to his car. He drove out South Park Street but at one point made a wrong turn and had to backtrack slightly. When he came to the hills, he had no trouble getting to the top. Once there, he parked near Zamora's patrol car and then looked into Zamora's car to see if there were any "implements of any kind with which the indentations and the fire could have been affected."[14]

Coral Lorenzen also reported that Zamora requested that Chavez come alone. According to her, "Chavez said Zamora felt that he was seeing something unusual and wanted a sympathetic and objective person to verify the object.... He [Chavez] was personally convinced that Zamora experienced what he claimed he did.... Chief Polo Pineda had said, simply, 'He's a good man.'"[15]

At that point that evening, it wasn't clear if there had been any other witnesses, if what Zamora had seen might not have been some sort of classified or black project being tested at the White Sands Missile Range or Holloman Air Force Base, or if it was something completely unknown, meaning something extraterrestrial. The sighting had lasted for only minutes, maybe less than two, and the creatures had been in sight for mere seconds according to Zamora's own statement, but there was hard physical evidence left behind. The bush that was nearly under the center of the craft was still smoldering, and there were imprints in the ground that suggested something heavy had set down there.

Chavez and Zamora began to search the ground at the landing site. Besides the smoking bush, there were several areas where they saw burned clumps of range grass. They found four impressions that had been pressed into the ground. These were wedge shaped, about 4 inches by 8 inches, and 3 to 4 inches deep. The local newspaper, the *El Defensor-Chieftain*, reported: "They did not appear to be made by an object striking the earth with great force, but be an object of considerable weight settling to earth at slow speed and not moving after touching the ground."[16] This also suggested that the impressions had not been excavated by Zamora in an attempt to fake the landing traces.

The landing pad imprints protected by rocks. The photo was taken within hours of the landing. Photo courtesy of the U.S. Air Force.

Chavez examined the bush that was near the center of the four landing pad impressions. While it was still smoking, Chavez said that it was cool to the touch. Rocks and grass had been seared, but there was no evidence of a flame; yet others would say that the flame from the craft had sliced the bush in half and Zamora was quite clear about seeing a flame.

There was one other point that would become important later: As the object lifted off, Zamora had seen some sort of symbol or insignia on the side of the craft. Using a scrap of paper, he sketched it before Chavez arrived and showed it to him while they were still standing on the landing site. Neither Zamora nor Chavez had ever seen anything like it. That scrap would turn up in the Blue Book files and become a point of contention among UFO researchers decades later.[17]

Additional Officials Arrive

Minutes after Chavez arrived, State Police senior patrolman Ted V. Jordan arrived. He was joined by undersheriff James Luckie and cattle inspector Robert White. All had apparently heard about the landing over the police radio and had driven out to see for themselves. Jordan had his camera and took pictures of the site while it was still light enough to see. At about 7:00 p.m., as the sunlight faded, everyone left. Chavez and Zamora returned to the police station.[18]

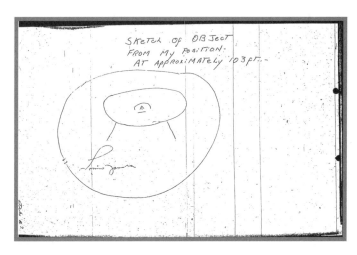

Drawing made by Lonnie Zamora within hours of the sighting, giving the relative shape of the object he saw on the side. Photo courtesy of the U.S. Air Force.

Here the sequence of events becomes a little muddy. Only later, with access to the Project Blue Book files and other information that recently became available, is it possible to straighten all this out. For now, to provide a proper look at the situation, it is necessary to examine the variations that have been published over the years. Accordingly, we see that some suggest that Chavez called Captain Richard T. Holder, who was the commander of the Stallion Site at the White Sands Missile Range and was the senior military officer in the immediate area. Though the main base was south of Alamogordo and more than 50 miles from Socorro, Holder lived in Socorro. His daily duty station was at the northern edge of the range, making Socorro closer than had he lived in Alamogordo.[19] There is something else implied by this call: Chavez obviously knew who Holder was and his connection to White Sands, where testing was accomplished on a variety of aviation-related projects, some of which were classified. Obviously, Chavez was thinking that Holder might be able to identify the craft Zamora had seen and let the authorities know that the project had been compromised to some extent.

Of course, as happens in many UFO cases, there is another explanation for Holder getting involved. Arthur Byrnes, Jr., an FBI agent in the area who had heard of the sighting, supposedly alerted White Sands, a call taken by First Lieutenant Hicks, who in turn tried to get in touch with Holder. Byrnes was quickly put in touch with Holder.[20]

According to Coral Lorenzen, it was Chavez who called Byrnes.[21] Jerry Clark, however, suggested that Byrnes had heard of the sighting over the police radio and apparently drove to the Socorro Police Station.[22] However it happened, Holder and Byrnes were the first two government officials to arrive on the scene, with the exception of other members of the local Socorro law enforcement agencies.

Ray Stanford, who wrote, *Socorro "Saucer" in a Pentagon Pantry*, suggested that after Zamora and Chavez had stayed on the landing site for more than an hour, they drove back to the police

station. Chavez, still convinced that Zamora had seen some sort
of experimental craft from White Sands, decided they needed to
contact the authorities there. Chavez called Byrnes, who in turn
called Hicks, who then called Holder. All of this took place just
after 7:00 p.m. By 7:10 the various notifications had been made,
however it might have happened. The exact sequence is of little
overall importance today. The names of all the players are documented in the Project Blue Book file on the case.[23] What is important is that all the players to this point had been assembled in the
Socorro Police Department.

Byrnes arrived before Holder, who got there at about 7:20.
Both men wanted to see the other's credentials. Satisfied that
each was who he said he was, Byrnes then introduced Holder to
Zamora. Both questioned him about what he had seen, searching
for the smallest detail during what was apparently a fairly extensive interrogation.

At some point during the questioning, Zamora, of course,
mentioned the beings that he had seen and the red insignia on
the side of the vehicle. Byrnes suggested that it might be wise
not to mention the creatures. The newspapers and some of the
people who heard about it might make fun of him for that, and it
was just something that might be best avoided. Holder said that
they should withhold the description of the symbol as well but for
other reasons. He thought that if others came forward to describe
the scene, they would be able to tell if the story was legitimate if
that new witness could describe the symbol correctly. It seems that
many who would be in and out of the investigation over the next
couple of days thought it was a good idea as well.[24] There didn't
seem to be any suggestion of an official cover-up at this point,
just two officials attempting to withhold certain facts with an eye
of determining who might have also witnessed the UFO and who
might be trying to climb on the bandwagon for his or her 15 minutes in the spotlight.

Holder later would tell the local newspaper, the *El Defensor-
Chieftain*: "After being appraised of the situation, I attempted to

determine whether White Sands Missile Range or Holloman Air Force Base had anything that might produce the conditions described. Neither...had an object that would compare to the object described. There was no known firing mission in progress...that would produce the conditions reported."[25]

It was sometime after this that Holder called for military police from White Sands to cordon the area. Using their flashlights, they made measurements and collected some samples. Holder, according to Clark, said, "I saw rocks that were normal on one side and charred on the other. There were bushes alive on one side, but when you'd touch them, the other side would flake to ash. When an object blasts off by rocket or jet propulsion, there's usually damage or debris in the area. But there was no indication of that type of disturbance."[26]

That wasn't all that happened that night. Once Holder and Byrnes finished interviewing Zamora and Chavez, they all returned to the landing site. According to Stanford, Byrnes and Holder rode in the same vehicle, and they picked up Sergeant Castle, the NCOIC [non-commissioned officer in charge] with the military police. They were the ones who made the measurements that night. Byrnes suggested they protect the landing gear imprints by surrounding them with rocks.[27]

While they were working to preserve the evidence, they found additional imprints. These were not as large or as deep as those made by the landing gear. One set was inside the perimeter set by the landing gear and roughly circular in shape. Speculation, given the location, size, and depth of these indentations, was that they were made by some sort of ladder. Zamora didn't report a ladder; given his location and the orientation of the craft it would have been hidden behind the object.[28]

The other set of impressions was 5 feet south of one of the landing gear indentations and outside the perimeter established by the gear. They were not well defined and, according to Ted Jordan, seemed to have been made by a person or persons with relatively small feet. He said that one of them looked "like a heel print with the instep over a small clump of grass."[29]

Stanford wrote, "All of those to whom I talked regarding them [the 'footprints'], who would venture an interpretation, felt that the group of soil indentations were shoeprints of two small humanoids Zamora had seen during his view from around 450 feet to the northwest."[30]

The problem, however, was that several people had already been walking all over the landing site. First, of course, were Zamora and Chavez, and then there had been other members of the local law enforcement community, and one of them had been taking pictures. Finally came the military, to cordon the area, and attempt to preserve it, but that might have already been too late. Human footprints were already obscuring some of the physical evidence.

If anyone had a thought about keeping the story under wraps, that idea quickly faded. There is a suggestion that someone had called one of the television stations in Albuquerque, but that didn't matter. On Saturday, April 25, the press had been alerted, and the nature of the investigation would subtly change.

Chapter 2:

The World of UFOs

The Lonnie Zamora sighting did not happen in a vacuum. For nearly 17 years, people had been sighting, reporting, and discussing flying saucers and then UFOs. There had been magazine articles, books, documentaries, and movies. Some of those movies, such as *Earth vs. the Flying Saucers*, were said to have been based on books, but only the words *flying saucers* had any relevance to the book on which it was based. The point is, by 1964 nearly everyone had heard of flying saucers or UFOs, but, of those, few thought it related to alien visitation and even fewer cared.

It is said that the modern era of UFO sightings began with Kenneth Arnold, a Boise, Idaho, businessman. Though I could argue it began years earlier with the Foo Fighters of World War II, for most Americans it started on June 24, 1947. Arnold, a private pilot, was on a business trip when he diverted, according to him, to a search mission that involved a lost military aircraft. As he flew over the area in Washington state, in the distance, in the direction of Mount Rainier, he spotted nine objects in a loose trail formation flying at high speed with an undulating motion. When he landed in Yakima, Washington, he told the reporters who had somehow heard about the sighting of the strange craft and were interested in what he had seen. He described the objects as moving with a motion like that of saucers skipping across the water. The shape, however, according to drawings that Arnold completed for the Army within days of the sighting, showed objects that were more heel shaped than saucer shaped. In later drawings, Arnold elaborated, showing objects that were more crescent shaped with a scalloped trailing edge than those heel-shaped things he had sketched earlier.[1]

Arnold's sighting didn't gain front-page status immediately, but stories about it appeared in newspapers a day or two later. It was, at that time, the story of an oddity without any real speculation about what he had seen. Arnold claimed later that he thought he had seen some sort of the new jet aircraft rather than something from outer space. This was the same sort of thing that Zamora had thought after the landing in Socorro. It was a black project and not an alien spacecraft.

According to the Project Blue Book files, Arnold wasn't the only person to see strange objects in the sky that day in that area. Fred Johnson, who claimed to be a prospector, reported watching five or six disc-shaped craft as they flew over the Cascade Mountains somewhat north of Arnold's location. He said the objects were round with a slight tail and about 30 feet in diameter. They were not flying in any sort of formation that he could see and, as they banked in a turn, the sunlight flashed off them suggesting a metallic surface. As they approached, Johnson noticed that his compass began to spin wildly. When the objects finally vanished in the distance, the compass returned to normal.

After learning of the Arnold sighting, Johnson wrote to the Air Force on August 20, 1947, saying:

Saw in the portland [sic] paper a short time ago in regards to an article in regards to the so called flying disc having any basis in fact. I can say am a prospector and was in the Mt. Adams district on June 24th the day Kenneth Arnold of Boise Idaho claims he saw a formation of flying disc [sic]. And i [sic] saw the same flying objects at about the same time. Having a telescope with me at the time i [sic] can asure [sic] you there are real and noting [sic] like them I ever saw before they did not pass verry [sic] high over where I was standing at the time. plolby [sic] 1000 ft. they were Round about 30 foot in diameter tapering sharply to a point in the head and in an oval shape. with [sic] a bright top surface. I did not hear any noise as you would from a plane. But there was an object in the tail end looked like a big hand of a clock shifting from side to side like a big magnet. There [sic] speed was far as I know seemed to be greater than anything I ever saw. Last view I got of the objects they were standing on edge Banking in a cloud.

It is signed, Yours Respectfully, Fred Johnson.[2]

Johnson was eventually interviewed by the FBI, whose report contained, essentially, the same information as the letter that Johnson had sent to the Army. The FBI report, found in the Blue Book files, ended by saying, "Informant appeared to be a very reliable individual...."

Johnson's sighting becomes important because it corroborates what Arnold reported and comes from an independent source. Of course, the problem here is that Johnson did not contact anyone about his sighting until after information about Arnold and what he had seen had been published in the various local and national newspapers. You can say that he was a contaminated source and the first line in his statement confirms that.

Even with the possible corroboration for Arnold and with Arnold's aviation experience, the Air Force eventually decided that Arnold had been fooled by a mirage, and, in the end, that was how they labeled the case.[3] Later others would suggest a formation of pelicans and some of the pictures of pelicans in flight resemble, to a great degree, the motion that Arnold described and the illustration that he had drawn.[4]

After the Arnold sighting, others began to report what they had seen to the various news agencies. In the days after Arnold, hundreds of people in the United States and thousands around the world mentioned similar sightings, with newspapers keeping a count of which states and which countries were involved. The importance here is that Arnold's sighting was the springboard for the news coverage that would follow.

Typical of those sightings was one made by the crew of a commercial airliner on the July 4th weekend. Captain Edward J. Smith was flying a United Airlines DC-4 near Emmett, Idaho, when his first officer, Ralph Stevens, reached down to flash the landing lights, thinking he saw another plane coming at them. Smith wrote:

> My copilot…was in control shortly after we got into the air. Suddenly he switched on the landing lights. He said he thought he saw an aircraft approaching head-on.
>
> I noticed the objects then for the first time.
>
> We saw four or five "somethings." One was larger than the rest and for the most part…right of the other three or four similar but smaller objects.
>
> Since we were flying northwest—roughly into the sunset we saw whatever they were in at least partial light. We saw them clearly. We followed them in a northwesterly direction for about 45 minutes.
>
> Finally, the objects disappeared in a burst of speed.[5]

According to the Project Blue Book file, Smith said that they never were able to discern a real shape. He said that he thought the craft were flat on the bottom and seemed to be irregular on the top. The objects seemed to be flying at their altitude and followed them for 10 to 15 minutes, but remained in sight longer than that.

The Air Materiel Command (which later had responsibility for investigating UFO sightings) opinion was that the event had occurred at sunset, which meant changing lighting conditions that were ideal for "illusionary" effects. The objects could have been birds, balloons, other aircraft, or pure illusion, though every member of the crew saw the same thing. The source of the objects was never identified.

The number and type of sightings continued to grow throughout the next couple days, with opinions about the source of the objects also growing. No one had a firm grasp on what was being seen or where they were coming from. In 1947, some of the suggestions were that they interplanetary as opposed to interstellar craft mainly because people were simply not thinking in terms of craft from planets beyond our solar system.

The number of sightings, which is to say the number that were reported, dropped significantly on July 9 when the Army and the Navy began a concentrated effort to suppress the stories. That just meant that sightings were no longer printed in the newspapers or reported on the radio. It didn't mean that the flying saucers had gone away, only that the reports of them were no longer considered news or more accurately were no longer reported because of the intervention of military authorities.[6]

For the next several years there would be a periodic report or someone would ask, "Whatever happened to those flying saucers?" Donald Keyhoe, a retired Marine Corps major, kept the story alive with periodic magazine articles and his claims that the Air Force knew more than it was letting on. He claimed there was a cover-up, but not many people were interested in his opinions or believed that the flying saucers were of any real importance—that is until July 1952.

The Washington Nationals (July 1952)

The Washington Nationals, as the sightings became known, began on July 19, 1952, but the country didn't learn about them until July 22. On that first Saturday night, July 19, pilots and crews of various airlines made multiple sightings of lights in the sky over Washington, D.C. Returns seen on the radars at Washington National Airport, Andrews Air Force Base, and Bolling Air Force Base suggested that weather-related phenomena were not the cause but that something tangible had invaded the airspace over Washington.[7]

Capital Airline officials said that they had learned from the airport radar operators at Washington National Airport that they had picked up unknown objects on their radars. Airline officials then asked the pilot of Capital Flight 807, Casey Pierman, to keep an eye out for anything unusual. Pierman said that he was between Washington and Martinsburg, West Virginia, when he and his crew saw seven objects flash across the sky. The lights were traveling at tremendous speed, and would move up and down and then suddenly slow until they were hovering. Pierman said, "They were like falling stars without the trails."[8]

The crew of another Capital Flight, Flight 610, reported that a single light followed them from Herndon, Virginia, to within 4 miles of National Airport. About the same time, an Air Force radar installation was tracking eight objects as they flew over Washington, D.C. This would be the only time that a military radar would track the objects, according to the documentation available.

One week later, almost to the hour, the UFOs were back, and the same crew who had watched them on the Washington National radar that first Saturday night was watching them again. This time interceptors were launched to identify the lights and the Pentagon's officer responsible for liaison between those investigating UFOs and those in Washington, D.C., Major Dewey Fournet, was present, as was the official Pentagon spokesman about UFOs, civilian Albert Chop.[9]

The sightings began at about 8:15 p.m. when the pilot and a member of the National Airlines flight crew saw several objects that they later described like the bright glow from the end of a cigarette. They were high overhead and they believed the objects were moving about a hundred miles an hour.

About an hour later the ARTC (Air Route Traffic Control) asked a B-25 crew in the area to investigate several radar targets that were near the aircraft. The crew saw nothing. They did report that every time they were told they had flown over one of the objects, they noticed they were over the same section of the Potomac River. Some would later consider this observation relevant.

Captain Edward Ruppelt, who was then chief of Project Blue Book, was told about the sightings, and he called Fournet, who lived close to the airport in Washington. Fournet, and eventually Chop, arrived at the airport's radar facility. Once the fighters were called in, Chop chased the reporters from the room citing the classified nature of the communications and procedures during the intercept. Reporters thought it was bunk, and Ruppelt would suggest the same thing years later, suggesting that ham radio operators with the right equipment would be able to listen to the radio traffic between the fighters.[10]

The radars were still "painting" the unknowns, showing them moving about 100 miles an hour and then streaking away at 7,000 mph. At 11:00 p.m. two fighters were scrambled from Newcastle Air Force Base. When interviewed years later, Fournet said, "The reports we got from at least one of the fighter pilots was pretty gory."[11]

This seemed to refer to the intercept attempt by Lieutenant William Patterson, who had been vectored toward one of the fast-moving targets. He spotted four white glowing lights and chased after them. He said that they were very brilliant blue-white lights.[12] They turned toward him and surrounded his aircraft. He called for instructions but received no clear reply. After a moment or two, the UFOs pulled away.

Chop added one point that was interesting: "The minute the first two interceptors appeared on our scope all our unknowns disappeared. It was like they just wiped them off. All our other flights, all the known flights were still there."[13]

As had happened the week before, as the sun came up, the unknown targets vanished from the scopes. There were a few anomalous targets remaining, but the radar operators identified them as weather related, meaning they were temperature inversions and the operators paid little or no attention to them.

Although there was a call to identify the objects quickly, including one from the White House, the answer finally supplied was unsatisfactory. The Air Force suggested it was the result of temperature inversions that had been over Washington on the nights that the radar showed UFOs. The one thing the sightings did was bring UFOs back into the public's attention. Newspapers, radio broadcasts, and even television mentioned the sightings.

By the end of the summer, with the Olympics as well as the presidential race catching media attention, UFOs no longer commanded front-page coverage. They disappeared except for the local angles as UFOs were still being seen and reported around the country. And, as had happened before, they slowly drifted back into obscurity.

The Levelland Sightings (November 2-3, 1957)

It was claimed, for a time, that the sightings in Levelland, Texas, and then at White Sands Missile Range hours later, were the result of the *Sputnik II* launch, but that information had not been made public until later that day, and no one in Levelland had heard the news. The first report was made by Pedro Saucedo, who called the Levelland sheriff, Weir Clem, to say that his pickup truck had been stalled when a large, glowing object had lifted off from a field near him. The object had a blue-green glow that faded into a red that was so bright it hurt to look at it. The UFO sat near the highway for about three minutes. Saucedo said that he felt a blast of wind that rocked his truck as the object disappeared in the east. Once the object was gone, his truck started and he found a telephone to call the sheriff.[14]

The spot where Pedro Saucedo's truck was stopped by the glowing UFO. Photo courtesy of the author.

Over the next few hours, witnesses in 13 separate locations in the area around Levelland and Lubbock, Texas, claimed to have seen the glowing red object that stalled their cars, dimmed their lights, and filled their radios with static. Typical of these sightings was that of Jim Wheeler, who saw a bright red object sitting on the road. He later told the NICAP investigator, James A. Lee, that the UFO was so bright that it cast a glow over the whole area.

As Wheeler approached the object, his headlights dimmed and his engine sputtered to a stop. As he started to get out of his car, the UFO rose into the sky. As it disappeared in the distance, the lights came back on and he was able to start his car. He called the police as soon as he could.

Ronald Martin told a similar story. He saw a red, egg-shaped object sitting on the road some 4 miles east of Levelland. As he drove closer, his headlights dimmed and finally went out. His engine stopped. He said the same things that Wheeler had said. When he started to get out of his car, the object lifted off rapidly. When it was gone, he could start his car and his headlights came back on.

The highway leading to Levelland, Texas, where the majority of the sightings were made on November 2-3, 1957. Photo courtesy of the author.

Even the sheriff, who ventured out to search for the object, saw it. In 1957, he said it was a streak of light in the distance, but he later suggested to friends and family that he had been much closer and had seen a great deal more. He said the Air Force investigator on the case, S/SGT Norman Barth, who came from Reese Air Force Base in Lubbock, had asked him to keep the details quiet.

In fact, family members suggested that Clem had told them that the day after the sightings, on a ranch outside of town, a

large, circular burn mark had been found. Although this information was gathered decades after the fact, there is some documentation in the Project Blue Book files that provide a point of
corroboration. There is a quote from Sheriff Clem made during
his interrogation by the Air Force representative. He said, "It lit
up the whole pavement in front of us [Clem had a deputy sheriff
with him] for about two seconds."[15]

Two hours after the sightings in Levelland, military police at
White Sands reported that they had seen an object land close to
them. Glenn Toy was one of those MPs who said that he was pa-
trolling up toward the Trinity Site where the first atomic bomb
was detonated, not all that far from Socorro.[16] Toy provided a
sworn statement to his commanding officer on the day of the
sighting. Toy said:

> At about 0238–0300 Sunday Morning [November 3, 1957]
> I, CPL X [Toy] and PFC Y [Wilbanks] were on patrol in
> Range Area when we noticed a very bright object high in the
> sky. We were proceeding north toward South Gate and ob-
> ject kept coming down toward the ground. Object stopped
> approximately fifty (50) yards from the ground and went
> out and nothing could be seen. A few minutes later object
> became real bright (like the sun) then fell in an angle to
> the ground and went out. Object was approximately sev-
> enty-five (75) to 100 yards in diameter and shaped like an
> egg. Object landed by bunker area approximately three (3)
> miles from us. Object was not seen again.[17]

Twelve hours later another patrol at White Sands, in a similar
location, reported that they watched a UFO. Although the Air
Force interviewed three of the four witnesses, they suggested the
men were young, inexperienced soldiers who might have been
caught up in the hysteria of the UFO sightings. Their reports
shouldn't be taken seriously and in fact, the Air Force decided
that one team had seen the moon and the other had seen Venus.[18]

But Toy said that he got a very good look at the UFO. "It landed right across the road from us," he said.[19]

The next day, the Levelland sightings hit the front pages and sparked a serious debate between the Air Force, who claimed that only three witnesses had seen the object in Levelland, and Donald Keyhoe, who claimed there were nine witnesses. Neither was right, but Keyhoe was closer to the actual number.[20] That became a major point of contention as the Air Force attempted to discredit the information that Keyhoe was publishing about these sightings.

In what might have been an important report as it would relate to the Socorro landing seven years later, a man, James Stokes, was burned by the close approach of a UFO. Stokes said that it was after 1:00 p.m., as he was driving between Alamogordo, New Mexico, home of Holloman Air Force Base, and El Paso, Texas, his radio began to fade out. He reached over to turn up the volume, but the radio was dead. At this point the engine began to sputter and finally died, and he saw other cars up ahead, all of them stopped with the drivers outside, pointing up at the sky. Stokes then saw the large, egg-shaped object that was coming toward them from the northeast. He said that it had a mother-of-pearl color; it was over the Sacramento Mountains and heading, more or less, southwest when it suddenly turned and passed over the highway. It made another sharp turn and again crossed the highway. It began to climb swiftly and finally vanished, not over the horizon, but apparently upward, into space.

Stokes said that when the object passed overhead, he felt some sort of pressure and a wave of heat. While standing there, Stokes took some notes so that he would have an accurate memory of what happened and what he had seen. He talked to two of the other witnesses, one man named Duncan and the other Allan D. Baker, who might have worked at the White Sands Proving Ground. According to Stokes, Duncan was from Las Cruces and had taken some pictures of the object, but searches for these men failed. The pictures have never surfaced, even with the publicity surrounding the sighting at the time in that area.

Once the UFO had disappeared, Stokes got back into his car. The engine started with no trouble and Stokes continued on to El Paso. On his return, the first thing he did was call his superior at Holloman, Major Ralph Everett, whose attitude seemed to be that it hadn't happened at Holloman, and because Stokes hadn't been on duty, and there was nothing in the inventory that could explain the sighting, there was no reason for Stokes not to say anything about what he had seen to those who asked.[21]

For several days, the sightings in Levelland and elsewhere were on the front pages of newspapers around the country. There was a large spike in the number of reports made to Project Blue Book. By the middle of December, the reports dwindled and the flying saucers fell from the front pages.

The Las Vegas UFO Crash

On April 18, 1962, according to Project Blue Book files, there was a radar sighting from Nellis Air Force Base just outside of Las Vegas, Nevada, but the information contained in that file mentioned nothing about eyewitnesses. The project card gave a brief summary of the sighting and then noted, "No. Visual."[22]

The problem for the Air Force was that the *Las Vegas Sun* reported on April 19, 1962, the day after the radar sighting, in a banner headline on the front page "Brilliant Red Explosion Flares in Las Vegas Sky." That article suggested dozens of eyewitnesses and even named some of them. In the lead paragraph, Jim Stalnaker, a reporter for the newspaper, wrote that a "tremendous flaming sword flashed across the Las Vegas skies last night and heralded the start of a search for a weird unidentified flying object that apparently had America's Air Force on alert."[23]

Stalnaker reported that Frank Maggio, a staff photographer, had seen the object. According to the newspaper, Maggio said that a series of bright explosions broke up its trail across the sky. It was a visual sighting of a bright light that seemed to be related to the radar tracks recorded out at Nellis.

That same article mentioned Sheriff's Deputy Walter Butt, who was in charge of the department's search and rescue team. The consensus seemed to be that the object was heading toward the east and there had been a final explosion near Mesquite, Nevada, on the Utah border. Butt took his team into an area between Spring Mountain and Mesquite, but nothing else had been reported to the newspaper.[24]

Butt said that they had searched the area in jeeps and, when the sun came up, had used airplanes. They didn't find anything of importance, except some ashes that he thought were probably part of a campfire started some weeks earlier by a hunter. When no one reported any missing aircraft, and they had run up against the fences of part of a Nellis gunnery range, they called off the search.[25]

At the AEC's Nevada Test Site was another man who also saw the object in the air. He said that it looked like a nuclear explosion but added quickly that it came from the wrong direction for that answer to be valid.

In Colorado Springs where the North American Air Defense Command (NORAD) is located, the information officer, Lt. Col. Herbert Rolph, said they had one report of a sighting as far away as New York.[26]

There is a handwritten note in the Project Blue Book files affecting all this. Lt. Col. H.C. Showers at the command post called "FTD [Foreign Technology Division] of the following event reported to the war room at the Pentagon."

The log entry said:

General [Laurence S.] Kuter (NORAD) took off and was climbing through 10,000 [feet] when he saw a "meteor" [quotes in original document] come out of orbit as 0319Z 19 April. He described the object as cherry red, clear green, with a long white and red tail. He estimated object near Colorado Springs and [the] AF Academy. USAF indicated reports coming in from Idaho, Utah, Arizona, 'OCD' 28th and 29th (??) Regions, Navy Aircraft, B-52 crew and DC-8 pilots. All reported alike in shape, color, and general direction of travel...south to north. An "Air Force Colonel" [quotes in original] reported that object [over] the western range—but there was no noise. Denver center [FAA flight center] reported at 0332Z that after 10–15 minutes after the first reports the trail could still be seen. No radar pick up reported as yet. Visual sightings only."

About 50 minutes later, just after midnight the command post got another report, this time from Lt. Col. James Howell, who wanted to report "numerous reports to the FAA and AFLC [command post] on the above sighting. It was observed in Los Angeles, Col. [Colorado], Montana; Kansas; Utah."

The Air Force, which had received most of the sighting reports, believed that one object was responsible for all the sightings. Officers at Stead Air Force Base near Reno, Nellis Air Force Base near Las Vegas, and at NORAD, all drew the same conclusion. The reports from Utah and Reno, Nevada, describe sightings made within 15 minutes of each other when corrected for the time zones and the fact that some of the sighting reports were filed using Greenwich Mean Time.

The Air Force file for the Nellis Radar sighting puts the incidence some 16 minutes after sightings in Utah and northern Nevada, but the official spokesman at Nellis said the Air Defense Command was alerted by the fire trail seen at approximately 7:20 p.m., or within a few minutes of the Utah sightings.

On September 21, 1962, Major C.R. Hart of the Public Information Office, responding to a letter from a New York resident, claimed that "the official records of the Air Force list the 18 April 1962 Nevada sighting to which you refer as 'unidentified, insufficient data.' There is an additional note to the effect that 'the reported track is characteristic of that registered by a U-2 or a high balloon but there is insufficient data reported to fully support such an evaluation.' The phenomena reported was not intercepted or fired upon."[27]

Reports in the Project Blue Book files clearly show that fighters had been launched and intercepts had been attempted. It could be argued that Major Hart did not have access to those reports and he had written only what he had been told. He wasn't lying or covering up, he just didn't have access to all the facts. He just didn't know.

His explanation also left something to be desired. He wrote that "track is characteristic of that registered by a U-2 or a high balloon." A balloon track would be made at the whim of the wind, reacting to the winds aloft, and a U-2 would have a track that showed intelligent control. A balloon track would look nothing like the track of a high-flying jet.

There is a variety of documentation of the sighting from the newspapers in the region including the *Las Vegas Sun, Los Angeles Times, Deseret News and Telegram, Salt Lake Tribune, Eureka Reporter,* and *Nephi News-Leader.* Additional documentation, including the reports created at the time, can be found in the Project Blue Book files.

The relevant point here, however, is that this sighting, though not gaining a national audience, was widely reported in the region from west Texas to Los Angeles. It demonstrated the Air Force interest in UFOs, suggested that something might have exploded, and with the information about the radar sighting, suggested something real.

~~~

This was the UFO world as it existed in 1964. In the 17 years before the landing in Socorro, there had been periods of extensive UFO coverage, and the idea of alien visitation had evolved to the point where there were millions who believed it. There were those who thought that many of the UFO sightings could be explained by black, government projects, and the idea of UFOs was used to hide that information. This theory has been grabbed by skeptics and even the CIA to explain away those sightings that are nearly impossible to explain.

When Lonnie Zamora saw the object landed in the arroyo south of Socorro, one of the things he thought was that it could be a government project. Sam Chavez believed this explanation as well. It was an idea that was pursued by those who investigated the case and one that was not found to be true.

Chapter 3:
The Other Witnesses

I have said in the past, and others have said in the past, that the problem with the Socorro landing is that it was seen by a single witness. Though it is true that Lonnie Zamora was a police officer and nearly everyone who was asked said that he was an honest man who was not prone to practical jokes and embellishing tales, it is also true that a good UFO case becomes a great case if there was more than a single witness.

But it turns out that this isn't actually a single-witness case. There are hints of other witnesses who remain unidentified to this day, and there are the names of two men from Dubuque, Iowa, who said that they had seen the craft as they were approaching Socorro late in the day on April 24, 1964. There are a couple of names of men who might have seen the same thing as it lifted off.

Throw in a couple of people who are known as "audio" witnesses, and the case becomes a little stronger.

Secondhand Sources

Opal Grinder was on duty as manager at the Whiting Brothers Gas Station on the main north–south highway through Socorro late on the evening of April 24. A car, described later as a light green Cadillac, stopped at the station. These were the days before self-service, when those working at the station pumped the gas, washed the windows, checked the oil, collected the money, and often engaged drivers in a bit of conversation while all this was going on. The car held five people: the driver, his wife, and three children. They were apparently on their way home, and Grinder said that he thought they were from Colorado.[1]

The driver, who had obviously stepped out of the car, told Grinder, "Your aircraft sure fly low around here." He said that an aircraft had nearly taken the roof of his car.

They were on the south side of Socorro, north of the airport and driving north on Highway 85 (later the route of Interstate 25) when the aircraft flew over them. The driver thought the craft was in some kind of trouble because he had seen a police car pull off the road and head in the direction of the craft.

Grinder thought the man might have seen a helicopter, but the man said it was not like any helicopter he had ever seen. Ray Stanford suggested the man and his family had seen an egg-shaped object that had smooth aluminum sides and seemed to be a little larger than his car. It was silhouetted against the setting sun. Stanford, in fact, added dialogue from the wife to the husband, suggesting she had pointed it out to him. However, in the various statements attributed to Grinder and in the affidavit he signed sometime later, there is no mention of the description or the craft or any additional details of the sighting from the driver or his family.

Grinder didn't understand the significance of what he had heard until the following Tuesday, when the then twice-weekly

Socorro newspaper, the *El Defensor-Chieftain,* published Lonnie Zamora's story. Then a search for the witnesses began, but they hadn't used a credit card for the purchase, and although Grinder's son had overheard the conversation, he didn't add much to it, other than saying that he thought the car had Colorado plates.

Dr. J. Allen Hynek also interviewed Grinder a day or so after the article appeared in the newspaper. Grinder told him the same story that he had given to everyone else when they asked. He added a couple of details, telling Hynek that the tourist had said, "Your planes fly awfully low here—one of them liked to knock me off the road just about when I was passing your sign coming into town." Grinder also said that he didn't pay much attention to the man because he (Grinder) was hurrying so that he could get to the bank before it closed at 6:00 p.m.[2]

The Air Force learned about the driver's sighting from the local newspaper and other media sources. Colonel Eric T. de Jonckheere, who was the deputy for technology and subsystems, wrote on May 28, 1964:

> News media and persons connected with various UFO organizations such as APRO [the Lorenzens] and NICAP [Ray Stanford] received word of the sighting and sent investigators to the scene. Newspaper accounts of the sighting had been much distorted with reports of little men running around and a rocket ship blasting off into space. The account of the sighting carried in the El Defensor & Chieftain (sic) dated Tuesday 28 April 1964 and the account by UPI representative in the Albuquerque Journal, 27 April 1964, are essentially correct. As a result of wide news coverage and public interest in the sighting Captain Hector Quintanilla, Project [Blue Book] Officer directed TSgt David Moody to assist in the investigation for the Air Force. Sgt Moody contacted Major Connor, the Officer at Kirtland AFB responsible for unidentified flying object investigations, and accompanied him to Socorro.[3]

The El Defensor and Chieftain [sic] carried an article indicating that an unidentified tourist traveling North on US 85 saw the UFO just before it landed. He also observed the police car heading up the hill toward the spot where the UFO landed. If this is true, the UFO not only disappeared in the direction of White Sand's (sic) but also came from the same direction. A telephone call to Mr [sic] Opal Grinder of Whiting Brothers Service Station indicated that he was the source for reporting that an unidentified tourist had observed the unidentified flying object. He verified that the information in the news article was correct.[4]

Whoever the tourist and his family were, they never came forward to tell exactly what they had seen, which seems strange given the national coverage of the story as noted by Colonel de Jonckheere. In fact, in a teletype message the Secretary of the Air Force Office of Information noted, "Numerous inquiries concerning Air Force investigation and evaluation of recent UFO sighting at Socorro, New Mexico, 24 April, continue to be received fron (sic) news media, from office of the President, and members of Congress."[5] This reinforces the idea that this was a big story at the time and that there might have been some pressure put on the Air Force to carry out a proper investigation. But it might also suggest something as simple as the tourist and his family didn't want to be subjected to the type of scrutiny suffered by Zamora. They might have wanted to avoid the Air Force investigation and the accompanying spotlight brought by the news media as well as the comments about their sanity, integrity, and intelligence from their neighbors and the rest of the country.

Additional Witnesses?

Ben Moss and Tony Angiola, when I spoke to them, said there were additional witnesses in the Socorro case. They said that three people had called the Socorro Police Department to complain about low-flying aircraft and the noise they were making at about the time Zamora was giving chase to the speeder. If true, this would be some confirmation of the Socorro landing. I asked if they had checked the police records for additional details and confirmation and verification of the story. The short answer from them turned out to be "no."[6]

That, however, was not the final answer. The Project Blue Book files contain a short report signed by Captain Richard T. Holder, who had been involved with the investigation from the very beginning on April 24. In that report he wrote, "Upon arrival at the office location of the Socorro County Building, we were informed by Nep Lopez, Sheriff's Office radio operator, that approximately three reports had been called in by telephone of a blue flame or light in the area. Initial sighting was made by Officer [redacted but clearly Zamora] at approximately 1750 [5:50 p.m.]."[7] Although the police department did not log the calls, or even write down the names of those people who had made the telephone calls, it does supply some confirmation of the sighting by somewhat independent sources. It is not as valuable as it might have been if the names had been obtained and interviews conducted, but it does confirm that others in the area had seen the object, or rather the blue flame in the sky, at about the time Zamora began his chase. We do not have the names, but we have documentation that the telephone calls were made.

Stanford, in his book, mentioned a telephone call that had been received by one of the Albuquerque television stations slightly before 5:30 p.m. The witness said that there was a shiny oval or egg-shaped object at a low altitude heading to the south, or toward Socorro. It wasn't moving very fast and the witness said that it resembled no conventional aircraft. Because it looked like nothing the caller had ever seen, he reported it to the television station.[8] Once again, the reporter from the station who provided Stanford with the information failed to get the name of the witness and Stanford doesn't supply the name of the reporter. It does suggest how these sorts of reports, of strange aerial phenomenon, were treated in 1964. It just wasn't important enough to even write down a name in case someone else called in with similar information.

There were also what Stanford refers to as auditory witnesses. According to him, he was in a restaurant in Socorro with radio reporter Walter Shrode on the evening of Wednesday, April 30, when he learned of two women who lived on the south side of Socorro. According to Stanford, Shrode introduced him to the women, who said that they believed what Zamora had said. Under Stanford's questioning about that, both women said they hadn't actually seen the object, but they had heard the roar from it. Not only that, the women claimed that their neighbors had heard the object as well and they had heard it twice. They had heard two different roars: when it landed and when it took off again, about a minute later. The women were not named in his book; Stanford said that they did not want their names reported publicly.[9]

Given the passage of time, it seemed that the need for anonymity might have passed. The names might yield additional evidence and, even after more than half a century, additional witnesses might be found. Unfortunately, Stanford failed to record their names and at this late date doesn't remember who they were. He told me they had been middle-aged at the time and doubted they were still alive.[10]

It would seem that if these two women had heard the roar, others would have, too, as they claimed. They suggested that their neighbors had heard it as well. Stanford said that he learned from the Socorro sheriff's office that hundreds had heard the roar of the craft landing and taking off. For some reason, he didn't attempt to talk to any of those people. Even if they hadn't seen a craft or the flame, it would have been valuable to have the confirmation from the independent sources.[11]

Named Sources

Robert Dusenberry, who worked for the Socorro Electric Corporation, said that he and two friends were in a car near the landing site late that Friday evening. They apparently saw the object as it took off. Jerry Clark learned of this in an interview that he conducted in 1995 with former law enforcement officer Ted Jordan. Dusenberry had not told anyone about his sighting until he talked to Jordan about it many years later.[12] This is important because there is a name associated with the information, so that it is not just another anonymous source. Jordan, in 1964, was a senior patrolman with the state police.

In a report that might be related to the case, but that was somehow overlooked by most of those investigating the Zamora sighting in 1964, is the story told by a master sergeant who was driving south from the Stallion Range Center at the White Sands Missile Range sometime between 8:00 and 8:30 p.m. He said that he spotted a blue light with orange at the bottom that seemed to be in the mountains west of his position, which would have put him south of Socorro about two or two and a half hours later. As the glow from the flame got brighter, his car engine died and his electrical system failed. The sergeant was a master mechanic who said that he had checked out his car to ensure it was in perfect working condition not long before the sighting. He got out of the car and watched the blue glow until it began to fade. His car then started again, apparently without him having to start it himself. When he arrived at his destination, he inspected the car again carefully but could find nothing wrong with it. Jerry Clark learned about this from Richard Holder when he interviewed him in 1995.[13]

Ray Stanford suggested there was another large group of witnesses who had never come forward publicly. He said that nearly every member of the law enforcement establishment in Socorro had seen UFOs and suggested that some of them had seen the one Zamora reported, but they had also seen how Zamora had been treated by the news media and by the "official" investigators either from White Sands, the FBI, or the Air Force. They wanted no part of that. Privately, they opened up to Stanford, though there is some evidence that they were known to those investigating the case but were never interviewed or never gave official statements.[14]

From the documentation available, it is clear that Zamora called State Police Sergeant Sam Chavez, asking him to come alone to the scene, but hadn't told him what was happening.[15] In an interview conducted the next day by Walter Shrode of local radio station KSRC, Zamora said, "From the time I saw this object, which I didn't know what it was, I placed a call to Sgt. Chavez of the State Police, called him to come out there and help me on this. And he said, 'Yes, I'll be right there, in about two minutes.'"[16]

When Zamora called him, Chavez had to turn a prisoner over to another officer and then got into his car to head out. He hurried out to the location that Zamora had given him, making a wrong turn that delayed him slightly. Unlike Zamora, Chavez said that his car had no trouble getting up the first hill and he stopped near Zamora's parked car.[17]

Shrode, in the interview, asked, "And he arrived just about two or three minutes after the object had taken off and left?"

Zamora said, "Well, the object was still about a couple of (unintelligible) up there when he arrived."

Zamora seemed to be saying that the object was still visible when Chavez arrived. But he also seemed to suggest that Chavez hadn't seen it. The Hobbs, New Mexico newspaper reported, "Zamora said that he called for help and State Police Sgt. Sam Chavez was on the scene within two minutes. By then the UFO was flying off towards the mountains. 'If he [Chavez] had just paid attention he would have seen it,' Zamora said."[18]

More Witnesses

According to one newspaper report, "The flame was spotted about 5:45 p.m. by other persons too. A sergeant with the New Mexico State Police said he saw the object on the ground in the desert."[19] Though the description—that is, of a sergeant with the state police—matches Chavez, it is also true that the police officer who saw the object on the ground was Zamora. This is most likely a mistake by the newspaper reporter and not confirmation that Chavez saw the craft. There simply is no evidence that Chavez was there before the object took off and, if he was, that he saw the object.

Stanford, on the radio in 2016, said that Chavez had confirmed to him that he (Chavez) had arrived after the object had taken off so he didn't get a good look at it. By the time he arrived, the craft was high in the sky, just about to disappear from sight when he saw it. Unfortunately, there is no record of this to support this claim. Statements by Zamora seem to suggest Chavez arrived in time to see the object, but Chavez himself left no verbal or written record about it. Stanford reinforced the idea that it was because the others had seen how Zamora had been treated and they had no desire to experience the same thing. They kept their mouths shut, and that included Chavez. The ridicule directed at Zamora might have been reduced with a second witness to the craft, even if it had been high in the sky before he saw it. And it would have added one more name to the roster of witnesses.

On the other hand, Zamora did try to alert other police officers in time to see something. Zamora called the police department's radio operator, Nep Lopez, and told him to look out the window. Unfortunately, the orientation of the office and the trees and terrain prevented Lopez from seeing anything at all. Coral Lorenzen, as did Hynek, reported that as the object took off, Zamora had called the police station to tell them about the object, but no one there had seen anything unusual.[20]

The best confirming witnesses (by that I mean the ones who told their story within days of the sighting and whose names were attached to it), were Larry Kratzer and Paul Kies. I learned of them when I was researching another UFO sighting and saw their story that had appeared in the Dubuque, Iowa, Telegram–Herald on Wednesday, April 29, 1964. It was one of those serendipitous things that pop up when researching UFOs. Others had also found the tale, but I wasn't aware of that.

According to what Kies told the Dubuque newspaper, he and Kratzer were in New Mexico, on Highway 60 a mile east of Socorro early in the evening, about 5:45 p.m. when they saw something shining in the distance.[21] Kratzer said, "We saw some brown dust, then black smoke—like rubbish burning—then a fire. The smoke hid the shiny craft as it flew away."[22] The object was hovering about 20 feet off the ground when they first saw it and then skimming away, across the desert.

Kies told the newspaper reporter that federal agents had cordoned the area and that government sources had denied they had any craft like that which Zamora had described. Both added some details and then mentioned that the exhaust of the craft had melted a pop bottle. These statements are problematic because they had only seen the craft in the air and had not been to the landing site to either see the cordon or the melted bottle. It suggests that they had either heard news broadcasts that gave some detail or had seen newspaper articles about the landing before they talked with the reporter from the Dubuque newspaper.

Ralph DeGraw, a UFO researcher living in Iowa, interviewed both men about their sighting about a decade and a half later. On May 11, 1978, he sat down with Paul Kies and recorded his conversation. The story shifts slightly from what had been reported in the newspaper more than 14 years earlier, but not enough to be worrisome given the passage of time and the way that memory works. He said that they were returning to Iowa after having left a boat in Quemado, New Mexico, because of car trouble when they had been there earlier. DeGraw said:

> [I]t was approximately 5:00 p.m. (Iowa time, or 4:00 p.m. New Mexico time)...when they reached a point approximately 1 mile southwest of Socorro. Suddenly Kratzer who was driving, pointed out of cloud of dust followed by black smoke which appeared to be ahead and slightly to the right of their position.... Kies estimated that it was about 1 mile distant and was coming from the ground...as they watched, a bright, shiny "reflection" appeared within the smoke... they continued on toward Socorro and that they moved at such an angle that the "reflection" was no longer visible.

Kies was not sure whether he had seen the reflection of sunlight (which was now low in the western sky) falling on the object on the ground or whether the object itself was emitting light. However, at the time, he felt that there must have been a junk yard in that area and that someone was burning tires and cutting up wrecked cars.... He at no time thought anything about UFOs.[23]

They continued into Socorro and stopped at a Chevron station to hook up the trailer lights. This was not the station managed by Opal Grinder, who had talked about five tourists in a Cadillac. Kies was driving Kratzer's 1964 Corvette, which would never be mistaken for a Cadillac. Kratzer thought he might have said something to the station owner about what they had seen but he didn't remember. Unlike Opal Grinder, that station employee never came forward, which suggests that Kratzer didn't say anything to him or what he said didn't connect with the story told by Zamora. With the lights hooked up, they continued crossing New Mexico, and somewhere near the Texas/Oklahoma border they heard a news report about the flying saucer landing.

Once they had arrived in Dubuque, they decided to tell the newspaper, because the Zamora story was still making headlines. DeGraw noted that they said the newspaper didn't get the facts straight, saying the men had seen the craft on Saturday rather than Friday and that they had been east of Socorro when they were west, driving east.

Kratzer had a little better description of the object than the one given by Kies. According to DeGraw, Kratzer said the UFO was a round or egg-shaped object that ascended vertically from the black smoke. He said that it was difficult to estimate size and distance given that the sighting had occurred so long ago. He couldn't tell how far away it was but thought that it was a half mile to a mile distant and flying at about a thousand feet.

DeGraw reported, "After climbing vertically out of the smoke, Kratzer said the object leveled off and moved in a southwest direction, disappearing in black smoke which he said was coming out of its underside."[24]

He also said that the craft was silver with a row of round, darker, mirror-like windows. And he said there was a red "Z" on the right side of the craft. There were about four windows visible on the side facing them and he believed that they circled the craft.[25]

Kratzer's statement, then, does not match the information that we have about the case. Zamora is the main source for the descriptions of the craft; he was the one who got closest to the object on the ground and he had the best opportunity to see it. He described that craft as having a smooth surface with no windows or signs of a hatch, even though he believed that the creatures had returned to the interior of the craft after they spotted him and he heard sounds like a hatch being closed. He did not describe the symbol as a red "Z," and you have to wonder how Kratzer would have seen it from the distance of more than a half mile if his estimate of the distance is accurate. Kratzer's statement doesn't even match that of Kies, who was with him in the car. Kies seemed to have seen less but according to the article, Kies was driving at the time.

Does this mean that we should reject both their statements about what they saw?

Clark mentions that there were problems with the testimony but just notes it, to let the reader decide what to think. It is clear from the article that appeared in the Dubuque newspaper that both men had heard of the sighting before they talked to the press, and Kies confirmed that when DeGraw interviewed him. I know of no investigation that attempted to determine if they had been in New Mexico at the time of the sighting, and, if they were, no one learned if they were in a position to see the object. Given the time that had elapsed prior to that interview—nearly a decade and a half—it is unlikely that any useful evidence would have turned up to prove that they were in New Mexico on that Friday in 1964.

I will note here that they couldn't have been aware of the Opal Grinder story, given the timing of their interview with the Dubuque newspaper. Grinder didn't come forward until the Tuesday after the sighting, and Kies and Kratzer were interviewed by the *Telegraph–Herald* in time for the Wednesday edition of the paper. Their story, as told to DeGraw more than a decade later, certainly suggests they knew the country around Socorro: where the highways lead and the best route from Socorro back to Iowa in 1964. Unless they had studied a map prior to DeGraw interviewing them, this is an interesting fact.

~~~

In the end, we are left with a number of alleged witnesses who did not leave a record of any kind. We don't know who the Colorado tourists were, but we do have the secondhand statements from Grinder about what they had seen. We don't know who the people are who called the police about the blue flame in the sky, but we do have some documentation to suggest this is true in the signed report by Holder and found in the Project Blue Book files. We don't know who the women were who told Stanford about hearing the roar and suggesting that their neighbors had heard it as well. We have nothing from any of the law enforcement personnel who were on duty that night, though we do have, again, secondhand information to suggest that some of them might have known more about the sighting and that some of them might have seen more than they were willing to tell either the official investigators or the civilian researchers.

Originally, like so many others, I had said that this was a single-witness case, but as we can see, it is much more than that. There is documentation to support additional witnesses, there is testimony to support that as well, and we do have two firsthand accounts from Kies and Kratzer. Unfortunately, their testimony leaves something to be desired, but it is on the record in the days that followed Zamora's sighting. There is, of course, the possibility that they were making it up because of what they had heard on the radio and read in the newspapers, though that seems un-likely, given the timing of all the events. Besides that, they were interviewed by DeGraw 14 years after they made their original statements and if they had made up their report that was the op-portunity to correct the record. They did not do that.

We are not quite back to where we started with only Lonnie Zamora as the witness. We have added to the testimony, though the additions are not as solid as I would like. Besides, there is another aspect to the case: physical evidence. Zamora said he saw something on the ground and there were landing traces from it, on the ground, seen within minutes of the departure of the craft. That adds another dimension to the story and suggests that what had landed was not an illusion, was not a hallucination, but some-thing real and heavy enough to leave its footprints.

Chapter 4:

The Investigation

It might be said that the investigation began when Lonnie Zamora broke off his chase of the teenaged speeder and turned toward the dynamite shack he thought might have exploded. It might be said that it began when Sergeant Sam Chavez of the New Mexico State Police received the call from Zamora and then drove out to the scene of the landing. Or it might be said that it began with the arrival of FBI agent Arthur Byrnes, Jr. and Captain Richard T. Holder at the police headquarters in Socorro. But it can be said with certainty that the investigation began within an hour of Zamora seeing the landed craft on the outskirts of Socorro.

The Project Blue Book files are in conflict on some of the minor points that do nothing to suggest that there is a hoax involved here. This concerns such things as the order in which radio

messages were received by various people and who then responded to Zamora's radio calls. What we learn is that Zamora, believing that he was seeing a wrecked car at first, radioed the station,
and told them that he was on the scene of a traffic accident and
that he would be outside his patrol car investigating.[1]

In a number of interviews conducted in the hours after the
landing, Zamora said that he had called Chavez privately and that
some of the radio traffic between Zamora and the police station
was monitored by other law enforcement officers. It seems to be
clear that Zamora requested the assistance of Chavez and asked
him to come alone. It is unclear how the request was made in days
before cell phones. Zamora had to have used the police radio and
that would suggest that others would monitor it, but the channel
used might not have been easily available to everyone with a police radio or one that was not monitored at all times.

Chavez, who had been fingerprinting a prisoner, told Zamora
that he would be there in two minutes. Chavez did question the
request to come alone and Zamora responded that he thought
he was seeing something strange. He thought it might be a black
project and was afraid that he might be violating government secrecy. He wanted a sympathetic person to verify the situation if it
turned out to be something different.[2]

Within minutes of receiving the call, Chavez pulled his car
up on the mesa and parked near Zamora. It is important to note,
once again, that Chavez had made a wrong turn, which delayed
his arrival at the landing site. This would become a point of contention during later investigations as the possibility that Chavez
had arrived in time to see the object in the sky was explored.

Zamora had also called the police headquarters to ask if anyone there could see the craft in the sky to the southwest. Given
the layout of the station and the vegetation around it, no one did.
But the call alerted others on the police radio net that something
unusual was happening on the south side of town. Other law enforcement officials including Under Sheriff James Luckie got into
his car to drive out to the site.[3]

While Zamora was waiting for Chavez, he walked down toward the landing site. He knew that Chavez would be there quickly so he didn't get very far, but he was close enough to see the bushes were still smoking.[4] This was obvious evidence that something hot had been there moments before and this would tend to corroborate his story of the landed craft that had taken off in a burst of flame. He then walked back up the hill toward his car and where Chavez had parked his.

When Chavez saw Zamora, he said, "You look like you've seen the devil."

"Well, maybe I have," he responded.[5]

Together they walked to the edge of the arroyo and watched the smoke rise from the bushes and the clumps of grass that were still smoldering. As they explored the landing site, they found impressions in the ground that suggested something heavy had been sitting there. These formed a rough quadrangle. The smoking bush seemed to be close to the center of those impressions and later precise measurements would bear this out.[6]

Luckie wasn't the only law enforcement officer who was intrigued by the radio call. State Police Senior Patrolman Ted V. Jordan and cattle inspector Robert White also decided to drive out to see what was happening. They all arrived not long after Chavez and parked near the other patrol cars. Chavez and Zamora briefed them on what Zamora had seen and what had happened after Chavez arrived. They all returned to the arroyo to inspect the ground where the craft had touched down. Jordan had his camera with him and took several pictures of the landing site, including the impressions in the ground. That film would later add an interesting dimension to the sighting.[7]

They all stayed on the scene until nearly 7:00 p.m.[8] and then returned to the state police headquarters. Once there, Chavez made a number of telephone calls. First, he called the local FBI agent, Arthur Byrnes, Jr., who also spoke to Zamora.[9] Byrnes, in turn, called the Stallion Station at White Sands and spoke to First Lieutenant Hicks, who, in turn, notified Captain Richard T.

Holder, who lived in Socorro. Minutes later, Byrnes called Holder and told him about the UFO sighting. Holder said that he would be there shortly and arrived at about 20 minutes after seven.[10]

The members of the local media learned about the sighting almost as soon as it happened. The newspaper *El Defensor-Chieftain*, published twice a week in 1964 and which wouldn't be out until Tuesday, did long interviews with Zamora and some of the government officials. The local radio station, KSRC, aired an interview with Zamora on Saturday, April 25. By the next morning, the story would be out.[11]

Both Byrnes and Holder interviewed Zamora at the station. Zamora told them about the people he had seen standing near the craft for only a few seconds and then about the symbol he had seen painted on the side of the object as it lifted off. Byrnes suggested that Zamora not mention he had seen any figures near the craft, saying that it would subject him to ridicule. Holder thought that Zamora should not describe the symbol. His thinking was that it would help them filter out imposters who might claim to have seen the object but who would be unable to describe the design.[12]

Having finished what could only be labeled an interrogation, and satisfied that Zamora was telling the truth as best he could, they decided they wanted to see the landing site for themselves. The various police officials drove in separate cars, and Byrnes and Holder headed out by themselves and stopped at the home of Sergeant Castle, who was the NCOIC (non-commissioned officer in charge) of the MP unit stationed at White Sands. He rode with them out to the landing site.

According to Holder, "Castle assisted in taking the enclosed measurements and observations."[13]

Once that had been completed, and once the impressions had been protected by placing rocks around them, everyone returned to the police station. Holder said that he and Byrnes completed their reports later that evening or early the next morning. Holder wrote, "By Request of the FBI, please do not refer to the FBI as participating in any fashion—use of local law enforcement authorities is acceptable."[14]

The next day the story was out nationally. Holder said that he had received a telephone call from a colonel who said that he was in the Joint Chiefs of Staff war room in the Pentagon who wanted to know if he (Holder) had prepared a report on the sighting. Instructed to read his report into the telephone, which had a "scrambler" (a device that would code the signal) attached, he had just begun when the connection was broken. Holder then called the war room, talked to the same officer, and finished reading his report. He often wondered, "Why in the world were they so interested?"[15]

Coral Lorenzen and APRO in Tucson, Arizona, learned of the sighting on the morning of April 25, when Arlynn Bruer of the *Alamogordo News* called her for a comment. Although the Lorenzens had plans and commitments for that day, they managed to make other arrangements and to leave Tucson at five that evening, arriving in Socorro about one the next morning. By 9:00 a.m., they were at the Socorro Police Department. Within the hour, they were being taken to the landing site by Chavez and Socorro Police Chief Pineda.[16]

Chavez explained everything to the Lorenzens, answering all their questions and helping them make measurements. They took samples from the bush that had been burned, the burned ground, and even inside one of the indentations. That finished, they returned to the police station and called Zamora. He agreed to meet them that afternoon.[17]

Their interview with Zamora didn't go quite as well as those with the other police officers. He was reluctant to talk but after Jim Lorenzen said that his questions would only take a few minutes, they all—which included the Lorenzens, Zamora, Luckie, and a reporter from the newspaper—went into the chief's office for privacy.[18]

Zamora explained, again, what he had seen and how he had reacted. He did tell the Lorenzens that he hadn't seen any "little

men." Coral Lorenzen pointed out that he had already told reporters about that, and his descriptions of them had been reported
on the radio and in the newspapers around the country. Zamora
then admitted that he had seen two figures that he thought of as
young boys or small adults standing near the craft. He said that
he could make out no features on them other than he thought of
them as little people.

They asked about the markings and Zamora said that he had
been told by an intelligence officer not to talk about it. He identified the officer as Holder, who was not an intelligence officer but
was assigned to White Sands. Jim Lorenzen called Holder, who
confirmed that he had made the suggestion as a way of identifying others who might have seen the same thing and rejecting
those who were making up a sighting for personal reasons or publicity. The Lorenzens thought that this was a good idea. However,
in the May 1964 issue of *The A.P.R.O. Bulletin*, they printed an
illustration that had the correct symbol on it.[19] To confuse the
issue, they also published an illustration that contained a different
symbol that has elements of the arc over an arrow head, but with
lines on the sides and bottom that make it look as if the symbol is
in a modified oblong box.

Lorenzen also reported that she had talked to Terry Clark,
who told them that the FBI man (Byrnes) had told Zamora not to
talk to newsmen about the little men. He received the same information: that it might detract from his report. Lorenzen thought
that this marked an attempt at censorship and that Zamora had
then retreated to the claim that he had only seen what he described as "white coveralls" with seeing anything else.[20]

The Lorenzens managed to hear about the creatures, though
Zamora denied having said anything about little people. The
Albuquerque Journal reported, "UFO Witness Sighs at Reports of
What He Supposedly Said" and also said, "Won't Tell Soul Next
Time." In the body of the article, it said, "Zamora denies he had
seen any little creatures around the object."[21]

In their investigation, the Lorenzens gathered some additional facts about the craft and the landing that matched those collected by others the day before. Coral Lorenzen wrote:

> The girder-like legs described by Zamora appeared to him to be 2–2½ feet long.... In reference to those "landing gear"—the tracks reveal that the object came down, gear extended to support it in a level position, and the "humping" of dirt on the outside of the tracks indicate that it was probably mounted a little with the landing and then displaced when the gear were withdrawn when the object took off.
>
> During the week following the Zamora incident, Socorro was literally overrun with UFO researchers as well as official investigators including Dr. J. Allen Hynek, the Air Force's Astrophysics Consultant. Lincoln La Paz, the famed meteoriticist of Albuquerque, made a statement or two in the press, as usual, and endorsed Zamora's reputation as an honest and reliable man. He had known Zamora for about 15 years. Hynek stated publicly his puzzlement concerning the fact that the Zamora object as well as other objects sighted in the area, were not picked up by radar, despite the fact that the area is literally "infested" with radar.[22]

Lorenzen did respond to Hynek's comment about the lack of radar confirmation. She wrote that the closest radar facility was at the Stallion Site. Holder was the man in charge there, and he said that the radars had been shut down by 5:00 p.m. on that Friday because no testing was scheduled that would require radar observation. She also suggested that other radars in the area, controlled by the Air Force or the FAA, for example, would have not "painted" the UFO because of its low altitude and low speed. The terrain and the distances to those other radars contributed to that problem. It would also seem that the development of stealth technology would suggest that large objects could fly through areas without producing a significant radar return.

Dr. J. Allen Hynek, the scientific consultant to Project Blue Book, and one of the investigators on the landing site within days of the sighting. Photo courtesy of CUFOS. Photo by Mark Rodeghier.

T/Sgt. David Moody was also in Socorro on Sunday (April 26).[23] Moody was assigned to Project Blue Book and had conducted other field investigations for the project for several years. Moody, along with Major William Conner, the Kirtland AFB public relations officer, who has also been identified as the local UFO officer, checked the landing site for radiation but didn't find any evidence of that. They apparently also attempted to find radar confirmation of the object but failed there as well, probably for the reasons stated above.

Hynek, of course, hadn't arrived in Socorro until Tuesday evening, April 28th, after being alerted by the chief of Project Blue Book, Captain Hector Quintanilla. The Air Force car taking Hynek from Kirtland Air Force Base in Albuquerque to Socorro had a flat tire. Hynek had to hitch-hike into town. Once there, he had the opportunity to interview Zamora and Chavez late that evening. They made plans for a reenactment of the events the next day. Hynek would later report that the area had been trampled by tourists and sightseers. He said, "The area certainly has been thoroughly messed up by tourists. There's nothing to see there now."[24]

But it seems that all was not well with Hynek and the police officers in Socorro. According to a memo Hynek wrote on May 20th, 1964:

> Found Zamora & Chavez were very anti-AF. I got rid of the AF people & got the story from them that night at the jail. (A slow process—they were not eager to talk at first.) The next morning we went & reenacted it at the spot. An NICAP (*National Investigations Committee on Aerial Phenomena*) person (Ray Stanford) was already there & and lent me some bottles for taking specimens. I have brought nothing.
>
> Z. is an unimaginative cop of an old Socorro family, incapable of hoax, and pretty sore at being regarded as a romancer. It took at least ½ an hour to thaw him out....
>
> The marks left on the ground: 4 rectangular scrapings as if a rectangular object had scraped along digging into the ground—deeper at the end. The gouging was done away from the center in every case. The arrangement was not regular, but the diagonals were perfectly at right angles.[25]

Ray Stanford, who at the time lived in Phoenix, Arizona, and was a member of NICAP, also arrived late on that Tuesday, much later than Hynek. He had talked to Zamora at some point prior to that, probably before he left Phoenix. Early on Wednesday morning, he called Zamora at home, only to be told that Zamora was still asleep. He called again about 30 minutes later and was told that Zamora was unavailable. Stanford finally just drove to the police station to try to find him.

Ray Stanford with *Propanoplosauras marylandicus* exhibit at the Smithsonian NMNH. Stanford was on the scene within days of the sighting and spoke to the principals, including Lonnie Zamora, the other police officers, and Dr. Hynek. Photo courtesy of Ray Stanford.

Zamora wasn't there. Stanford talked to the morning dispatcher, Mike Martinez, and was told that Zamora had seen two figures in white and that one had turned toward him and "sorta jumped." Martinez also said that Zamora was to the point that he didn't want to talk to anyone about what he had seen given his treatment by some of those who had interviewed him over the last several days and some of the things that he had seen written about him in various newspapers.

Stanford said that Zamora had promised to meet him, and Martinez finally volunteered that Zamora was on the south side of town. Stanford pointed out that this could only mean one thing and asked that Martinez use his radio. Chavez answered the call but said they didn't want anyone else out there while Hynek was on the scene investigating. Hynek apparently broke in and said to let Stanford come out, but that he was to come alone.

Hynek apparently welcomed Stanford to the site and they discussed, briefly, some evidence from another case. Zamora pointed out where the object had come from and how it had exited the area while Hynek took some pictures. Finally, Hynek said that he wanted to collect some samples but he had nothing in which to collect them. Stanford had brought some vials and offered to let Hynek use them. I have no idea why Hynek wished to collect samples. According to Holder, he gave all that material (that is, the samples he had collected) to Hynek. Holder apparently retained nothing once Hynek and Moody arrived.

While Stanford was collecting samples, Hynek said that he wanted to find some of the paper or other material had been burned by the craft landing and taking off. The only paper in the area looked as if it had been outside for a very long time and had nothing to do with the UFO landing. Both Chavez and Zamora mentioned that the curiosity seekers and other tourists had cleaned the site of anything useful that had been there. This means, of course, by the time Hynek arrived in his capacity as the scientific consultant and Stanford arrived as the NICAP representative, much that might have been useful had been taken away by those who had no real official standing. They were souvenir hunters and anything they picked up was lost to the official investigation.

Stanford listened as Hynek asked additional questions. He wondered if the landing gear marks might not have been created by prospectors. Zamora said that they corresponded to the locations where he had seen the landing gear touch down.[26]

Stanford was standing with Hynek, Zamora, and Chavez near one of the imprints when Zamora pointed to a broken stone inside the imprint with markings on it. Zamora thought that the landing gear might have hit the rock, scraped it, and broken it, leaving small metallic traces behind. Hynek didn't seem impressed with it, but Stanford thought there might be some sort of physical evidence on it that could be tested.[27]

Stanford related the discovery of the rock in a slightly different fashion. He said that Zamora had spotted the broken rock,
pointing it out. Stanford wrote, "I tried to conceal my interest in
Zamora's discovery. I reasoned, if the object's landing gear had
pressed so hard on a rock to break the edge of it, there must be
some trace, even if minute, of metal or foreign substance scraped
off onto the surface of that rock!"[28]

Stanford noted Hynek's lack of interest in the rock. He believed that if he expressed an interest, Hynek might take custody
of it and then, by default, the Air Force would end up with this
possibly important bit of physical evidence. Stanford then told
Hynek that he was supposed to be at a press conference at the
motel and, to distract them even further, asked if they would like
to see some UFO slides that he had brought with him.

Not long after the press conference in a local hotel room finished, Hynek returned to Albuquerque to catch a plane back to
Evanston and Northwestern University. With Hynek gone and
the police officers occupied with their official duties, Stanford
returned to the landing site. The rock was still there. He began
to photograph it from various angles before he removed it and
repeated the photographic process afterward so there would be
complete documentation about the rock. He wrapped the rock in
newspapers thinking that if anything fell from it, it would fall into
the paper. Stanford wrote: "I pushed surface dirt into the large
cavity where the rock had been. If this were a policeman or intelligence officer [who had driven up as he pried the rock out of the
ground], and if he should venture down into the ravine and see
the fresh hole, trouble might be generated by his asking what I
had removed. After all, there might be some legal technicality by
which authorities could ensnare me."[29]

Once he had succeeded in getting the rock to his car, Stanford
drove back into Socorro for dinner with radio station reporter
Walter Shrode. It was during this dinner that Stanford was introduced to the two women who heard the UFO on April 24.

On Thursday, April 30, Stanford was able to interview Zamora. The first thing he asked was about the press conference the day before. He said that Hynek had told the reporter that Zamora had not been told by anyone to say nothing about the symbol he had seen.

According to Stanford, Zamora's response was emphatic: "No! I didn't tell him that."

Zamora then said the same thing that he had told the Lorenzens on Saturday: "Yes, I'd say someone told me it would be best if I don't tell about the shape on the side...."

But then Zamora seemed reluctant to answer any questions, not even telling Stanford the shape of the craft which had already been widely reported. Zamora said that they might not want him to say anything about that.[30]

The "they" in all this is probably Byrnes and Holder, though neither had any real authority to stop Zamora from talking to anyone about it. What is more likely here, given some of the things that Zamora had said previously and things he would say later, is that he was tired of answering questions and he was tired of the whole thing. He wished he had never said anything about it and wished it would just go away.[31]

Stanford didn't have much more time in Socorro. But before he could leave, one of the other members of the police force, holding a copy of the *Albuquerque Journal*, said that Hynek had called Zamora a liar by saying that no one in the Air Force had told him not to talk about the sighting. Stanford pointed out that those who had suggested that Zamora withhold details weren't in the Air Force, but in the Army and FBI. But he added that, in the press conference the day before, Hynek had not qualified the statement in any way.[32]

After his aborted interview with Zamora, Stanford left town.

Although the police officer had said, according to Stanford, that Hynek had better not return to town because he "might get his butt chased right back out," Hynek did return on August 15th. He told those in Socorro that he was traveling from Las Cruces to

Boulder on some sort of inspection of observatories and, because
the route took him through town, he decided to stop to ask a few
additional questions.

According to Hynek's report, "Socorro Revisited," the object
of his visit was to "obtain an overview of the feelings and opinions
about the Zamora sighting of April 24th, after several months had
passed, and to find out if the principals had any afterthoughts or
changes which they wished to make to their story, how they were
now regarded by the townfolk (sic), and what if any was the official
opinion."[33]

There is nothing new in the report. Hynek interviewed a number of local residents who said that Zamora was a reliable source
and that they believed him. Hynek wrote, "Although I made
a distinct attempt to find a chink in Zamora's armor, I simply
couldn't find anyone with the possible exception of a Mr. Philips[34]
who has a house fairly near the site of the original sighting, who
did anything but completely uphold Zamora's character and reliability, and I again talked with people who had known him since
childhood."[35]

Hynek visited the landing site again and saw that the indentations were still visible. He talked to various participants in the
sighting and aftermath, but didn't seem to conduct any real interviews. He noted that Holder "is still quite enthusiastic and really
fairly enamored of the idea of strange crafts."[36]

He did make one stop that could have relevance to later enqui-
ries about the landing. He wrote:

Before we left, we called Dr. Wartman, the retiring president
of the New Mexico School of Mine's [sic], who had nothing
further to offer. Before our visit with Captain Holder, on
coming back from the site, we visited a Mr. Philips who lives
fairly close to the site of the alleged landing. Mr. Philips
had been in his back yard just over the hill from the sighting place, and maintains that he heard no loud roar and
has remained skeptical about the whole thing. He claimed

that if there had been an explosion such as Zamora claims to have heard, he (Philips) certainly would have heard it. However, this does not necessary follow, because Zamora was directly down wind from the gully, there was a very strong southwest wind blowing, and the gully is on the opposite side of the hill from where Mr. Philips was listening.... He was the only person we talked to, however, who tended to disbelieve Zamora's veracity."[37]

Hynek returned to Socorro in March 1965, but the trip was a replay of his last one. He talked to a number of people but learned nothing that had not been in his "Socorro Revisited" report written months earlier.

The official investigations had ended with Hynek's last visit to Socorro. There had been civilian research conducted by the Lorenzens and Ray Stanford. In the years that followed, others took an interest in the case but there was no additional intensive investigation until the early 21st century when Ben Moss and Tony Angiola decided to see if they could learn anything new.

They did interview Ray Stanford, who told them that Chavez had arrived in time to see the object in the sky. Then Stanford added that he hadn't learned that from Chavez himself but that every member of the Socorro law enforcement establishment he talked to said that Chavez saw the object.[38]

Moss and Angiola also talked about the symbol seen on the side of the craft and suggested reasons that the case wasn't a hoax. Using Project Blue Book files that Rob Mercer had located, radio and television footage about the case, and their interviews with Stanford, they concluded, as did those with Blue Book, and that there is no terrestrial object or project that would account for the sighting. That is the way it has been for more than half a century.

Chapter 5:
Other New Mexico UFO Reports

Prior to the UFO report made by Lonnie Zamora, there had been a single sighting in New Mexico in April. The UFO was seen over Texas, Wyoming, Colorado, and New Mexico. The Project Blue Book files labeled it as "astro," which in this case meant meteor and, given the descriptions and the wide area of the report, that doesn't seem all that unreasonable. After Socorro there were a number of landing reports and other sightings made in New Mexico and a few in other states that were similar to what Zamora had claimed.

Within hours of Zamora's sighting there was another landing in New Mexico, this one in La Madera, northwest of Espanola, which itself is near Los Alamos.[1] According to the documentation available in the Project Blue Book files and other sources,

Orlando Gallegos had gone outside to chase away some horses when he saw an object sitting on the ground about 200 feet away. He said that he was afraid to get any closer. When he first saw it, there was a ring of blue flames erupting from jets around the bottom of the object. Later he would suggest that the blue flames were tinged with orange. He heard no sound, and as he watched the flames died. Unlike Zamora, he didn't see anyone or anything around the craft.

Gallegos returned to the house to tell his father and the rest of the family what he had seen. They either laughed at him or were all too frightened to go back to look, but Gallegos himself went back out twice to verify his sighting. He said that it appeared to be made of bright metal without windows. It resembled a butane tank that was as long as a telephone pole. Finally, he gave up and went to bed. The next morning it when he went out to look again, the object was gone.

There was more information found in the Project Blue Book file. According to an article there:

[H]e noted an unusual craft resting upon the ground in a gravel area some 200 feet distant. The UFO was reported to be the length of a telephone pole, with a circumference of 14 feet. Rings of blue flame emitted from jets about its underside....

The next morning, however, they all examined the landing area, noticing the ground to be still fumy from the previous night.

State Police Captain Martin Virgin [sic], upon checking the charred area, noticed that the rocks present within the center of that landing site were cracked, and a bottle nearby had melted. Green brush in the surrounding area had been set afire, evidently from intense heat. Four depressions and unusual "paw-prints," resembling those of a Mountain Lion, were also seen.

The Air Force, although having sent investigators into the area, has thus far remained silent on their findings, if any.[2]

That next afternoon, according to Coral Lorenzen, as reported in *The A.P.R.O. Bulletin*, as Gallegos was heading back home in La Madera, he heard about the Socorro landing. He stopped in Espanola and told police officer Nick Naranjo about the UFO. He then told the same tale about what he had seen to State Police Officers Marvin Romero and David Kingsbury.

State Police Captain Martin E. Vigil learned about the sighting from the other police officers and in turn sent another officer, Albert Vega from Ojo Caliente, to the landing site. When Vega reported that something unusual was at the scene both Vigil and Kingsbury joined him.[3] Vigil would later say:

> At the time [about 7:30 pm.], the ground was still smoldering and badly scorched. Officer Vega advised that he had observed four impressions on the ground, one of which was quite clear, the others having been obliterated due to windy weather conditions. Officer Vega stated that this depression was approximately eight by twelve inches in size, about three or four inches deep, sort of "V" shaped at the bottom.
>
> There were also oval shaped, or "cat-paw like" markings around the scorched area. These were approximately three and one-half inches in diameter.[4]

Vigil added some detail in his conversation with Coral Lorenzen. According to her, when he arrived on the scene he saw that the area was still hot and smoking. There was glass that looked as if it had been melted. He said that there was an area about 35 or 40 feet in diameter that was scorched and smoldering.

One of the police officers, Kingsburg, took color photographs, "which ARPO obtained but which showed nothing."[5]

Martin would confirm to others that there had been something out near that house. He told the United Press International, "There was definitely something there."[6]

Vigil also told Lorenzen that Major William Connors, the public affairs officer from Kirtland Air Force Base who had been in Socorro, had traveled to La Madera to interview Gallegos. Interestingly, Hynek, who was in New Mexico investigating the Socorro case at the time, apparently couldn't get permission from the Air Force to travel north to interview Gallegos.

In a letter dated April 27, 1964, Major John C. McNeill, quoted from an Officer of the Day report on the same date:

> AFSC Command Post called at 1645 [4:45 p.m.] relaying a UFO report as follows: At approximately 0130 local time near Espanola, N.M. on 26 April a Ranger's son observed an object emitting flames and noise. His father sent him back to bed. The next morning the Ranger and his son investigated the area near where the object was sighted. The grass was burned and still smoldering and there were footprints in the vacinity [sic]. They notified the state police and Kirtland AFB. The prints were similar to those reported on the 25th April at Socorran [sic], N.M. Personnel from Kirtland are at the site now.[7]

Doyle Akers, a reporter for the *Santa Fe New Mexican*, also examined the spot. He wrote:

> At the scene itself the charred area was a peculiar shape, like two overlapping circles. It was about 20 feet across. Large rocks within the area showed evidence of extreme heat, while others within a few feet weren't damaged at all.

• •

A soft drink bottle had melted with another five feet away was intact.... An attempt to set fire to a chamisa brush nearby failed.[8]

There was another sighting in that area about the same time that Gallegos saw his object. According to Lorenzen, "a glowing object which 'buzzed' two unidentified men in a car near La Madera Sunday morning. This sighting was made to State Police before the Gallegos sighting came to light."[9]

Vega also remembered that he had found a group of drunken young people who had been at a dance in Ojo Caliente. According to Vega they would have passed near La Madera, but they had seen nothing. When he found the landing spot it was still smoking and he told Dick Thomas, "That area wouldn't start burning from a match or cigarette. You'd have to have some kind of gasoline or chemical to make it burn like that. But I don't think anybody would be out starting a fire at 1 o'clock in the morning."[10]

The Air Force did investigate, and did reach a conclusion. They believed the sighting had been inspired by a fire set on a dumping ground. According to the project card in the Project Blue Book files, "Witness reported seeing an obj emitting flames. Police called to investigate. No noise. Obj stationary. Light suddenly went out. Much publicity following Socorfo [sic] sighting. Witness had been drinking heavily.... Area where light was used as a dumping area. Burned spot at this location."[11]

Their conclusion: "Fire in Dump."

In 1970, in a United Press International report, there was a quote from Emilio Naranjo, who was the sheriff in Rio Arriba County in 1964: "Our investigation showed that three or four young boys had been washing a car at the river and started a fire to burn the rags they had used. That was the flying saucer Gallegos saw."[12]

There seems to be no sign of an Air Force investigation. The case file is thin, made up of copies of articles from newspapers and UFO organization publications. There are no indications of where the idea that there was a dump in the area came from; it might simply be the reference to the soft drink bottles found in the area. There are no reliable sources to suggest that Gallegos was drunk that night, no names attached to the boys washing a car and setting rags on fire, and no reasonable explanation for the case. Coming so close as it did to that from Socorro, it seemed to add a note of credibility to the La Madera case, but it also seems that much of the information missed the mainstream press of the time and the thin case files suggests that the Air Force was uninterested in the report.

Holloman Air Force Base UFO Landing

The Zamora sighting did seem to inspire others. That is not to say that these new witnesses were inventing their tales, only that they were now reporting what they had seen because there was an interest in these sightings. It could also mean that there were additional unidentified craft flying around New Mexico and that, too, explains the surge in sightings.

In what was, in the beginning, a somewhat mundane sighting with a possibility of a landing has grown into something more grandiose over the years. On April 30, 1964, nearly one week after the Zamora sighting, an unidentified pilot of a B-57 bomber was on a routine mission near the Stallion Site (a site that Captain Holder headed up on the White Sands Proving Ground), when he called his mission control, asking if he was alone.

They asked, "What do you mean?"

The pilot said, "I've got a UFO." He then said, "It's egg-shaped and white."

He couldn't see any markings and said that he was going to make another pass at it. He turned and flew over the area where he had seen the object and reported, "It's now on the ground." At that point communications with the control was lost.[13]

There seems to be no additional information about who the pilot was, how many of the crew might have seen the UFO, and if any sort of attempt to reach the UFO was made by those on the ground. Lorenzen apparently didn't follow up on the sighting and the case does not appear in the Project Blue Book files except as "information only."

During that limited investigation conducted by Lorenzen, and in communication with Terry Clarke of Alamogordo radio station KALG and Arlynn Bruer, a reporter for the *Alamogordo News,* it was learned that an airman had told others of a UFO in a guarded hangar at Holloman Air Force Base, which is not far south of Socorro. Clarke had said that an airman shopping in downtown Alamogordo had told several people in one of the stores about the UFO. A day or two later the airman returned, saying that he had been mistaken about the UFO. He said there was nothing like that at Holloman. He had been told by officers at the base to go back and explain the situation.[14]

Lorenzen speculated that the airman's tale of the UFO was probably truer than not. She wrote that she doubted the Air Force would have the ability to capture a flying saucer. She thought that the airman might have heard about the landed UFO and seen a guarded hangar on the base, and leaped to a conclusion about a UFO in a hangar. If the story wasn't true, there seemed to be no reason for the officers at Holloman to order the airman to retract the story. If it wasn't true, why should they care?

But the story doesn't end there, and it gets even bigger. Rumors began to spread that the landing had not been in the desert of the White Sands Missile Range, which is co-located with Holloman, but on the base proper. The alien craft had actually landed on the airfield.

Then, in early 1973, Robert Emenegger and Allan Sandler said they had been approached by Air Force officers asking if they would be interested in a documentary on a secret U.S. government project that dealt with UFOs. When the men suggested they might be, they were shown photographs and films of UFOs and the occupants of them.[15]

They said they were invited to Norton Air Force Base,[16] where the head of the Air Force Office of Special Investigation (AFOSI) and Paul Shartle, who was a security officer at Norton, met them. Emenegger and Sandler were told that there are been a landing at Holloman in April 1964, or maybe in May 1971; the exact date was never made clear. The landing had been by prior arrangement, suggesting there was communication between the Air Force and the occupants of the UFOs. The landing was filmed, as would be expected, and Emenegger and Sandler were promised several hundred feet of film for their documentary. Then, suddenly, permission was withdrawn. It was the political climate around Watergate that caused the trouble, at least according to the reports being made.

Emenegger told the tale of the Holloman incident in his 1974 book, *UFOs Past, Present and Future*:

> We are in the operations tower at Holloman Air Force Base at the landing field.
>
> We hear, over an intercom, a voice: "Check list April... Charlie four standing by." From within the tower, we hear a control operator giving some data to a pilot: Wind, north-easterly—two knots. Temperature sixty-eight degrees, visibility ten miles and clearing." Behind the operator's voice, airmen are making small talk about the lousy coffee.
>
> The day is clear. It's about 5:30 a.m. Traffic is light; one recon plane is on the field ready for takeoff when the tower phone rings and Sergeant Mann is given a report of an approaching unidentified craft.
>
> We shift to the radar hut. On the scope several blips appear as the radar scans to the sky. The radarman leans into his phone: "I'll repeat it again—unidentified approaching objects—on coordinate forty-niner—thirty-four degrees southwest following an erratic approach course."[17]

After watching the object, and attempting to identify it, they alerted the base commander, identified in the scenario as Colonel Horner. He wanted to know if the aircraft had been warned about entering Holloman or White Sands restricted airspace and wanted to know if Edwards Air Force Base in California had been contacted. Edwards was where many advanced design aircraft were tested.[18] Then two fighters were alerted, and launched to intercept and escort the unidentified craft from the restricted area.

There was a helicopter with cameramen, a technical sergeant, and a staff sergeant who had their equipment with them and were able to take several feet of film of three unidentified objects. One of them broke away from the other two and began a rapid descent. By coincidence, there was a second crew, this one using a high-speed camera to record a test launch in the White Sands area. They exposed some 600 feet of color film of the landing.

The UFO hovered for a moment, and then touched down on three landing gear. A hatch opened and one being, then a second and finally a third stepped out. They wore tight-fitting flight suits, and had a blue-gray complexion, widely spaced eyes, and large pronounced noses. They wore some sort of helmet or head piece of a rope-like design.

All of this is a reconstruction of the "real" events that supposedly happened and part of the film footage shown to Emenegger and Sandler. It seems that some of those reading Emenegger's book believed that the reconstruction presented was accurate, and it is possible that the landing at Holloman reported by Lorenzen in 1964 and the publication of Emenegger's book led to the conclusion that the event had happened as described. What had begun as a landing that had no names attached to it other than those in the Alamogordo area who had attempted to verify the rumors became much more than it should have been.

But there is an addendum to all of this. Timothy Good, as he was preparing his book, *Alien Contact*, said that he had verified some of the information. During the syndicated program *UFO Cover-Up? Live*, Emenegger, interviewed for the show, had said,

"What I saw and heard was enough to convince me that the phenomenon of UFOs is real—very real." Good said that Emenegger had told him the same thing.[19]

Paul Shartle, the former head of security and chief of requirements for the audio visual program at Norton, said:

> I saw footage of three disc-shaped crafts. One of the craft landed.... It appeared to be in trouble because it oscillated all the way down to the ground.... A sliding door opened, a ram was extended, and out came three aliens.... They were human size. They had odd gray complexions and a pronounced nose. They wore tight-fitting jumpsuits, thin headdresses that appeared to be communication devices, and in their hands held a translator, I was told. The Holloman base commander and other Air Force officers went out to meet them."[20]

You might say that Shartle giveth and then taketh away. He also said, "I was told it was theatrical footage that the Air Force had purchased to make a training film."[21] The overriding fact in this is that he did confirm the existence of the film.

Later still, Richard Doty, who had been in the AFOSI, mentioned to Linda Moulton Howe that the Holloman Landing had taken place on April 25, 1964, some 12 hours after Lonnie Zamora had seen the landed craft near Socorro. This, according to Doty, had been an error on the part of the alien flight crew. The craft was not supposed to land in Socorro but at Holloman some distance to the south. Doty had now provided a third date for the landing, but Doty's credibility suffered with his involvement in the MJ-12 controversy, questions about the end of his association with the AFOSI, the completion of his military career, and his association with Bill Moore. All that means is that his confirmation of the Holloman landing is not particularly persuasive.

More New Mexico Sightings

There were a number of additional sightings in the hours and days after Zamora saw the landed UFO. Few of them were either reported to the Air Force or made their way into the Project Blue Book files as "information only" cases, which was a way of acknowledging their existence without having to do anything about them. For example, from *The UFO Report,* a newsletter that reprinted UFO information, published in summer 1964, came a sighting from Socorro that a trucker driver, Napoleon Green, and his wife had seen two egg-shaped objects about 5:30 p.m. on April 27 about 17 miles north of Socorro.

According to the newspaper article noted in *The UFO Report,* Green said, "I wasn't going to report it because I didn't want to believe my eyes."

His wife dived beneath the dashboard after seeing the objects that were moving as fast as a jet and about half that size with one following the other. They were shining brightly in the setting sun, but there was no visible smoke. They were in sight for about two minutes before disappearing over the eastern horizon.[22]

In Hobbs, New Mexico, on April 28, several children said they had seen a white, circular object hovering over the city before it moved off toward the northeast.

Another report on the same day and at the same time came from two unidentified adults who were about twelve blocks from where the children had made their sighting.[23]

In Las Cruces, also on April 28, a state police officer, Paul Arteche, and four employees at the state port of entry on Interstate 10 south of the city, sighted a luminous object moving in a jerky motion. A private pilot said he had seen the same thing between 10:00 and 10:30 p.m.[24]

There were other sightings as well. Newspaper reports on April 28 included information that was sketchy at best and certainly not as spectacular as with the Zamora or the Gallegos sightings.

George Mitropolis of Albuquerque said that he had seen a "silver looking" object. It disappeared over the mountains.[25]

According to Socorro police officer Bill Pyland, an unidentified 18-year-old girl said that she had seen a fire in the hills to the southwest of Socorro on Sunday night, April 26, 1964. She said that she approached to within 200 or 300 feet of the fire when she saw something in flames. She left the area to report it to the police who searched the area but found no sign of a fire and nothing out of place.[26]

The question always becomes: What inspired all these sightings? Was it a reaction to Zamora? Were there more objects flying around and therefore more sightings? Were people now looking up and therefore seeing things that they wouldn't have noticed before? Was it that they knew where to report their sighting or that the newspapers now took those sightings seriously and reported them? Or were people seeing things that were mundane and misidentifying them? Or did it give people an idea and lead to them inventing their sightings for reasons of publicity or because they thought there was money to be made?

The Hoaxes

A number of stories were reported in the newspaper that might have had their inspiration in the Zamora tale but that were not based on reality. One that seemed to get the biggest play was that of 10-year-old Sharon Stull, who said that she had been burned by a UFO. The story was somewhat reminiscent of that told by James Stokes in November 1957. Stokes said that he was traveling toward El Paso, Texas, from Holloman Air Force Base when his radio faded and his car stalled near Orogrande, New Mexico, which is not all that far from the gate to the White Sands Missile Range.

Stokes said that he noticed other cars stopped along the side of the road and pulled in behind them. Outside there was some sort of object flying overhead, into and out of the clouds. When the object finally disappeared, his car started normally and he continued his trip to El Paso. That evening, he noticed a slight burn on his face and arms, as if he had been out in the sun a little too long. When he was interviewed later that evening by Terry Clarke and the Lorenzens, they all noticed a slight reddening of Stokes's skin. Two days later, when he was examined at the Holloman base hospital, there was no sign of the burn. It is clear from their reporting of the incident that the Lorenzens and Clarke believed that Stokes was telling the truth about what he had seen and the burn he had suffered. Neither the Lorenzens nor Clarke found a real reason to dismiss Stokes's sighting. Although there were other witnesses to the sighting, according to Stokes, none have ever come forward or been located.[27]

With the case of Sharon Stull, who was burned on the face while watching an egg-shaped craft on April 28, the same can't be said. The Lorenzens were involved almost from the beginning, interviewed the various principals, and came to their conclusions that seemed to be the opposite of what they normally discovered.[28]

According to the story, Stull had come home for lunch and then walked back to school. While there with her sister Robin, she saw the white, egg-shaped object flying overhead. She pointed it out to the other children but they all seemed to be uninterested. She continued to watch it for about 10 minutes as it circled around before she headed in to class.[29]

When she got home that evening, Stull began to complain about some pain in her eyes. She was taken to the hospital, treated for sunburn, and sent home. Although her neck and hands had been exposed, there were no burns reported there.

Coral and Jim Lorenzen traveled to Albuquerque to interview the girl and her family. They talked to the doctor, calling him from the Stulls' house, and learned that the burn would be about the same as that after eight hours of exposure to the sun.

Continuing the investigation, they interviewed Lieutenant Jolly of the Albuquerque Police Department. He told Jim that the other children who were cited as witnesses said that they hadn't seen anything at all. Those other children included Stull's sister.

Lorenzen reported that Stull's mother seemed more interested in "parlaying her daughter's experience into money." Stull's mother actually called Lonnie Zamora, questioning him about what he had seen. Lorenzen wrote:

> During the conversations with Mrs. Stull, she consistently called the one TV announcer a "good friend" and the Doctor their "family doctor." The truth of the matter was that the TV announcer had not seen the Stulls since he had got help for them in January [they had arrived in Albuquerque from Los Angeles in January without money], until the burn case came up. The Doctor had never seen the Stulls until he was called in to take case of Sharon, as a result of the "burn" from the UFO.
>
> One thing notable during the visit with the Stulls was that the story tended to get more involved and "stickier" as the Lorenzens expressed their interest in the minute details. Mrs. Stull did all the talking, except to occasionally say to Mr. Stull, "Isn't that right, Max?"...to which he would give an affirmative answer. The L's [Lorenzens] had a difficult time questioning Robin (never did succeed there) and Sharon. Mrs. Stull repeatedly had suggested they not talk too much about the case, and their rights were being trod on.[30]

Although the Lorenzens were firm believers in alien visitation and were among the first to embrace the idea of alien abduction, they were quick to close this case. Coral Lorenzen wrote, "The whole thing was preposterous and the Lorenzens were hard put to understand the kind of people who would attempt to perpetrate such a fraud."[31]

The Air Force investigation of the case doesn't seem to have been very extensive. On the project card, they wrote, "Extensive news accounts of sighting flying saucer with green men. Witness

12-year-old girl. Supposedly burned by ray guns from obj. Seen from school yard. Noon recess."[32]

This does provide an insight into the thought process among the Project Blue Book staff in 1964. Sharon Stull was 10, and she said nothing about seeing any sort of being, including "little green men," nor anything about ray guns. Their investigation seemed to have been based solely on what Coral Lorenzen had published, what the newspapers in Albuquerque published, and what various other UFO group newsletters reported. They did write the case off as "imagination," and in the master index as a "hoax." This seems to be a case in which they arrived at the correct conclusion but took the wrong road to get there.

In the same Blue Book file with this tale is information about another UFO incident, which also has its own folder. Whereas the Albuquerque case is labeled as "imagination," this one, from Edgewood, New Mexico, is labeled as a "hoax." According to the newspapers, Don Adams told law enforcement officials that he had seen an object about a hundred feet off the ground. He said it appeared to be a fluorescent or glowing green-colored object about 25 feet long.

He said that he had driven under the UFO and his car stalled. He got out, grabbed his revolver, fired six shots, reloaded, and fired another six. The first six, he said, hit the object, but it had begun to move to the north so he didn't know if the next six did. At any rate, the bullets apparently had no effect on the craft.

The Project Blue Book card said, "Police investigated. Witness was drunk but no arrest could be made for discharging firearm because witness was on own property. Witness regarded as unreliable and case judged to be a hoax."

There is nothing in the Blue Book files and nothing in the UFO literature to suggest that this case was anything but a hoax. It is another example of the Air Force getting it right, though it seems they only communicated with the local police but given the information, there seemed to be no reason to investigate further.

During that same month of April, the Albuquerque newspapers reported on a man who claimed to have seen flying saucers five times. He also said that he had talked with the alien crew twice. The man, Apolinar A. (Paul) Villa said, "I don't know why they picked me. I'm just an ordinary working man."[33]

Villa did provide some predictions about the coming year, which was 1964 to 1965. He said that we should expect "large-scale" volcanic activity. More importantly, he said there would be a "catastrophic" war between China and Russia that would involve many of the Asian nations. We now know that these did not come to pass, which said something about the reliability of the information.

He said that the aliens came from the "far-distant galaxy of Coma Berenices, imaginably far distant from here."[34] That, of course, is a star cluster in the Milky Way and not a distant galaxy.

Villa did take photographs of the alien craft, and copies of those photographs were obtained by the Air Force. The photographs were taken on June 16, 1963, and analyzed by the Air Force.

Captain William L. Turner, chief of the Air Force Photo Analysis Division, wrote in his official report, "All [Villa's] photographs have a sky background with an unobstructed view of the object. It seems unlikely that anyone photographing a UFO from several angles would have all good, clear unobstructed photographs of the object."[35]

It might be suggested that Villa was just a very good photographer, or he might have been lucky, which would explain the clear shots. Turner, however, provided some other information that seemed to prove the case for a hoax. He wrote:

Photograph #7 shows the UFO at close range with a leafless branch on the left side of the print, passing behind the object. Two twigs from this branch are readily visible on the right side of the object and in good alignment with the main branch. It does not seem possible that these twigs are from the tree on the right which is further away. Therefore, the object is between the branch and the camera. The object is estimated to be 20 inches in diameter and seven inches high.[36]

Turner also noted that in photographs numbers 1 and 2 "the object appears to be a sharper image than the near and far trees. This indicates the UFO is between the near trees and the camera."[37]

Given that the photographs are hoaxes, and given Villa's somewhat shady background, it would seem that the Air Force analysis is once again verified. Other UFO researchers have come to the same conclusions. The newspaper reported that Villa's home had burned down but he had no insurance, he accidentally shot himself in the arm and he had been through a bankruptcy. Though it could be argued that all these events are just bad luck, it does suggest something about the man.

Analysis

It could be argued that Lonnie Zamora's sighting inspired these other reports. Some of them actually occurred before Zamora but weren't reported until after the media told his story. Some of them, especially that by Orlando Gallegos, seemed to hit the media about the same time. It is interesting that Gallegos reported the same sort of landing gear impressions that Zamora had seen. This one fact doesn't seem to have been co-opted by Gallegos, because when he made his report, that facts of Zamora's sighting weren't widely known. Others, including the local sheriff, saw the impressions, which verifies their existence.

Other cases were just sightings of objects in and around the Socorro area or along the highway that ran from El Paso in Texas up through Albuquerque. The trouble is that once the Zamora landing had received national attention, it is impossible to determine if that inspired others to report strange things they had seen, if they began to search the sky for something to see and misinterpreted natural phenomena, or as show, some were just inspired to make up something.

Chapter 6:
Other "Unidentified" Occupant Sightings

It has been a matter of faith in the last few decades that there was a single UFO sighting that involved entities in the Project Blue Book files that was labeled as "unidentified."[1] That statement is untrue. There are other cases in which the witnesses reported entities that were labeled as "unidentified," but there are many more such reports that were dismissed as "psychological problems," meaning that the investigators did not believe that an alien craft was seen or that the crew of that craft had been spotted by the witnesses. The Air Force thought the people had mental problems if they saw any extraterrestrial entities and sometimes just reporting the craft on the ground was enough for the Air Force to reject the sighting.

These sorts of cases, which involved alien beings and which Dr. J. Allen Hynek had labeled as "Close Encounters of the Third Kind," were rare. As demonstrated with the Lonnie Zamora landing, those who said they had seen creatures from inside the craft outside it, or described beings that were humanoid but not necessarily human, faced an additional problem of credibility. Not only were they claiming to see a craft that didn't seem to have been manufactured on Earth, but now they were claiming to see sentient beings that had not been born on Earth. It added to the ridicule factor, and FBI agent Arthur Byrnes had advised Zamora not to mention seeing creatures for his own protection. As we know, that advice came too late to be of any use to Zamora.

Pittsburg, Kansas (August 25, 1952)

Twelve years before Zamora burst on the scene, William Squyres[2] of Frontena, on his way to Pittsburg, Kansas, said that he had seen, through the windows of a landed craft, "a man" he thought was controlling it. The man was facing forward, toward the edge of the object. The windows were blue that seemed to get darker as time passed.

Squyres said he was driving to work at about 5:30 in the morning on August 25, 1952. He was north of Pittsburg, when he saw an unknown object hovering over a field. He later told Air Force investigators that he began slowing down and he reached a point where the object could be seen out the right-hand window, so he stopped. He said that the hair on the back of his neck stood straight up when he saw it.

Attempting to keep the UFO in sight the whole time, he got out of his car and moved toward the field where the object hovered. He said that after he had shut down his engine, he could hear a deep throbbing sound coming from the craft. When he got to within 150 feet of the object, which he estimated was about 70 feet long and about 12 feet high, it began to lift off. Then veering off into the strange, he said, according the Blue Book file, it looked like an airfoil, which suggested it had the shape of an airplane wing, and there were small propellers around the perimeter, each about a foot in diameter and rotating in a vertical position.[3] It was a dull aluminum in color and had a rather weathered look about it. Squyres said that it was oscillating back and forth about 12 feet above the ground.

Nearly every other description of the craft suggests another shape, a more conventional shape. Hynek, using one of the Air Force reports, wrote that Squyres had described it as "platter shaped, meaning that it was shaped like two platters or bowls put together one over the other, rim to rim."

A newspaper article reported that "Squyres described the saucer as being as long as Broadway is wide downtown [in Pittsburg] and about two thirds as wide as long. It had the shape of two platters placed together."[4]

That changes the description slightly, as another Air Force report quoted by Hynek, said, "He described the object as platter-shaped; by this [he meant to say] [brackets in original] that it looked like two platters or bowls had been put together by reversing one platter and placing it over the first one."[5]

As in the Zamora case, there was physical evidence of the craft's passing. According to the Project Blue Book files:

General area under the exact location was pressed down and form a round 60' diameter impression, with grass in a recognizable concentric pattern. Loose grass lay over the top of the impression as if drawn in by suction when the object ascended vertically at high speed.... Area is extremely dry at present. Grass showed where Squyers (sic) had walked in to a fence and stopped. Squyers said that as he neared it, the object rose vertically to about the altitude that airplanes fly and then accelerated tremendously, straight up into the broken clouds. The sighting lasted about half a minute.[6]

According to the newspaper, "Squyres was driving along the road about dawn when he noticed the saucer hovering near the ground about 100 feet west of the road. As Squyres stopped his car in wonderment at the vision, the saucer rose straight up to disappear in the sky. The backwash of the object whipped the grass and weeds on the ground, according to the report."[7]

In 1952, Squyres had no way of contacting anyone about the sighting from his car. There were no cell phones, and he didn't have a two-way radio. He drove to the radio station, KOAM, and told fellow employees L.V. Baxter and D. Widner what he had seen. They all returned to the landing site some six hours later, at about 11:35 that same morning. Both Baxter and Widner saw Squyres's path to the fence marked by the bent grass and the depression in the tall grass left by the craft.[8]

Another man, Robert E. Greene, visited the landing site some five and a half hours after that, just after 4:00 p.m. that same day. He saw the depression that had been described by the others, though it was now less distinct than it had been. He collected samples of the grass and the soil from where the UFO hovered and from a point some 200 yards away as controls. He submitted some of it to the Air Force for analysis.

Though there are good descriptions of the craft and the landing area, there is little mention made of the pilot. He seemed to be human, and Squyres never said anything to suggest he was anything other than human. He said, "I definitely saw a human being through the window." He was convinced that the object was "piloted by humans, and not some men from Mars."[9]

About the only other thing he did say about the man was he seemed to be frenzied in his activities inside the object. He could see the occupant's head and shoulders through the clear glass of the front of the UFO. He said that in the mid-section, through the blue-tinted windows, there was a lot of activity or movement but he couldn't tell if that was caused by the occupant because there seemed to be no pattern to the movement.

The Project Blue Book file does contain a note about the soil samples taken by Greene, which, of course, confirms that he had been there and had taken samples, but little else. In a short, one-paragraph report, the Air Force technicians said that they had found no radiation, burning, or anything that suggested the grass might have been under stress. There was no indication that the control samples taken in other areas of the field varied from those taken under the craft. Unlike the Zamora case, there was no evidence of burning, and the witness said nothing about a flame as the craft lifted off.

There is another interesting aspect to this case, which undermines the idea that there was nothing classified in the Project Blue Book files. There is a notation that reminds all that there is a regulation that requires all cases that have unknown causes or that have no plausible explanations have information withheld.[10] The cases are not to be discussed with those who do not have the proper clearances while those case that had been identified or had a plausible solution could be discussed with anyone and everyone including members of the media.

Hynek, in his book, gives a glimpse into the attitudes at Project Blue Book at the time of the sighting. He wrote, "My skepticism was so great at that time that I was quite willing to dismiss it as a hallucination."[11] He was willing to overlook the physical evidence that something landed, and he was willing to dismiss the testimony of the men who had seen the landing site and the depression in the grass because he didn't believe that UFOs were alien craft. He was willing to believe that Squyres believed he had seen what he had reported, but he was unwilling to accept the idea that there was no good explanation for it. By the time he got to Socorro 12 years later, his attitude was beginning to change.

Temple, Oklahoma (March 23, 1966)

Slightly less than a year after Lonnie Zamora reported seeing two figures near a landed UFO in New Mexico, William E. Laxson, who worked at Sheppard Air Force Base near Wichita

Falls, Texas, was driving to work early on the morning of March 23, 1966, when he spotted a bright light off to the right. At first, he believed that it was a truck stopped in the far lanes of the highway, but as he approached, he saw a large, what he called a "fish-shaped" craft blocking the road.[12]

Laxson stopped, got out of his car, and began walking toward the object, which was lighted by both his headlights and four bright lights on its side. He thought he was looking at a C-124 without wings but soon realized that he was not looking at any conventional aircraft. The object, according to Laxson, was about 70 or 80 feet long and more than 12 feet high. He could see no sharp edges on it and believed it was resting on some sort of landing gear, but he could only see a single strut. There was a round window divided into four sections that was located about halfway between the front and rear of the craft. Near the front was an open hatch that had a ladder leading up into it. Although he could see inside and there were bright lights on, he could see no detail.

Underneath the craft, Laxson saw a single entity who appeared to be wearing a baseball cap. According to Hayden Hewes, who interviewed Laxson within hours of the sighting, "He [the being] must have heard my car door slam, because he crawled up the ladder in a big hurry. When the door shut, it sounded like metal hitting metal."[13]

Laxson provided a description of the "human." He was about 5 feet 9 inches and weighed about 180 pounds. "He had a fair complexion and was wearing a mechanic's cap with the bill turned up. I got the impression he had three strips arching over his shoulder, something like a master sergeant. I got the impression he was 30–35 years old...he was wearing either coveralls or a two-piece suit that looked like green-colored fatigues."[14]

As did Zamora, Laxson saw markings on the side of the craft. He said that they looked like a "T" over "L" with a four-digit number that he said was either 4738 or 4138 under the letters.

After the "man" got into the craft, it began to rise with the sound like that of a high-speed drill. Laxson said that as it took off that the hair on the back of his head stood up.

Laxson wasn't the only witness. Two miles down the road he found a parked truck. He asked the driver, C.W. Anderson, if he had seen anything. Anderson said that the craft had followed him for about 20 miles; he had been watching it in his rearview mirror. He also said that he had pulled over to get a better look at it and that it had then landed. Anderson confirmed the story to both the Air Force investigators and local newspaper reporters. He didn't, however, fill out the long form (AF Form 117) that the Air Force used to gather information on sightings.[15]

Another truck driver, Bob Stroll, said that he had seen a bright light in the same area about the same time, that is, about 8 miles south of Temple, Oklahoma. No other details were offered, but it did add a third, independent witness to the report.[16]

Laxson, who worked as a civilian for the Air Force and who knew what sort of aircraft were in the inventory, both military and civilian, said that he had never seen anything like it. He added that he was convinced that it was some sort of terrestrial craft though he could not identify just what conventional craft it might have been. Like so many others it seemed that he believed he had seen something from a black or classified project.

J. Allen Hynek provided some additional information about the case in his book, *The Hynek UFO Report*:

Various organizations were contacted around the Temple area for a possible experimental or conventional aircraft. The observer [Laxson] stated that he thought the object was some type of Army or Air Force research aircraft. All attempts at such an explanation proved fruitless, since there were no aircraft in the area at the time of the sighting. Although there are numerous helicopters and other experimental [aircraft] in the area, none could be put in the area of Temple at approximately 0500, 23 March 1966.

• •

Because of this factor the case is listed as unidentified by the Air Force.[17]

Here was a case in which three men, at three separate locations, saw the same object at about the same time. Only Laxson reported seeing any sort of crew, and he thought that crewman looked to be human. This is another of those cases in the Project Blue Book files that include a description of an entity associated with the craft that was accepted at face value by the Air Force investigators. Like the Lonnie Zamora case, the main witness thought it would some sort of black project, but no evidence for that has ever surfaced.

Berlin, Germany (June 17, 1950)

In the United States, this case was reported to the Air Force but had been routed through the CIA in 1952. It included the description of the alien creatures seen in connection with some sort of alien craft. According to Hynek, the information came from a former mayor of Gleimershausen, close to West Berlin, and was filtered through intelligence officers. Hynek reported the story came from a Greek newspaper on July 9, 1952.[18] The date of the sighting, according to other research and documentation, was June 17, 1950. Hynek accepted the report at face value and indicated it was in the Project Blue Book files, but I was unable to confirm this as I began my research.

A number of others have also attempted to find the reference in the Project Blue Book files but have failed to locate it. This suggestion that it was in Project Blue Book has been repeated a number of times. The problem for all of us is that it is not found under the proper date or the proper location. It is found in March 1952 and is listed as "Additional Reported Sightings (Not Cases)," and is listed as Hasselbach, Saxsoni. It is case 1087 in the Project Blue Book index. This explains why it had been so difficult to locate but ultimately found.

The witness, Oskar[19] and his 11-year-old daughter, Gabriella, provided sworn testimony in front of a West German notary, Dr. Oskar Krause, which seemed to have inspired the intelligence officers and a number of newspaper reporters to investigate further.[20] According to some accounts, Linke was said to have described the object as "resembling a huge flying [sic] pan." Better translations of the original German suggested he said it was an "oval warming pan," which doesn't have a handle. It was about 15 meters (50 feet) in diameter and landed in a forest clearing in what was then East Germany.

He told the notary, during his sworn statement, "While I was returning to my home with Gabriella, the tire on my motorcycle blew out near the town of Haselbach.[21]...Gabriella pointed out something that lay at a distance for about a hundred and forty meters away...since it was twilight, I thought she was pointing at a young deer."[22]

He said that he had left his motorcycle near a tree and walked into the forest. As he approached the object, which he now realized was not a deer but two "men who were not more than forty meters away.... They seemed to be dressed in shiny, heavy metallic clothing...like people wear in polar regions."[23] They were stooped over and were looking at something laying on the ground. He later said that one of the men had a lamp on the "front part of his body, which lit up at regular intervals." This sort of description would be reported in other cases such as the Brooksville, Florida, case more than a decade and a half later (detailed in Chapter 7).

Linke continued to walk toward the men and until he was about 30 feet from them. He watched the two men as they seemed to communicate with one another with hand and arm gestures. He couldn't hear them speaking or making any sound.

He would later say he wasn't sure if the figures were human or humanoid. In response to a question asked by Dr. Leon Davidson, who interviewed him about the sighting, he said, "It is difficult to say whether the two forms who stood in front of the object and then flew off were men. I would say they could also have been other creatures since their (manner of) locomotion was a glide, similar to that of bears."[24]

He noticed the UFO looked like a warming pan with two rows of holes along the side, about 12 to 15 inches in circumference. The space between the holes was about 18 inches. There was a black, conning tower like that of a submarine on top that was 10 feet high.

Linke said that at that point, as he had reached the ridge and was lying on the ground watching, his daughter called to him because he had been gone for about 25 minutes. The two men jumped at the sound of the girl's voice. They disappeared inside the conning tower. The side of the object that had holes had opened and began to glitter. It was a green that turned red and at the same time there was a hum. Some have interpreted these lights as flames on the side, which might have given rise to Gabriella's description of a "ring of fire."[25] As the brightness and the hum increased dramatically, the tower began to slide down into the center of the object and the whole craft began to rise, spinning like a top.

There was a cylinder at the bottom, according to what Linke said. As it hovered a few feet off the ground, surrounded by that ring of flames, the cylinder on the bottom disappeared into the craft and then reappeared on the top. As the rate of climb increased, Linke and his daughter heard a whistling sound, like that of falling bombs. It then turned toward a neighboring town, continuing to climb as it disappeared.

Others who lived in the area said that they had seen the object in flight but thought it was a comet or meteor. Georg Derbst, a shepherd, said that he was about a mile and a half from Linke's position when he thought he saw "a comet bounce off the earth."[26]

A sawmill watchman, whose name has been lost, told Linke that he had seen what he thought was a low-flying comet. It flashed away from the hill where Linke and Gabriella had seen the object.[27]

As with the Zamora case, Linke said that he went over to where the craft had been and there found "a circular opening in the ground and it was quite evident that it was freshly dug. It was exactly the shape of the conical tower." He found physical evidence of the passing of the UFO but there wasn't any real investigation of the landing site.

And as was Zamora's, his original thought was that he had seen some new Soviet craft rather than something that had been made on another planet. He said, "I confess that I was seized with fright because the Soviets do not want anyone to know about their work." In fact, he was so frightened by this prospect that he said nothing about any of it until he had defected to the West with his family years later. He suggested that the final motivation for his defection was his fear of the Soviet reaction if they learned what he had seen in the forest.

The problem here, of course, is that the Hynek claimed that this had been part of Project Blue Book. Neither he nor any member of the Blue Book team would have had the opportunity to interview the witness or his daughter given that at the time of the sighting they lived behind the Iron Curtain in East Germany. Hynek's information clearly came from the CIA document, but it is unclear why he thought it part of the main Blue Book file. The CIA document, according to him, was originally classified as secret, which meant that storage of it required a safe. Most of the Blue Book material was unclassified and didn't require a safe.

Hynek offered no real analysis of the report. He wrote, "One of the more interesting but isolated Air Force 'Unidentifieds' came to Blue Book in the form of a (then) secret CIA Document."[28] It suggests that the CIA thought the case interesting, but it could be that the CIA agent who found the newspaper article about the landing forwarded it because it dealt with UFOs and the possible observation of alien beings. There is nothing to suggest the CIA connection was anything more than forwarding the report, and the classification might have been nothing more than a protection for the transmission system rather than an evaluation of the sighting, suggesting an importance to the case that it did not deserve. At any rate, Hynek thought enough of it to publish the information and others have looked into it sporadically. It is not one of the major cases in the UFO literature, though it seems to be more reliable than so many others.

Analysis

All these cases have elements that are similar to those described by Lonnie Zamora. All of them mention landing traces left by the craft that others saw later. Each of them had entities seen with them, and in the Berlin case, the creatures seemed to react in the same way as those did in the Zamora case. In other words, there were two humanoids outside the craft and were startled by the appearance of the witnesses.

Each of them seems to be internally consistent, and there were others who either saw the craft or who saw the landing traces left by it. In these cases, there are multiple chains of evidence from the sighting, to the landing traces, to the analysis of material from the landing sites. Unfortunately, nothing that could be suggested as evidence of alien visitation was found. The soil, rock, and plant samples were simply unexceptional.

In the end, there is no explanation for what was seen. The craft seemed to have otherworldly capabilities, but the entities seen seem to be more human than alien. Even more than half a century after the sightings, and after all the investigation into them, the source of these craft has never been found. If a black project, either Soviet or American, was responsible, no link to it has ever been discovered. Without that, these cases add to the body of the inexplicable.

Chapter 7:
Psychological Solutions

B ack in the early days of UFO investigation, at the beginning of the Air Force's Project Sign, and on through its various incarnations, witnesses who reported seeing the occupants of the spacecraft were almost universally written off as having psychological problems or were virtually ignored with one-page entries. It seems that while the official investigators were quite willing to accept the testimony of strange craft seen at a distance in the sky, if that craft approached the ground or if the crew happened to be visible, then there was clearly something wrong with the witness's ability to identify mundane objects and with his or her mental capabilities.

We've already looked at the very few cases in which these labels were not applied. Now we'll take a look at a few cases in which they were applied and cases relegated to almost nonexistent entries because creatures were reported. I freely admit that some of these sightings are truly weird, but the witnesses seem to be sincere in what they say and what they claim—which, of course, doesn't mean that the report is grounded in reality only that the witness or witnesses truly believe what they are reporting.

Flatwoods, West Virginia (September 12, 1952)

One of the first of the occupant or creature reports to reach Project Blue Book was made from Flatwoods, West Virginia, on September 12, 1952. The Air Force file on the Flatwoods case contains a project card, that form created at ATIC (Advanced Technical Intelligence Center) that holds a brief summary of the sighting, what the solution is if one has been offered, and other such easily condensed data and very little else. According to the project card, the Flatwoods sighting was solved by the meteor that had been reported over the East Coast of the United States on September 12. In fact, the only reference to anything suggesting a creature was on the ATIC Project Card where there is the note about the "West Virginia monster, so called."[1]

All this presents a curious problem. Clearly the Air Force had heard of the case, and just as clearly had written it off as a very bright meteor. There is also a note that the meteor (or meteoroid, for those of a precise and technical nature) landed somewhere in West Virginia (becoming a meteorite).[2] Apparently, the Air Force believed that the "landing" of the meteorite was enough to inspire local residents to imagine a creature on the ground. And, apparently, they believed that the meteorite would account for all the reports of physical evidence by the witnesses.

Ufologist and biologist Ivan T. Sanderson, writing in his UFO book, *Uninvited Visitors,* was aware of both the Air Force explanation and the meteorite that had been reported. Sanderson wrote:

[W]e met two people who had seen a slow-moving reddish object pass over from the east to west. This was later described and "explained" by a Mr. P.M. Reese of the Maryland Academy of Sciences staff, as a "fireball meteor." He concluded—incorrectly we believe—that it was "traveling at a height of from 60 to 70 miles" and was about the "size of your fist."...However, a similar, if not the same object was seen over both Frederick and Hagerstown. Also, something comparable was reported about the same time from Kingsport, Tennessee, and from Wheeling and Parkersburg, West Virginia.[3]

The whole story of the occupant sighting, as it is usually told, begins with several boys playing on a football field in Flatwoods. At about 7:15 p.m., a bright red light "rounded the corner of a hill," crossed the valley, seemed to hover above a hilltop, and then fell behind the hill. One of the boys, Neil (or sometimes Neal) Nunley, said that he thought the glowing object might have been a meteorite. He knew that fragments of meteorites were collected by scientists and might be valuable, so he suggested they all go look for it.[4]

As they watched, there was a bright orange flare that faded to a dull cherry glow near where the object had disappeared. As three of the boys started up the hill, toward the lights, they saw them cycle through the sequence a couple of times. The lights provided a beacon for them, showing them where the object was.

They ran up the main street, crossed a set of railroad tracks, and came to a point where there were three houses, one of them belonging to the May family. Kathleen May came out of the house to learn what was happening and where the boys were going. Told about the lights on the hill, and that "a flying saucer has landed," she said that she wanted to go with them. Before they left, May suggested that Eugene Lemon, a 17-year-old member of the National Guard (which has no real relevance to the story, but is a fact that is always carefully reported) went to look for a flashlight.

They found the path that lead up the hill, opened and then closed a gate, and continued along the winding path. Lemon and

Nunley were in the lead with May and her son Eddie, following, and they were trailed by others including Ronald Shaver and Ted Neal. Tommy Hyer was in the rear, not far behind the others as they climbed the hill.

As they approached the final bend in the path, Lemon's large dog, which had been running ahead, began barking and howling, and then reappeared, running down the hill and obviously frightened. Lemon noticed, as the dog passed him, that a mist was spreading around them. As they got closer to the top of the hill, they all smelled a foul odor. Their eyes began to water.

Some of them reported that they saw, on the ground in front of them, a big ball of fire, described as the size of an outhouse, or about 20 feet across. It was pulsating orange to red. Interestingly, although it was big and bright, not everyone in the tiny party saw it.

Kathleen May spotted something in a nearby tree. She thought they were the eyes of an owl or other animal. Nunley, who was carrying the flashlight, turned it toward the eyes. What they saw was not an animal, but some sort of creature, at least in their perception. The being was large, described as about the size of a full-grown man. They could see no arms or legs, but did see a head that was shaped like an ace of spades. That was a description that would reoccur with all these witnesses. No one was sure if there were eyes on the creature, or if there was a clear space on the head, resembling a window, and that the eyes were somehow behind that window and behind the face.

Lemon reacted most violently of the small party when he saw the object. He passed out. There was confusion, they were all scared, and no one was sure what to do. The boys grabbed the unconscious Lemon and then ran back the way they had come.

They finally reached May's house. Inside, they managed to bring Lemon back to full consciousness. They called others, and a number of adults arrived at the May house. The group, armed with rifles and flashlights, headed back up the hill, to search for the strange creature. None of the men seemed to be too excited about going up the hill, and in less than a half an hour, they were back, claiming they had found nothing at all.

Still others, including the sheriff, eventually arrived at the house. Most didn't bother to mount any sort of search that night, and the sheriff, who was clearly skeptical, refused to investigate further than talking to May and the boys. It is important to note here that the sheriff had been searching for a downed small aircraft reported to him earlier that evening. He found no evidence of an aircraft accident and no one reported any airplanes missing. The relevance of this will become clear later.

Two newspaper reporters, apparently from rival newspapers, did at least walk up the hill, but they saw nothing. They did, however, note the heavy, metallic odor that had been described by May and her group, which provided a partial confirmation of the story.

A. Lee Stewart, Jr., one of the editors of the *Braxton Democrat*, convinced Lemon to lead them back to the spot of the sighting. Given Lemon's initial reaction, it says something about the kid that he agreed to do so. They found nothing and saw nothing but did smell that strange odor. Stewart returned early the next morning and found what he said looked like skid marks about ten feet apart heading down the hill. He said that a large area of grass had been crushed.[5]

The next day, there were follow-up investigations. During some of these additional trips up the hill, it was reported that they had found an area where the grass had been crushed in a circular pattern. Sanderson, who visited the scene a week later, said that he and his fellow investigators were able to see the crushed grass and a slight depression in the ground.[6] No one bothered to photograph this reported physical evidence, which is one of the problems that seem to flow through UFO research. People don't take basic steps to ensure evidence is preserved in some fashion, even if it is just a photograph.

Sanderson pointed out that the other physical evidence that had been reported—skid marks on the ground, an oily substance on the grass, and the foul odor—might have been part of the environment. The type of grass growing wild in that area gave off a similar odor, and the grass seemed to be the source of the oil. Sanderson said that he couldn't find the skid marks and knew of no one who had photographed them.

Gray Barker, a UFO researcher, also arrived a week later and coincidently, on the same day as Sanderson, found others to interview. He talked with A.M. Jordan, Neil Nunley's grandfather, who said that he had seen an elongated object flash overhead on the night of the landing. It was shooting red balls of fire from the rear and it seemed to hover before it fell toward the hilltop.[7]

Barker also interviewed Nunley, whose description of the craft disagreed with that of his grandfather, though he did say the object seemed to stop and hover before falling to the hill. I wonder if the disparity came from the different perspectives of the witnesses. Sometimes the angles from which something is viewed seems to change the shape of the object and the direction in which it appears.

When this story is reported, it always seems to end here, with the one group, led by May and Lemon, seeing the strange creature or entity. The investigations, carried out by various civilian agencies, always fail to find any proof. Many believe that if there was some corroboration—if someone else, not associated with May and her group, had seen the creature—it would strengthen the report.

Several years later that corroboration seemed to be found. A men's magazine carried another story of the Flatwoods monster written by George Snitowski, as told to Paul Lieb. According to the article, George Snitowski was driving in the Flatwoods area with his wife, Edith, and their infant son, on September 13, 1952, when he saw the thing on the ground.[8]

Snitowski didn't say anything about his tale until two or three years after the fact. He then told it to an officer of the civilian Flying Saucer Research Institute, who published the account in the magazine. Looking at it from that point of view—that is, a tale told long after the national publicity that was provided for May and the others—there certainly is the hint that Snitowski was influenced by those articles. There is no proof he was, only the very real possibility.

Snitowski was, according to his story, returning home with his wife and their baby when, near Sutton, West Virginia (not far from Flatwoods), his car engine stalled. He tried, but couldn't get it to start. Because it was getting dark, he didn't want to leave his wife and baby alone on the semi-deserted highway if he walked for help. He thought they would wait for morning, and then he would walk the 10 or 12 miles to the closest town, if someone didn't come along to give them a hand before then.

Snitowski said that a foul odor began to seep into the car, making his wife cry and gagging the baby. Snitowski didn't know what this odor was but suspected it might be from a nearby sulfur plant burning waste. It was then that a bright light flashed overhead. Both Snitowski and his wife were confused by it. He said later that, looking down into the woods after the light flew over, he could see what he thought of as some kind of dimly lighted sphere. He said that the light had a soft violet hue to it, and while soft, it was blinding to the eyes. He rolled down the window to get a better look when the odor they had noticed earlier became even stronger.

Snitowski finally got out of the car and started walking toward some woods where he believed the earlier light flash had originated. He said the odor almost stopped him as it became much stronger. He said that he then stopped, leaned against a tree, and threw up. Inside the tree line sat the sphere some 200 or 300 feet away. He couldn't make out any details. He thought that it was floating above the ground rather than resting on it. There was no visual evidence of a landing gear.

As he moved deeper into the woods, closer to the sphere, he said that his legs began to tingle, almost as if they had gone to sleep. Still sickened by a foul odor, and barely able to walk, he began to retreat, stumbling back toward the car. He neared the road and stopped, again leaning against a tree.

His wife screamed then, and Snitowski yelled, "Edith, for God's sake. What's the matter?" He rushed toward the car and saw she was pale with fright.

She was unable to speak and Snitowski saw, leaning against the hood of the car, a strange creature. He couldn't see it well because of the lack of lighting around the area, but he thought it was 8 or 9 feet tall, and was generally shaped like a human, with arms and a head attached to a bloated body. It was silhouetted against the violet glow of the sphere.

Snitowski reached the car, climbed in, and grabbed a kitchen knife that he had in the glove box. He forced his wife down to the floor and begged her to silence the crying baby. He didn't know what to do and said that the odor was now overpowering. But then, out of the corner of his eye, he saw the object, the sphere, beginning to climb erratically into the sky. It stopped to hover several times and eventually disappeared. Suddenly it swooped, then climbed upward in a bright, dazzling light, and vanished. When he looked outside the car, the creature had disappeared.

Not knowing why, Snitowski tried to start the car now that the object was gone. Without trouble the engine started. They drove away, found a motel, and checked in. The next morning, they heard about the sighting from Flatwoods, but neither wanted to tell authorities what they had seen several hours later. Snitowski said that he didn't want his friends and neighbors to think that he or his wife was crazy. Besides, he didn't have any evidence about the creature or the UFO, and they were far from home. There was only his story, corroborated by his wife but no other witnesses.[9]

If his report is true, and there is no way, today, to learn if it is, then it makes a nice corroboration for the Flatwoods case. The problem, however, is that the Flatwoods case was national news the day after it happened, and Snitowski had said he heard about the landing. At that point, the story was contaminated because an investigator could never be sure that Snitowski, or anyone else who came forward with a report, hadn't been primed by the story as published in the newspapers, heard on the radio, or even seen on television.

These two reports, by Snitowski and by those in Flatwoods, were not the only ones made about that strange, tall, smelly, creature. About a week earlier, according to an investigation conducted by two Californians, William and Donna Smith, a 21-year-old woman who lived about 11 miles from Flatwoods said that she had seen the creature that gave off the horrible odor. She was so upset by the encounter that she was hospitalized for three weeks. Like Snitowski, she wasn't interested in publicity at the time, so when the report from Flatwoods made the news, she elected to remain silent. There was no corroborating tales to support her.[10]

As happened with the Zamora sighting, continued research produced others who said they had seen something strange that night. Alice Williams said that about 7:00 p.m. she saw a slow-moving, glowing object at a low altitude west of Charleston, West Virginia. She, along with Clarence McClane and his wife, said they saw ashes falling to the ground as the object seemed to come apart in the sky.[11]

Woodrow Eagle, who was nearing Sutton, West Virginia, not all that far from Flatwoods, said that he had seen what he thought was a small airplane crash into a hillside. He turned around and then stopped at a service station to call the sheriff. The sheriff drove to the site, but he didn't find the downed aircraft.[12] This was the case the sheriff was investigating before he headed out to May's house.

The trouble here is that both these witnesses—Williams and Eagle—were apparently members of a group that included Sanderson, and Sanderson had called others in that group to investigate the Flatwoods landing. Given that, a good case for cross-contamination can be made. It doesn't mean that there was any confabulation involved, only that these witnesses were not completely independent of other another as it seemed before those connections were made.

Years later, in the mid-1990s, Kathleen May Horner was interviewed about the sighting. She told investigators that the two men who everyone thought were newspaper reporters were, in fact, government agents. She also remembered that a local reporter received a letter from some unidentified government agency that revealed the creature was some sort of rocket experiment that had gone wrong that day. There had been four such "rockets" and all of them fell back to earth.

The government agents were able to recover all but one, and that one had been seen in Flatwoods. It must be noted here that there is no corroboration for this story of government intervention and that it did not surface until 40 years later.[13]

There are few points of corroboration for this tale, even among those who were together that night. The descriptions of the craft in flight sound more like a bolide—that is, a very bright meteor. Newspapers from other communities in the region report on just such a meteor. P.M. Reese from the Maryland Academy of Sciences suggested the red fireball was relatively slow moving and 60 to 70 miles high.

And we know that meteors can seem to climb, though that is an optical illusion, that they can seem to hover briefly, and that they can seem to maneuver, again optical illusions. The witness testimony here is not sufficient to reject a meteor, especially when it is remembered that the object was seen over a large region, suggesting something that was very bright and very high. People looking up into the night sky are simply unable to judge height and speed with any degree of accuracy. A meteor of sufficient size and brightness was seen that night.

Even if we reject, for whatever reason, the theory that any of the Flatwoods witnesses saw a meteor, we can look at the descriptions and how they vary. Even those who trekked up the hill report things differently, from the color and shape of the craft to even whether anything was sitting on the ground. Sanderson reported that the object was black but glowing red and shaped like the ace of spades, but Barker said it was spherical and some of those he interviewed said they hadn't seen it at all.

Jerry Clark reported that the witnesses stuck to their stories but that doesn't mean what they saw was grounded in our shared reality. That they were truly frightened only suggests they were telling the truth about what they thought they saw, but not that they saw an extraterrestrial being.

After I reviewed the literature on this, I am struck by the disparity of the witness descriptions and how these sorts of things can be overlooked. I am surprised that there are descriptions of physical remains, but there is little to document any such evidence. I am struck by the number of witnesses who said they saw the bolide and that the bolide was what everyone saw. And yes, many believe that a bolide has landed close by when it has either burned out and not touched down or it landed hundreds if not thousands of miles away. In fact, several bolides have been reported to authorities as aircraft accidents, just like the one the sheriff investigated that night.

This case seems to be the result of the bolide and the hysteria brought on UFO sightings that were headline news around the country, including the impressive sightings from Washington, DC. It seems that those who climbed the hill, believing they were going to find a landed flying saucer, talked themselves into the hysteria, and when they saw something in a tree with eyes that glowed in the light of their flashlights, convinced themselves they had seen an alien creature.

No, this isn't a perfect resolution. It makes too many assumptions. But the evidence for a UFO sighting and a landing with an alien creature, or maybe some sort of an alien robot, is very weak at best. Given the timing of the sighting, given the lack of physical evidence, given the conflicting witness statements, and given the well-known bias of the original investigators, there isn't much left here.

In the end, the terrestrial explanation is more likely the correct one here. I'm not completely sold on it, but it seems that the preponderance of the evidence suggests that. Until something changes, that's probably where it is going to stay.

Kelly-Hopkinsville, Kentucky (August 21, 1955)

On August 21, 1955, the Sutton family in the Kelly-Hopkinsville area of southern Kentucky reported that their farm house had been assaulted by small alien entities. The attack lasted through most of the night, with the men shooting at the aliens with their shotguns, rifles, and pistols. Eventually the family was driven from the farm and headed to the Hopkinsville Police Station in two cars. They said that it all started around 7:00 p.m., when Billy Ray Taylor had gone out to the well for a drink of water. He ran back into the house to say that as he was bringing up the bucket, he had seen a flying saucer, saying he thought it had landed in a gully behind the house.[14]

Illustration of the creature seen by the witnesses during the night siege at Kelly-Hopkinsville. Photo courtesy of the U.S. Air Force.

According to various sources, including the Project Blue Book files and Isabel Davis and Ted Bloecher, at about 8:00 p.m., one of the dogs started acting up, barking loudly. Taylor and Lucky Sutton went to the back to see what had disturbed the animal. As they got there, the dog ran under the house and wasn't seen again until the next morning. They saw a small figure approaching from the fields behind the house, something that was glowing and about 3 1/2 feet tall. It had an oversized head, floppy, pointed ears, and glowing yellow eyes that were bigger than those of a human. It looked as it was made of silver, and had long arms that ended in talons and reached almost to the ground.

The two men ran inside for weapons, one grabbing a .22 caliber pistol and the other seizing a shotgun. When the creature neared to within 20 feet, both opened fire. The being, apparently struck more than once, flipped over backward and then ran to the side of the house as if to get away. Not long after that another creature, or maybe the same one, appeared at a side window. J.C. Sutton shot at it through the screen with a 20-gauge shotgun and it reacted in the same fashion. When struck by bullets, it did a flip and disappeared.

Sutton and Taylor decided they needed to go back outside to see if they had actually hit anything. As Taylor stepped off the porch, the others saw a claw-like hand reach down. Sutton pushed past him into the yard and opened fire with his shotgun, knocking the creature from the roof.

Taylor yelled that there was another one in the tree. Both men fired at it, knocking it out of the tree. Rather than falling, it seemed to float to the ground. When it landed, it jumped up and ran off. Another, or maybe one of those that had been on the roof, came around the corner of the house, and still another appeared. It became clear that their weapons had no real effect on the creatures and the men retreated to the house. When they heard a tapping up on the roof, they stepped into the backyard, again firing at the creature. It was hit but rather than falling to the ground, it floated to the fence, where it perched for a moment.

There followed a period of calm during which there were no more sightings and no more attacks on the house. But the creatures returned periodically, almost as if teasing those in the house to see if they would be shot at again. The creatures seemed to be playing some kind of game, but the purpose was lost to those in the house. Finally, at about 11:00 p.m. everyone in the house abandoned it and headed for the Hopkinsville Police Station.

The reaction of the law enforcement officers at the station wasn't the typical reaction of those confronted with a story of creatures from a flying saucer. All of them seemed to take the report seriously. The Hopkinsville police radioed the Kentucky State Police, which ordered its officers on patrol to head out to the Sutton farm. The chief of police, Russell Greenwell, at first thought it might be a joke played by his officers, but was quickly convinced it was not.[15] Other police officers involved at some point were named T.C. Gross, Dorris Francis, and Gray Salter. All of them, along with Greenwell, eventually drove to the farm.

Though it seemed that the sighting might have been limited to those at the farmhouse, just as the Zamora sighting seemed, at first, to be limited to Zamora standing on a ridge overlooking the arroyo, there were witnesses to other strange things. One of the state troopers said that he had been 2 or 3 miles from Hopkinsville and had seen several "meteors" fly over with a sound "like artillery fire," which is not all that uncommon with big, bright meteors. He did see two of those meteors as they passed over heading in the general direction of the Sutton farm. The trooper said that the objects, whatever they were, hadn't been like any meteors he had ever seen.

Once everyone had arrived back at the farm (that is, the Sutton family and the law enforcement officers), the police conducted a thorough search of the house. The Suttons refused to enter the building until the search had been completed and were told that there were no one and nothing inside. Chief Greenwell would later say that he had looked for signs that everyone had been drinking but found no evidence of that. Years later, an Air Force officer,

Lieutenant Colonel Spencer Whedon, would hint that drinking had been a major factor in the case.

The search turned up little in the way of evidence. There were holes in the screens made by the bullets, and law enforcement officers did find a luminous patch of material near the fence where one of the creatures had landed after being shot. According to the newspaper story, the Suttons and Taylor claimed to have fired more than 100 rounds of .22 caliber ammunition at the creatures, assuming they were talking about the standard 50-round boxes.[16]

One of the policemen involved in the search said that he had seen greenish light in the distance, in the woods near the house. Other officers were sent in search of the light but found nothing extraordinary. According to the newspaper, the only excitement was when one of the MPs (military police) stepped on a cat's tail while inside the Sutton house.[17] This suggests the involvement of the Army in the initial investigation; however, the military men could have been Air Force. That point is not clarified in the newspaper, and anyone in a green fatigue uniform would be considered Army by almost everyone.

The attacks, or rather the visitation, didn't end there. Glennie Lankford, part of the Sutton clan, said that sometime after 2:30 a.m., she had seen one of the little men with its hand on the window screen. The glow from the creature had alerted her to its presence. She called to other members of the family and Lucky entered the room. He fired at the being but missed. The creatures reappeared several times over the next few hours, the last time being just before the sun came up.[18]

Because a UFO had been seen, and because the creatures were apparently alien, there were those who believed that Project Blue Book would be involved in the investigation. Those at Blue Book apparently had no real interest in the sighting, although the files do contain documents that suggest one active duty officer, and possibly more, did some sort of investigation but all of that was unofficial. No real, "official" investigation began until two years later, and that seemed to be in response to an article that was going to be published in a national magazine that featured the case.

Without any sort of physical evidence except for the bullet holes in the house and the window screens, and the luminous puddle found by law enforcement, there wasn't much proof that the Kelly-Hopkinsville tale was true. Most of the people who heard about it were quite skeptical. The press, which included the radio news reports, reflected that attitude. The Air Force did issue a statement about it not long afterward, telling all who would listen that they were not investigating and that there was no basis for investigating. In other words, the case was so unimportant that the Air Force wasn't going to waste its time or limited resources on a family of "drunken hicks" who thought that alien beings had landed near their farm house and attacked them throughout the night.

Some two years later, in a letter from ATIC at Wright-Patterson Air Force Base, to the commander of Campbell Air Force Base and available in the Project Blue Book files, Wallace W. Elwood wrote: "This Center requests any factual data, together with pertinent comments regarding an unusual incident reported to have taken place six miles north of Hopkinsville, Kentucky on subject date [21 August 1955]. Briefly, the incident involved an all-night attack on a family named Sutton by goblin-like creatures reported to have emerged from a so-called 'flying saucer.'"[19]

Later in the letter, Elwood wrote: "Lacking factual, confirming data, no credence can be given this almost fantastic report. As the incident has never been officially reported to the Air Force, it has not taken official cognizance of the matter."[20]

And that sort of says it all for the Air Force and its investigation. If there is no official report, even if it is aware of the case, it has no obligation to investigate and, in fact, can ignore it. Carmon Marano, who was an officer with Blue Book, confirmed this attitude in a 2017 interview.[21] Over the course of Project Blue Book, it did collect information from a variety of "unofficial" sources, such as newspapers and private UFO group newsletters, but other than sticking the information in a file folder and labeling it, did nothing with it unless pressed to do so by adverse publicity or some sort of official inquiry from those higher in the chain of command.

Another witness, whose name has been redacted from the file, might have seen a similar object in the sky several months earlier. A letter dated September 17, 1957, adds another note to the story. According to that letter, signed by Captain Robert J. Hertell:

Briefly, Mr. [name redacted] and a negro handy-man [who was not named] employed by him had observed an unidentified object streak across the sky, perform several abrupt changes of course, and finally disappear in the direction of Bowling Green, Kentucky. They observed this object for several minutes. I think that another witness or two present that were guests of Mr. [name redacted] at the time. Since Mr. [name redacted] was a very prominent citizen of the area, and the senior member of the largest local law-firm, and since the description of the object and its maneuvers was very accurate, some credence was lent to the story. We therefore reported this incident in accordance with AFR 100-1, by Confidential Message.[22]

Whatever the Air Force opinion or policy, the Kelly-Hopkinsville matter was assigned to First Lieutenant Charles N. Kirk, an Air Force officer at Campbell Air Force Base. He apparently conducted a six-week investigation before sending the reports and interview transcripts on to ATIC on October 1, 1957. He researched the story using the Hopkinsville newspaper from August 22, 1955, to September 11, 1955.[23] He also had a letter from Captain Hertell, a statement from Glennie Lankford [the matriarch of the Sutton family and who had been there throughout the night] and a statement given to Kirk by Major John E. Albert [who unofficially investigated the case in 1955] and a copy of an article or statement written by Glennie Lankford.

Although it has been suggested that there is no evidence that any military personnel were involved with the exception of the MPs, Hertell, in his report, wrote, "As for the report that the affair was investigated by two Air Force Officers from Campbell Air Force Base, I don't beleive (sic) that there is any fact in this."[24] Then, as if to contradict himself, he wrote, "I beleive (sic) that a couple of our officers may have gone down-on their own—to view the place, as I heard some talk of this at the time, but Colonel Donald McPherson, the Base Commander certainly never ordered any official investigation, to the best of my knowledge."

To further complicate this, Hertell continued, "I seem to remember Captain Bennett saying something about going down to see the spot, but since he is still stationed there, surely you have already questioned him regarding this matter." There is nothing in the files to suggest that this was the case, that is, no one at ATIC ever questioned Bennett about what he might have seen at the Sutton farm.

And then, to contradict what he had written earlier, Hertell said, "The only other officer who may have looked into this matter was the Deputy Base Command, Major Ziba B. Ogden.... I remember the two of us talking about the incident, and he could possibly have been sent to the scene by Col. McPherson, in an unofficial capacity, without my knowing about it."

This unofficial investigation and statement provided some interesting information about the case. The Air Force was claiming that the case had not been officially reported and therefore the Air Force was not obligated to investigate. It seems that here we get lost in the semantics of the situation and the question that begs to be asked is: Why not, because it seems that some sort of report had been sent to the Air Force given the documentation in the Blue Book files?

Or is that the case? Lieutenant Kirk, in his report in 1957, sent a copy of the statement made by Major John E. Albert on September 26, 1957, to ATIC. The very first paragraph seems to suggest that notification was made to Campbell Air Force Base, which should have, according to regulations in effect at that time (1955), qualified as a report in official channels. The regulation is quite clear on the point and it doesn't matter if anyone in the military believed the sighting to be a hoax, a hallucination, or the real thing, regulations required an investigation, now that it was in official channels.

In the statement, Albert said:

On about August 22, 1955, about 8 A.M., I heard a news broadcast concerning an incident at Kelly Station, approximately six miles North of Hopkinsville. At the time I heard this news broadcast, I was at Gracey, Kentucky on my way to Campbell Air Force Base, where I am assigned for reserve training. I called the Air Base and asked them if they had heard anything about an alleged flying saucer report. They stated that they had not and it was suggested that as long as I was close to the area, that I should determine if there was anything to this report. I immediately drove to the scene at Kelly [for some reason the word was blacked out, but it seems reasonable to assume the word is Kelly] Station and located the home belonging to a Mrs. Glennie Lankford [name redacted], who is the one who first reported the incident. (A copy of Mrs. Lankford's statement is attached to this report).

Albert's statement continued:

Deputy Sheriff Batts was at the scene where this supposedly flying saucer had landed and he could not show any evidence that any object had landed in the vicinity. There was nothing to show that there was anything to prove this incident.

Mrs. Lankford was an impoverished widow woman who had grown up in this small community just outside

of Hopkinsville, with very little education. She belonged
to the Holy Roller Church and the night and evening of
this occurrence, had gone to a religious meeting and she
indicated that the members of the congregation and her
two sons and their wives and some friends of her sons', were
also at this religious meeting and were worked up into a
frenzy, becoming emotionally unbalanced and that after
the religious meeting, they had discussed this article which
she had heard about over the radio and had sent for them
from the Kingdom Publishers, Fort Worth 1, Texas and
they had sent her this article with a picture which appeared
to be a little man when it actually was a monkey, painted
silver. This article had to be returned to Mrs. Lankford
as she stated it was her property. However, a copy of the
writing is attached to this statement and if it is necessary,
a photograph can be obtained from the above mentioned
publishers.

There are a number of problems with the first couple of para-
graphs of Albert's statement, but those are trivial. (For example, it
wasn't Glennie Lankford who first reported the incident, but the
whole family who had traveled into town to alert the police. They
drove two cars so that no one was left behind with the creatures
still in the area for all they knew.) The third paragraph, however,
is filled with things that bear no resemblance to reality. Lankford
was not a member of the Holy Rollers, but was, in fact a member of
the Trinity Pentecostal Church. Neither she, nor any of the family,
had been to any religious services the night of the "attack." She
couldn't have heard about any article on the radio because there
was no radio in the farm house. And there was no evidence that
Lankford was ever sent anywhere for any kind of article about flying saucers and little creatures. In other words, Albert had written
the case off almost before he began his "investigation" because
of his false impressions and the false information. He provided
no source for the allegations about the Langford's activities that
night. Apparently, he was only interested in facts that would allow

him to debunk the case and was not interested in learning what
had happened during the night. He had no official standing, at
least according to the statements that appear in the Blue Book
files, he was not acting on specific orders by a higher authority
but only a rather vague suggestion, and he had just interjected
himself into the case by calling Campbell Air Force Base with
the information he'd heard on the radio which, ironically and as
mentioned, put the case into official channels.

Further evidence of this is provided in the next paragraph of
his statement:

It is my opinion that the report Mrs. Lankford or her son,
Elmer [Lucky] Sutton, was caused by one of two reasons.
Either they actually did see what they thought was a little
man and at the time, there was a circus in the area and
a monkey might have escaped, giving the appearance of
a small man. Two, being emotionally upset, and discussing the article and showing pictures of this little monkey,
that appeared like a man, their imaginations ran away with
them and they really did believe what they saw, which they
thought was a little man.

It is interesting to note that Albert is not suggesting that the
witnesses were engaged in inventing a hoax. Instead, with absolutely no evidence whatsoever, Albert invented the tale of an escaped monkey that fooled the Sutton clan. That does not explain
how the monkey was able to survive the shots fired at it by the ter-
rified people in the house, especially if it was as close to the house
as the witnesses suggested. With shotguns, pistols, and rifles being
fired at the "little man," someone should have hit it and reported
that they had, in fact, hit it, but there was apparently no injury to
the creature.

But Albert wasn't through with the little monkey theory.
According to him:

The home that Mrs. Lankford lived in was in a very run down condition and there were about eight people sleeping in two rooms. The window that was pointed out to be the one that she saw the small silver shining object about two and a half feet tall, that had its hands on the screen looking in, was a very low window and a small monkey could put his hands on the top of it while standing on the ground.

The final sentence of Albert's account said, "It is felt that the report cannot be substantiated as far as any actual object appearing in the vicinity at that time." It was then signed by Kirk.

What is interesting is that Albert and then Kirk were willing to ignore the report of the object because there was nothing to substantiate it. But, they were willing to buy the monkey theory, though there was nothing to substantiate it, either. They needed a little man for the family to see and shoot at, and they created one because a monkey might have escaped from some mythical circus in town.

Glennie Lankford might have inspired the little monkey story with her own statement provided to authorities. In a handwritten statement signed on August 22, 1955, she wrote:

My name is Glennie Lankford age 50 and I live at Kelly Station, Hopkinsville Route 6, Kentucky.

On Sunday night Aug 21, 55 about 10:30 P.M. I was walking through the hallway which is located in the middle of my house and I looked out the back door (south) and saw a bright silver object about two and a half feet tall appearing round. I became excited and did not look at it long enough to see if it had any eyes or move. I was about 15 or 20 feet from it. I fell backward, and then was carried into the bedroom.

My two sons, Elmer Sutton aged 25 and his wife Vera age 29, J.C. Sutton age 21 and his wife Aline age 27 and their friends Billy Taylor age 21 and his wife June, 18 were all in the house and saw this little man that looked like a monkey.

The Air Force seized on her description and turned it into a possible solution, suggesting, with no justification, that the Suttons had been attacked by a monkey that was immune to shotgun and rifle fire. They postulated a nonexistent circus for it to have escaped. They overlooked the evidence of the case, dispatched someone to look into it unofficially, and then denied that they had investigated it at all. The best way to debunk something was to offer any solution to it no matter how ridiculous that solution might be. To their way of thinking, any solution is better than no solution and people would only remember that the case had been solved though they might remember the tale of the monkey. They rarely remembered what that solution might have been.

Skeptics have attacked the case in the decades since the event. They have suggested that there was no military there the next day, but it is clear from the documentation that Albert was there the next day and, given his statement, he arrived fairly early in the morning. They have said that neighbors heard no more than four shots and that there was evidence of only two shots fired inside the house. But, of course, if the men were outside, then the bullets would have been lost in the distance. There is evidence of shots being fired through screens, and Davis and Bloecher reported a bullet hole in one of the window casings. The number of shots fired, according to the newspaper the next day, would have been in excess of 200 but that seems to be a little high.

Skeptics have also said that the little man, or men, was, or were, barn owls. Such owls, according to the skeptics, are nearly as big as the little men reported. But according to various bird-watching guides, they aren't nearly as big as the creatures reported by the Suttons, and it doesn't seem that they would have stayed around if they were being shot at. In fact, given that a shotgun was used and the distance to the target wasn't all that great, there should have been remains of one or more of the owls for the police or sheriff to find.

This is one of those bizarre cases that involves some very disturbing information that isn't easily explained. However, there is no real evidence to support the case other than the testimony of those involved and the observations of the law enforcement officers who were on the scene later.

The Tin Can Man (October 23, 1965)

In a case that had originally been explained in the Blue Book files as an "astro," in this case Venus, we now found it later changed to "psychological." Someone had scratched out the original explanation on the project card and penciled in the new conclusion. The file consisted of the standard Blue Book form that has been filled out by the witness, Jerry Townsend, and a teletype copy of a newspaper article that appeared in the St. Paul, Minnesota, newspaper.

According to J. Allen Hynek, on October 23, 1965, a radio announcer was driving near Long Prairie, Minnesota (though the Air Force mislabeled it as Lone Prairie) at about 7:15 p.m., when he rounded a bend in the road and spotted a rocket-shaped object sitting on the pavement. He said that it was 30 or 40 feet tall, 10 feet in diameter, and sitting on its fins just as all the rocket ships ever shown in movies or on television have been. As he approached his car engine died, the radio faded, and the headlights dimmed. He said that he tried to start his car but failed. Then, according to the report he filed with Project Blue Book:

> I then got out of my car with the idea to go up to it and try to rock the center of gravity and topple it over so that I would have the evidence right there in black and white. I got to the front end of my car and stopped with no further interest in going further because three little "creatures" came from about behind and stood in front of the object. I think they were looking at me.... I was quite fascinated

with what I saw.... I felt that if they could stop my car, they could surely do something worse to me and I wanted to live to tell the story so that the people of the United States would know that there were things of this nature. I can safely say that we "looked" at each other for about three minutes. Then they turned and went under the object and a few seconds later, the object started to rise slowly. After it was about one quarter mile high (this is only a guess), the light went out and my car engine started to run again (I did not have to tough the starter), and my headlights came on. I looked at the area that it had been sitting on over and could see no evidence that it had been on the ground. I then drove to the Todd County Sheriff's Office [Sheriff Jim Bain and police officer Lavern Lubitz] and reported what I had seen to the sheriff. He went back out to the spot and could not find anything on the road that would show they were on the ground. That is what happened.

Hynek said that he personally investigated the case "via the telephone." He said that there were confirming witnesses to the object's take-off. Several raccoon hunters, according to the sheriff, had seen "a light in the sky" at the time the object took off.[25] There were apparently four other witnesses who might have seen the object take off. Although there was no radar confirmation of the craft, other witnesses in nearby towns had seen it, including the sheriff in Anoka.

Hynek's account does not describe the creatures, but several others did. According to Coral Lorenzen, who spoke to Townsend in the days after the sighting, "When he got to the front of the car three little creatures which looked like tin cans on tripods and about six inches tall, came from behind the object. They had no discernible features. Townsend stopped in front of his car with no intention to go closer. He said that although he could detect no features, he felt the creatures were watching him."[26]

Although Hynek reported that there had been nothing found on the road, that was not confirmed by Lubitz: "The only thing we found were three strips of an oil-like substance on the road.... They were about a yard long and four inches apart, all parallel with the road. I don't know what they were and I've looked at a lot of roads and never saw anything like them before."[27]

Other, named witnesses were also located. Ray Blessing, who was 14 at the time and using his reflector telescope that night, said that at about 7:00 p.m. he had seen a "Buck Rogers-like thing" fly by. This was about 15 minutes before Townsend saw a similar shaped craft on the road.[28]

Jim Bain, whose father had been the sheriff in 1965, provided some interesting detail. In an email written on October 15, 2015, Bain said that he was the son of the sheriff and his father would get together with another sheriff, John Stack of Morrison County. Bain said that he had been in the sheriff's office on the night that Townsend came in with the tale of seeing a spaceship. His immediate reaction was one of disbelief, but according to what he wrote later:

My father went out to the site but he called the civil defense director at the time to ride with him.... The director said he would bring his Geiger counter. When they got to the site the marks were visible and distinct and highly radioactive.... A couple of weeks after this siting [sic] a gentleman from the government came and was talking to my father.... This was not unusual for me to just walk in his office...if my father wanted me to leave he would say so but on this night he had so [sic] reason for me to leave. The conversation was basically over this space ship landing however in the conversation my father brought up another gentlemen [sic] who had directly seen the space ship but would not let his name be used. After bring[ing] this up they called the second individual and he agreed to speak to [the] government investigator.... When we got to the home [where the witness

lived we found] the hunter, his wife, son and investigator...
[he said]. "We had just let the dogs out and they took off
across the field when this space ship came over them and
lite up the ground like it was day.[29]

Though there isn't much in this account, it does put a government investigator into the story who was obviously not from
the Air Force. An Air Force investigator would have been in uniform, and nothing in the Blue Book suggests any real Air Force
investigation. It does mention a space ship but gives no detail. It
happened on the same night as Townsend's encounter, near that
location and time.

Although it seems that the original idea—that there was a single witness—doesn't seem to be borne out, just as happened in the
Zamora case. The investigation turned up other witnesses to an
object in the sky, to lights near the ground, and even to a sighting
of a similar object in the sky about the time of the original sighting. It would have been better for the witnesses to be located prior
to the publicity, but the fact they reacted to that publicity doesn't
render their testimonies completely moot. It does suggest possible
contamination, and all who look at the story need to acknowledge
that fact.

Analysis

It is clear from the documentation available that by the time
of the Zamora sighting the Air Force did not accept the idea of
alien visitation. It worked very hard to ignore sightings in which
alien creatures were reported, often labelling witnesses as having psychological problems without bothering to interview them.
In some cases, it sent its standard forms to witnesses, and if the
seven-page document was not completed and returned, it was another excuse not to investigate the case or label it as "Insufficient
Data for a Scientific Analysis," which is no explanation at all. It
does keep the report out of the "unidentified" category.

We also see that the Air Force has attempted to hide its interest in a case by failing to officially investigate. Instead, it relied on the services of other officers, sometimes in other branches of the military, who, it could be suggested, were operating on their own. Though reports were furnished to Blue Book, because there was nothing to show an official investigation, the Air Force could avoid dealing with the case.

Finding the witnesses wouldn't have been difficult, had the Air Force wanted to interview them. Local newspapers published the names and details of the sightings. Rather than dispatch an officer from Wright-Patterson Air Force Base to learn the facts, it just collected the newspaper clippings, decided that the witness had psychological problems, and let it go at that. The Air Force had a solution, one that many would believe, simply because "everyone" knows there is no alien visitation and anyone seeing a flying saucer has to be a little bit nuts.

If that didn't work, they could always invent a solution as shown in the Kelly-Hopkinsville sighting. Glennie Langford said the creatures they had seen were about the size of a monkey, and the creatures then became monkeys from some mythical circus.

Important here, however, are the descriptions of the creatures. They are not those you would expect as portrayed in science fiction, though the 1957 film *Invasion of the Saucermen* seems to have been inspired by the descriptions offered by the Suttons. They are not the greys that would become the standard in later years. These were truly weird little beasts that only vaguely resemble humans, which is to say that had two arms, two legs, and two eyes on one head.

Just like in Socorro, there is an impression that the sightings are single witness. But they are not. For those who paid attention, the names of other witnesses and documentation were available. As happened all too often, the ridicule factor inhibited if not actually prevented a proper investigation.

Chapter 8:

UFO Symbols

Within hours of Lonnie Zamora telling Army Captain Richard Holder and FBI Agent Arthur Byrnes about the symbol he had seen on the craft he had spotted, he was advised to keep that information to himself. It wasn't that they were thinking about keeping the information classified for any reason other than they thought they would be able to weed out copycat sightings by asking what symbol had been seen, if one was reported. It would allow them to eliminate the fakes. Even the Lorenzens agreed that it was a good idea, but they hadn't thought it through. Symbols reported on or associated with UFOs had been around almost from the beginning of the modern age, so withholding Zamora's was not unlike locking the barn door once the horse had been stolen.

The First Alien Symbols?

What some have suggested as the first example of alien symbols came from the Roswell crash story, but no one talked about those symbols until after 1978. According to the story, Major Jesse Marcel, Sr., had brought a box of metallic debris home with him after he had been to the field near Corona, New Mexico, where something truly strange had fallen. He would say that it was wreckage from a flying saucer and that he wanted his son to see it.

As they were handling the material, Jesse Marcel, Jr., found what he said looked like an I-beam, and there were raised, purple symbols on it. Marcel, Sr., said that his son might have been the first person to have ever seen alien writing.[1]

Dr. Jesse Marcel, Jr., holding a replica of the I-beam that he had seen in the wreckage his father brought home before driving to the Roswell Army Air Field. He described the symbols as purplish and resembling geometric figures. Photo courtesy of the author.

Both Marcels would describe what they had seen, but their descriptions wouldn't exactly match: Marcel, Sr., suggested that the small structure was square and that the writing, such as it was, did not look all that strange. It was straight lines set at various angles. There wasn't much to it. Marcel, Jr., suggested that it had been embossed on a small structure like an I-beam made of purple-colored geometric symbols. Because it was a foreign, possibly alien written language, there was no rationale for the symbols, which is to say nothing that would give a hint as to what they meant.[2]

There are hints of other alien writing that predated what the Marcels had seen. In 1891, Helene Smith, who was a medium among her other talents, said that she could speak and write Martian. Skeptics suggested that her Martian language seemed to be based on French.[3] Of course, in 1891, many people believed that Mars was inhabited. It wasn't until the late 20th century that the true nature of the Martian landscape was realized and landings on Mars proved that it contained no life, plant or other animal.

During the Great Airship sightings of late 1896 and the beginning of 1897, there were suggestions of alien writing having been found. In April 1897, it was reported that one of the airships had hit a windmill near Aurora, Texas, and exploded, showering the area with metallic debris and, apparently, some samples of alien paper. The metal was collected, but it seemed that no one hung onto any of it. The same can be said about the paper, some of which might have been taken from the body of the alien. It was said to be covered with hieroglyphics that no one could read and that no one described. That seemed to indicate that there were no recognizable characters on the papers. No one was able to produce any of it when UFO investigations of the case began in the early 1970s. All that means is that we have testimony about alien symbols and a vague suggestion of what they looked like but no real description of them.[4]

Ashland, Nebraska (December 3, 1967): Uniform Symbols

Former police officer Herbert Schirmer said that he had seen a landed UFO near Ashland, Nebraska, in 1967. He told fellow officers and then investigators working with the University of Colorado UFO study known as the Condon Committee that the object had been on the ground for about 20 minutes. He had, at first, thought it was a truck, but as he approached, he saw red lights that were blinking through windows of what appeared to be a disc-shaped craft hovering about 6 feet off the ground. It climbed slowly, passed over Schirmer's car, and then shot straight up and disappeared.

That would have been the end of it, but Schirmer, along with his superior, Bill Wlaskin, and investigators for the Condon Committee, including Doctor Leo Sprinkle, met in Boulder, Colorado, to explore the case. Sprinkle was there to observe and to use hypnotic regression if it could be verified that there had been a period of missing time, an indication of alien abduction.

Convinced that Schirmer had experienced a short period of missing time, Sprinkle hypnotized and learned that a "white, blurred object" had exited the UFO. Schirmer and this object communicated telepathically after the power in his car had failed. Schirmer refused to give details of that communication, believing it was wrong for him to talk about it.

Sprinkle would later, in his summary of the session, suggest that the white, blurred object was a living being, and Schirmer would add details after the hypnosis. Schirmer thought the craft was powered by some combination of electric and magnetic power or force that could control gravity. Though he said he couldn't talk about the encounter until later, he did suggest that the craft he saw belonged to a sister ship that was like an aircraft carrier and that it was based on Venus or Saturn, but they were from another galaxy.

The Condon Committee had a somewhat skeptical conclusion about the case: "Evaluation of psychological assessment tests, the lack of any evidence, and interviews with the patrolman left the project staff with no confidence that the trooper's reported UFO experience was physically real."[5]

Whereas the reality of the sighting is debated by skeptics, UFO believers, some members of law enforcement, and some of the scientists who worked on the Colorado study, the important part of the case, for those of us interested in symbols, revolves around Schirmer's description of the UFO occupants. He said that the beings were about 4 1/2 to 5 feet tall, with heads that were long, thin with gray-white skin, and catlike eyes. They wore silver gray helmets, each with a small antenna on the left side.[6] The uniforms and gloves were the same color, and at the left breast of each suit was the symbol of a winged serpent.[7]

Schirmer's winged serpent wasn't the only one that has been reported. Folklorist Dr. Thomas "Eddie" Bullard reported beings similar to those seen by Schirmer had similar symbols on their uniforms and had been reported in a Florida case. In his research, he wrote:

> The sample offers only 10 cases, half worn by humanoids and only two by humans. For all their scarcity the insignia reveal surprising consistency when compared. Betty Andresson saw an image of a winged Phoenix on the beings' shoulder. Herb Schirmer and Bill Herrman each saw a winged serpent. Filiberto Carenes a serpent on a chalkboard while Gerry Armstrong found an image of a winged serpent on a chalkboard after an encounter. Less compelling similarities occur among three other cases where the symbol is a triangle or boomerang figure and a chevron pointing to the right. The remainder includes a figure combining the nuclear symbol with the Star of David, a UFO in flight, and an unspecified emblem. Harry Joe Turner reported that his beings had numbers on their faces, again for no apparent reason.[8]

These were not symbols seen on the craft, but symbols that were associated with UFO sightings and abduction reports. The problem, however, is that even though the reports seem to be independent of one another, the UFO and abduction researchers were in communication with one another. The independent reports might not have been quite so independent.[9]

Antonio Vilas-Boas (October 16, 1957): Symbols Inside the Craft

Vilas-Boas, who was working the family farm and who would later become an attorney, said that he saw a red star, or what he thought of as a red star, approaching. It continued to descend, and Vilas-Boas saw that it was an egg-shaped craft with a red light in front and a rotating cupola on top. Three legs came from the bottom as it prepared to land. Vilas-Boas tried to get away on the tractor, but the engine quit. He leaped from it and tried to run but was caught by several short creatures in gray coveralls and helmets. Four of the creatures were able to drag him to their ship.[10]

Inside, he was stripped, washed with some sort of liquid or gel, and taken through a hatch into another room. Above the hatch, which is important to us, were a number of red symbols. Vilas-Boas said that he was able to memorize them and draw them for investigators. They have been reproduced at number of websites and in a number of magazine articles.

Blood was drawn by a device placed on his chin. He was then taken to another room occupied by a naked female who had white hair on her head but bright red hair under her arms and in the pubic area.[11] He felt sexually drawn to the female and they had sex. When it was over the female pointed to her belly and then toward the sky, apparently letting him know that she would become pregnant and their child would be raised on another world.

His "task" finished, he was shown around the ship. He tried to steal a small instrument to validate his tale, but the aliens saw him take it and made him surrender it. When the tour ended, he was taken from the ship, which then took off. He had been gone for four hours.

The story, because of its bizarre abduction and sexual content, was labeled a hoax by skeptics and many in the UFO community. Although it seemed that the story had been around since February 1958, the first mention in print seems to be in 1962. Interestingly, the story does contain details that were mentioned in a magazine article that appeared in November 1957, or at the height of the UFO wave of sightings, including the landings around Levelland, Texas, that involved an egg-shaped craft that glowed red. What this means is that information had been circulated around Brazil prior to Vilas-Boas's story surfacing.

The important point here is that Vilas-Boas did talk of symbols painted on the craft, though they were inside rather than out, and they had been red. Although interesting in relation to what Zamora had reported, it is more of a coincidence than corroboration.

Brooksville, Florida (March 2, 1965): Recovered Documents

This case, labeled as a hoax by the Air Force, began in the early afternoon of March 2, 1965, and resulted in the recovery of two pages of alleged alien writing. John Reeves said that he had been out searching for snakes and was in the scrub lands near his home when he spotted a flying saucer sitting in a clearing. A domed disc, he described as reddish-purple and blue-green in color, was sitting on four legs. It was between 20 and 30 feet in diameter by Reeves's estimation, and was about 6 feet high.

As he crouched in the scrub brush near the craft, a movement on the far side of it caught his attention. Reeves would describe a being as a "robot" with some sort of glass dome on top, which could have been a helmet, about 5 feet tall with a darkly tanned face and wearing a silver-colored suit that might have been made of canvas. He could see the face through the glass on the helmet, and said that the eyes were widely set and that it had a very pointed chin. It carried a cylinder on its back and was wearing a skull cap of some kind.

Reeves said that he tried to "hunker down" in the bushes, but the creature, or robot, apparently spotted him. It watched him for a minute, or a minute and a half, reached to its left side, and then raised a small, black object, which it pointed at Reeves. The object flashed twice, panicking Reeves, who tried to flee. He tripped and fell, and the robot flashed the object at him again.

The creature turned and walked back to the ship. Using a stairway at the bottom of the craft, the robot entered the ship. That done, and to what Reeves would later tell investigators for NICAP, "a lot of little blades around the rim of the saucer started to move.... It made a whooshing sound,"[12] the stairway retracted, and then the four legs retracted. It rose rapidly into the cloudless sky and was gone in something like 10 seconds.

With the object gone, Reeves inspected the clearing. He found indentations of the landing gear, a large number of dumbbell-shaped footprints, and wadded-up sheets of paper. The paper was very thin, but very tough and was covered with strange writing that Reeves described as Chinese.

He then walked over to the service station and convenience store run by his friend John Wells and told him about his encounter. Wells would later say that he had no trouble believing his friend.

That evening Reeves talked to another friend, Estes Morgan, who would say that Reeves had been shaken by his encounter and to prove his tale, showed Estes the thin paper.

Estes decided to call the local television station, but they were not interested. In fact, they were less than cordial in their rejection of the story. The local newspaper, a weekly, did interview Reeves. They also contacted the owner of the Brooksville radio station WWJB, who also seemed interested in the story.

The station owner, William Johnson, called McDill Air Force Base to relay the information. With the story now told to various media and authorities including the Air Force, Reeves, with a couple of others returned to the landing site.

Early in the afternoon of the day after the sighting, or about 24 hours later, the Air Force arrived. First Lieutenant Edward R. Goettl and three enlisted men met Reeves and Johnson at the radio station. Eventually they drove out to the landing site and took pictures of the markings, prints, and papers.

Goettl, in his official report, wrote, "The paper Mr. Reeves claims he found at the landing site is similar to silk span paper used to build model airplanes."[13]

It's clear from the tone of his report that he didn't believe Reeves, and, in case that was somehow obscured, he noted that Reeves was "of doubtful" reliability.

Everyone returned to the radio station and the Air Force took off. Johnson, however, had been working the phones, and there were reporters from other, larger cities waiting to interview Reeves. The next morning, there was even more interest in the story. People flooded into the scrub land and obliterated any evidence that might have been there so that further investigation would be impossible.

With even more people believing Reeves, investigators from both the civilian world and the military arrived. Lieutenant Goettl, with an NCO and a man with PhD, were there. NICAP was represented by Robert M. Snyder and Robert S. Carr. As can be expected, the Air Force team still thought of it as a hoax and the NICAP investigators, though maybe not accepting everything that Reeves said as totally reliable, began their investigation with the attitude that it was not a hoax.

There was more hoopla during the next few days. Reeves was being advised by Johnson, who might have been protecting his interests in the story. At any rate, the ripple was spreading further and further with Reeves in the center. Attention was focused on him.

As happens in these sorts of tales, someone arranged for a lie detector test conducted by David Allison. (I'm somewhat ambivalent about them. There is a segment of the population who can beat them and there are others who seem to be so nervous about them they fail even when telling the truth. And, there are methods to beat the "box," though I doubt that Reeves was sophisticated enough to have been able to do that.) The polygrapher said that the tests he conducted convinced him that Reeves was not telling the truth.[14]

And as happens in these sorts of tales, a second test was arranged, this time by an NICAP member who was also a polygrapher. The NICAP representatives, Snyder and Carr, when they reviewed the tapes made of the first session, were convinced that Allison had done a poor job. E.J. Edwards talked to Reeves, and tested him in Orlando. Edwards, as could be expected, said, "John F. Reeves has answered all pertinent questions truthfully, regarding the experience he had when he stated he saw a UFO and occupant on March 2, 1965 at Brooksville, Florida."[15]

What happened to the papers that Reeves found? The Air Force had the paper analyzed and concluded that the paper was made up of leaf fibers from a number of plants, but they didn't identify any of the plants. In fairness, it must be pointed out that all they did was analyze the paper and had no expertise in identifying the specific plants that might have been used in the manufacture of the paper. It would seem to me that the Air Force would then change their point of attack and attempt to pinpoint the types of plants. Terrestrially based plants would tend to rule out an extraterrestrial explanation, but the Air Force never did that.

At the end of March, a Project Blue Book press release announced its conclusion that Reeves had invented the story. It was a hoax told by a lonely man. The Air Force suggested that "[t]he holes which were purportedly caused by the landing gear were straight and appeared to have been scooped or dug as opposed to indentations caused by an object of any sizeable weight."[16]

The Air Force also claimed to have deciphered the "hieroglyphics" on one page. The message was, according to the Air Force, "Planet Mars, are you coming home soon? We miss you very much. Why did you stay away too long?"[17]

That was to be expected from the Air Force, and, naturally, NICAP disagreed with those conclusions. Reeves asked for the return of his papers and the Air Force dispatched two officers from McDill Air Force Base to hand-carry them to him. If that was to convince people that the Air Force had returned the papers, it didn't work. Johnson called the NICAP representatives and said that the papers returned were not the ones the Air Force had been given.

While I was in the area in the summer of 1968 finishing the Army's helicopter pilot training at Fort Rucker, I visited the sheriff's office and talked to the deputies who were involved in the case. One of them said that Reeves was an honest man who had bankrupted himself when he owned a trailer park by forgetting to collect rents and buying food for those who couldn't afford it. Reeves didn't treat the business as a business but more as a philanthropic operation.

And the deputy told me that the papers returned by the Air Force were not the ones Reeves had given. He said that they had cut a tiny piece from one and when they touched a match to it, it erupted like flash paper. The papers returned by the Air Force didn't have the same feel, nor did they react the same way.

I was a little concerned about this. Here is a little bit of material that might be of extraterrestrial origin and these guys are cutting it up and setting it on fire. But, one of the easiest tests of anything is to see how it reacts to heat. I have no reason to suspect the deputy was lying to me about it, and the actions, given the circumstances, seem to be reasonable. What would be the purpose of lying about it?

The story of the switch wasn't something that would be obscure in the summer of 1968 when we were there. It had been around from almost the very beginning.

There is more to the Reeves story. Although the first story was fairly down to earth, but from that point on, and as the interest in Reeves began to evaporate, he came up with new and better wrinkles. He said that he'd had another sighting and had again encountered the robot. He would eventually claim a trip in the saucer, a six-hour voyage that took him to the moon. He walked the surface, without benefit of spacesuit or supplemental oxygen.

Back on the ship, they flew around to the dark side of the moon and Reeves saw people living there. By his count, there were 18 people along a stream flowing down a mountain, though by 1968, the backside of the moon had been photographed by various terrestrially launched spacecraft.

Once back on Earth he was told they would come back, and two months later he took another ride. This time they went to Venus. Reeves returned with a Venusian flag. They, of course, didn't call their world Venus. To them it was Moniheya. And the surface temperatures, hot enough to melt lead, didn't seem to bother them or Reeves.

Although the Reeves case is extreme and it is difficult to believe in any life on Venus, let alone a society that would invent flags as we have done on Earth, there are some interesting parallels between Reeves and Zamora, which I point out merely because of the coincidence.

Both men came upon a landed craft and saw the occupants on the outside. Reeves described a robot and Zamora suggested something more human. Both craft left landing traces, though in Zamora's case the impressions seemed to have been pressed into the ground and with Reeves it seemed they had been excavated.

Importantly, both men had been alone when they saw the craft, and it seemed that there were no other witnesses. In Socorro, Captain Holder reported that police officials told him three people had called the station to report the blue flame in the sky in the minutes before Zamora reported the craft on the ground. In Brooksville, John Wells said sometime later that after the story was reported, three different people had said they had seen the same thing at the same time and at the same place.

Zamora, however, did not have repeated UFO sightings, did not travel to other worlds, and only saw a single symbol. Reeves did all those things and reported them to those who would listen.

I had thought that my contribution to the Reeves case was the statements made to me by the deputy sheriff—something that was interesting when I heard it, but something I later learned was not all that rare. Apparently, a number of people did believe the papers returned by the Air Force were different than those it had taken away.

I was told by the deputies how to find the clearing where Reeves had made his sightings. I was warned that the sand was soft and I'd get stuck if I wasn't careful. So, I found a place to park and walked up. There was nothing to see, other than the concrete top of some concrete slab that seemed to be the top of a buried bunker that had strange symbols painted on it. They didn't match those on the papers that Reeves had found, and a number of people were able to decipher the message. It had nothing to do with Reeves.

I did drive by Reeves's house, but I didn't stop. He had erected a 23-foot obelisk to commemorate his first encounter with the aliens. He also built a wooden saucer and took to wearing a jumpsuit. Later, on the site where the UFO allegedly landed, he placed a plaque that said, "The spaceship that took John F. Reeves to planet Moniheya, millions and millions of miles from Earth, landed here October 5, 1968."

Had it not been for the deputies telling me about the papers and that they were not the same as those that had been surrendered to the Air Force, I could write this off as a hoax. But like so much in the UFO field, there is always that confounding factor and nothing is as simple as it seems.

Symbols on the Outside of the Craft

There have been other sightings in which the witnesses claimed to have seen a symbol or words on the outside of the craft. Two women in Texas who reported they had seen something strange knew what it was. UFO had been written on the side.

In Spain, on February 6, 1966, several people claimed to have seen an object over Madrid. There were many witnesses to this, including Jose Luis Pena, who said he approached the craft and said that it was enormous. Spanish UFO researcher Antonio Ribera wrote to Jordan and received a long reply including the information that on the underside of the object he saw a large symbol that looked like reversed parentheses, which meant that rather than forming a lens shape, they looked more like slender

"Cs" back-to-back with a vertical bar between them. The symbol seems to resemble that from the astrological table used to designate Pisces (which might have no relevance here but would to some Christians).

Mock-up of the craft reported to have crashed near Kecksburg, Pennsylvania, in December 1965. There were strange symbols around the bottom of the craft. Photo courtesy of Stan Gordon.

On June 1, 1967, there was another sighting, which included photographs taken by an unidentified young man. In one of these pictures, the symbol was photographed. The main difference was a horizontal bar that connected the three vertical bars. Unfortunately, the man who took the photographs was never found.

For a short time, the sightings were thought to be valid, given the number of independent witnesses and the photographs of the object. But then messages from alien creatures from a planet called UMMO began to appear. Fernando Sesma, president of the Society of the Friends of Space, announced that a ship from UMMO would land soon. Although there were many messages and members of the Society, there was no actual evidence to prove the case. Jacques Vallee suggested that the whole affair took its inspiration from a short story that had been published in 1941. The point here, however, is that the photographs, which showed the symbol, have been shown to be a small model and renders further discussion moot. The majority of those involved in UFO research suggest the case is a hoax.[18]

There is one case from the 1960s that is not a hoax and that did provide information on symbols seen on the outside of the crash. On December 9, 1965, an object was seen in the sky, left a smoke trail, and was seen plunging into a wooden area near the Pennsylvania town of Kecksburg. Unlike many sightings, this one was made by hundreds of people, and many saw the debris and an object that came down in the woods. Dozens arrived at the scene shortly after the object crashed.[19]

In was sometime after 6:30 p.m. that Francis Kalp called Greensburg, Pennsylvania, radio station WHJB to say that she had seen an object or fireball fall into the woods near her house. John Murphy, the news director, who was in the middle of his nightly news broadcast, interrupted that to interview Kalp about the "breaking news."

Murphy thanked Kalp for the story and then called the state police, who in turn attempted to call Kalp. Her line was busy but the operator broke in, telling her to call the state police. The county emergency center was activated and volunteer firefighters searched the woods, all based on the telephone calls that Kalp had made.

There were other witnesses, including Bob Blystone, who was 15 at the time, and Mary Keto. Blystone saw an orange jet trail at low altitude, and saw a round object glide slowly to the treetops. Keto saw a fireball hovering over the trees with blue smoke coming up.

Murphy, having finished his news broadcast, drove to Kecksburg. Shortly after he arrived, two state police cars and Kalp arrived. A state fire marshal, carrying a yellow Geiger counter, was also there. Murphy attempted to interview Carl Metz, the fire marshal, who had been down in the woods, but Metz told him to talk to the Army. That surprised Murphy, because it was the first time that anyone had said anything about the Army.

Murphy then drove to State Police Troop A barracks, where he saw both soldiers and airmen, in uniform. One of them, a first lieutenant, told Murphy he didn't know much. Murphy also talked with Captain Dussia of the Pennsylvania State Police, who told Murphy, on the record for the radio report *Object in the Woods*, "The Pennsylvania State Police had made a thorough investigation of the woods. We are convinced that there is nothing whatsoever in the woods."

Dussia and others were about to return to the woods, and Murphy said that he was going with them. Permission was denied, repeatedly, and the officials took off with Murphy left behind. He said after that confrontation that it was the last time that he saw any military personnel in the area.

A few civilians did manage to get to the center of the woods. Stan Gordon of the Pennsylvania Association for the Study of the Unexplained (PASU) found a firefighter, Jim Romanski, who had entered the woods before the military and the state police sealed them off. Romanski, according to what Gordon learned, had reached a streambed and found the object. It had crashed through the trees, cut a furrow in the ground, and came to rest partially hidden.

Romanski said that he approached it and saw that it was acorn shaped, some 9 to 12 feet in diameter with a gold band around the bottom with writing on it. Romanski told David Templeton of the *Pittsburgh Press* that the writing looked like "ancient Egyptian hieroglyphics." The characters were broken and straight lines, dots, rectangles, and circles.[20]

Using Romanski's description of the object, along with that of another man, Bill Bulebush, who had managed to get close to the downed object, a monument was erected near the spot where the craft fell. Painted on it are the symbols as remembered by the witnesses. Interestingly, the symbols, though described as Egyptian, look more like those that had been seen by Vilas-Boas when he was inside the alien ship that had abducted him.

They also resemble, to a lesser extent, the symbols drawn by Jesse Marcel, Sr., decades after he had seen one of the small I-beams that he had picked up while on the Brazel ranch in July 1947. His son, Jesse Marcel, Jr., had drawn them as more geometric symbols rather than the lines drawn by his father.

Marcel, Sr., had been dispatched by 509th Bomb Group commanding officer, Colonel William Blanchard, to the ranch managed by W.W. Mack Brazel after Brazel had visited the Roswell, New Mexico, sheriff, George Wilcox, complaining about a field filled with metallic debris. Accompanied by a counterintelligence corps officer, Sheridan Cavitt, Marcel spent the better part of a day picking up debris to be transported back to the base, 65 or 70 miles to the southeast. It was when Marcel stopped at his home to show the material to his wife and son that they spotted the symbols on one of the small pieces of debris.[21]

In the search of symbols that have been reported on UFOs, seen inside the craft, or related to over material recovered in relation to UFOs, the symbol seen by Zamora remains unique. There have been suggestions that the symbol most widely reported was not the correct one and that the one suppressed at the suggestion of Captain Holder has appeared on other craft. The solution to this can be found in the history of those symbols, which we'll look at next.

Chapter 9:
What Symbol Did Zamora See?

The controversy about the true symbol seen by Lonnie Zamora started almost from the moment he returned to the police station and spoke to Captain Richard Holder, an Army officer, and the FBI agent there, Arthur Byrnes. Holder thought—as well as others, it seemed, including Jim and Coral Lorenzen of the Aerial Phenomena Research Organization (based in Tucson at the time)—withholding the true nature of the symbol would be useful in weeding out copycat sightings. If those copycats described the wrong symbol while claiming to have seen the Zamora craft, then those investigating the landing would know that the new report was a confabulation.

To those outside the investigation of the Socorro sighting, the symbol that has been reported in many books, magazines, and documentaries is the one that appears repeatedly in the Project Blue Book files. That symbol is a red arc over an inverted "V" with a line from the apex of the "V" down, giving it the look of an arrowhead with a horizontal line underneath. There has been a challenge to this idea catching fire recently, with a number of UFO researchers suggesting that we have all been misled on orders from a member of the intelligence community. This isn't true, but it has the makings of a nice conspiracy.[1]

Briefly we'll review what happened on April 24, 1964. According to what Lonnie Zamora told government officials, Captain Richard Holder and FBI agent Arthur Byrnes, within minutes of the object departing the area, he found a scrap of paper and drew a symbol on it that he had seen on the side of the object: an arc over an arrow head with part of the shaft attached and a single line beneath the symbol. Zamora wanted to remember exactly what it had looked like and, as a good police officer, wrote down the observation as soon as possible on that scrap of paper. According to what he said at the time (within an hour or so of returning to the police station), he had made the illustration before his friend Sergeant Sam Chavez arrived on the scene.[2]

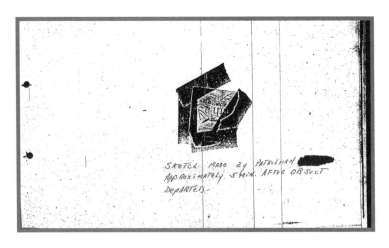

The scrap of paper that Zamora used to draw the symbol he had seen just minutes after the craft departed. It was found in the Project Blue Book files. Photo courtesy of the U.S. Air Force.

Once it was dark, everyone who had driven out to the landing site after hearing Zamora's radio call returned to the police station. At that point, Holder and Byrnes began their interrogation of Zamora and, given the descriptions in the Blue Book files, it can only be called an interrogation. During that time, it seemed they had Zamora draw additional pictures of what he had seen, and one of those included the symbol. As he had done with the smaller picture, on the scrap of paper, Zamora signed his name to those illustrations.[3]

During the discussions with Zamora, it seemed that Holder suggested that it might be a good idea to withhold this bit of information. Holder's motivation seemed to be that found in many investigations: withhold a critical piece of information to weed out those who might try to leap on the bandwagon.

Within 48 hours, Jim and Coral Lorenzen were in Socorro and had the opportunity to interview Zamora. Although somewhat more reticent to talk because of what had transpired in the time between the sighting and the time the Lorenzens arrived, Zamora did sit down with them. During the interview, Zamora was convinced to tell the Lorenzens about the creatures that he had seen near the object, but when it came to the description of the symbol, he wouldn't budge.[4] It would seem that alien creatures would be of more importance than a symbol on the side of a craft, but Zamora said that Holder, who was the officer in charge at the Stallion Site on the White Sands complex, had asked him not to talk about it and he wasn't going to talk about it. Byrnes had merely suggested that he not mention the creatures to spare him (Zamora) a little grief by those who might find tales of alien creatures in the New Mexico desert a little difficult to believe.

In the May 1964 issue of *The A.P.R.O. Bulletin*, on page 2, there is a drawing of the object based on descriptions provided by Zamora. It includes the symbol that Zamora had drawn within minutes of the object departing. Ironically, the illustration had appeared in the Socorro newspaper, the *Defensor-Chieftain*, days earlier, but the symbol had yet to be added to the drawing.[5]

In the official Blue Book files is a report prepared by Major William Connor, allegedly the public relations officer at Kirtland Air Force Base and who had the additional duty as the UFO officer, who, as part of his duties, had driven Hynek around New Mexico in April 1964. Connor was reporting on an interview with Zamora that he had either conducted or witnessed. On page 3 of that document, he included an illustration of the symbol that resembled those that Zamora had drawn himself.[6]

There is another source for this particular symbol: Rick Baca, who, as a 14-year-old in 1964, was commissioned to draw the craft within two weeks of the sighting. According to Paul Harden, a Socorro resident who spent years researching the case and who is or was friends with many of the principals in the case:

> The mayor at the time, Holm "Pappy" Bursam, asked Lonnie to prepare a full statement so it wouldn't come back and bite him or the City later. Part of that statement was the attorney [the paralegal in the city attorney's office] had his son, Ricky, then a school student, draw the image with Lonnie sitting...providing the description. So that image was drawn with Lonnie's description and approval...and it was taken to the Socorro *Chieftain* newspaper office to show Hynek—which had used the newspaper as sort of his office. It was photographed and published.[7]

This was the illustration that had been published in the newspaper with the symbol missing and published by APRO with the symbol intact. Baca retained the illustration. According to Harden, and confirming what had been said, Hynek had asked that the symbol either not be added to the drawing or removed for publication. Hynek "didn't want the symbol published to taint future reports."[8]

Rick Baca explained more about the illustration that appeared in both the Socorro newspaper and *The A.P.R.O. Bulletin*. He said that Zamora had visited the city attorney, worried about his job and the affect the sighting might have on it. Baca's father was a paralegal working in the office while Zamora was there. With the elder Baca taking notes, Zamora described the situation, the craft, and the symbol he had seen. With permission, Baca shared the information with his son, who then completed the drawing, but it did not have the symbol. Later, Zamora saw the drawing and said that it matched what he had seen. Using a red colored pencil, and with Zamora guiding him, Baca added the symbol to the craft.[9] In other words, with no motivation other than making the illustration as accurate as possible, and without worrying about making the symbol public, Zamora had it added and approved the design. It was the arc over the arrow rather than the inverted "V."

Much more recently, Rich Reynold, who operates the *UFO Conjectures* blog, said that he had interviewed Zamora's wife about a decade ago. She told him that the symbol with the arc over the arrowhead was the correct one. There is no reason to believe that she didn't know the truth and no reason that she would have lied about it at that late date.[10]

There is one other source on this: Ray Stanford. In a letter to Dick Hall, dated May 3, 1964, Stanford wrote that the correct symbol was the one that Zamora had drawn on the first night. Stanford wrote, "I advise not letting out the real (as told in the tape by Mike Martinez) description of the symbol on UFO, as if person(s) claim UFO 'contact' with an "A" or "A" (here he drew the one with the three bars through it) on side we can suspect a hoax."[11]

That inverted "V" was apparently the one given to the news media. A story published on April 30, 1964, by the *San Antonio Express* among other newspapers, reported that "[w]itnesses to the craft seen by Zamora said it was marked with a red inverted V with a line or several lines horizontally through the V."

An Associated Press story dated April 29, 1964, which might have been the inspiration for the *San Antonio Express* report, suggested that Hynek was one of those additional witnesses. It reported, "The scientist [Hynek] also discussed the markings that

Zamora said he saw on the side of the object, a red, inverted V with bars through it."

The story was also reported on April 29, 1964, in the *Dubuque Telegraph-Herald*: "Officer Zamora said the object he saw last Friday night was a brilliant white. He said there was a red marking on it like an upside down V with three lines across the top, through the middle and at the bottom."

Taking this even further, Stanford said that he had recorded, on tape, a conversation with Socorro police dispatcher Mike Martinez, who told him that Zamora described the design as "un 'V' invertido con tres lineas debajo," meaning "an inverted 'V' with three lines beneath it." That interview was recorded in the police station and is difficult to understand given all the background noise.[12]

At about this same time in Socorro, Hynek was interviewed by Walter Shrode at KSRC radio and said, "He [Zamora] described it to me as an inverted "V" with a sort of bar across it."[13]

This statement by Hynek seems to be at odds with the idea that there was an inverted "V" with three lines through it. Hynek had said one line, but it was unclear if he meant above the "V" or through it.

The best way to resolve this particular problem would be with an illustration. There is a handwritten letter by Hynek dated September 7, 1964, in the Project Blue Book files. Ray Stanford made a big deal out of his "discovery" of the letter on August 3, 2013, and in an article found on Bill Chalker's blog on June 4, 2014, Stanford wrote, "James Fox asked to take that photo of me holding an important Hynek letter I had just found discovered in the National Archives Socorro file."[14] These are, of course, the Project Blue Book files that have been available for public review since the mid-1970s.

The symbol in the letter is not the one that Stanford had been pushing as the real one. It has a horizontal bar over the apex of the inverted "V" and two other bars inside the legs that don't touch those legs. It doesn't corroborate any of the versions that have been offered. The argument could be that Hynek hadn't actually seen any drawings of the symbol but was basing his descriptions on what he had heard, or he was attempting to remember something that hadn't struck him as all that important in the first place.

As if this whole thing wasn't complicated enough, there are the problems raised by what is something of an unofficial Blue Book file. As the project was being closed, a great deal of information was being destroyed. Lieutenant Carmon Marano, an officer assigned to the project, thought that the material should be preserved, so he collected it.[15] Part of that material was a thick file on the Socorro landing. In that file, there were two handwritten cards that were probably notes made from a newspaper article, given the wording. There is no reference for it, which makes the whole thing problematic. One seems to be a copy of the first but written more carefully and legibly. That notation includes an illustration that shows the inverted "V" with the three bars through it.

This does seem to be problem with no resolution, given the documentation available. But a careful examination of the facts provides a conclusion for us. The documentation seems to be overwhelming and points to a single conclusion based on a review of all the evidence.

To recap briefly:

- In the Blue Book files, there is an illustration of the craft drawn by Zamora that includes the symbol with the arc over the arrowhead. Zamora signed that illustration.

- In the Blue Book files, there is a scrap of paper which shows that same symbol. Zamora said he had drawn this symbol on it within minutes of the craft leaving and he signed that one as well. Though you can argue about a break in the chain of custody, it is clear that the symbol on the scrap available matches others drawn by Zamora.

- Jim and Coral Lorenzen interviewed Zamora within 48 hours of the sighting and published a long article about the case in *The A.P.R.O. Bulletin*. That same symbol is used on one of the illustrations, though a second stylized symbol is used on another illustration in that same issue. Neither of them resemble the inverted "V" with the three lines drawn through it.

- Rick Baca, working with information provided by Zamora, given in the city attorney's office, produced an illustration of the craft. The symbol on that illustration was added later, under the direction of Zamora.

- Ray Stanford, in a letter to Dick Hall, confirmed the arc and arrowhead symbol as the correct one but also mentioned that the symbol of the inverted "V" with the lines through it was the "faked" one given to the press. The letter was written not long after the events in Socorro in 1964.

- Rich Reynolds, who interviewed Zamora's wife around 2006, was told that this symbol was the correct one— that is, the arc over the arrowhead.

- Hynek, in a confidential interview with Isabel Davis on May 20, 1964, included this symbol as the correct one. He did mention the inverted "V" with the lines through it, but noted it was from the newspapers. It is clear that at that time, Hynek was aware of which symbol was correct and which one had appeared in the newspapers.

On the other side of the argument:

- There are newspaper stories printed on April 29 and 30, which seem to be based on an Associated Press story in which Hynek seemed to suggest the inverted "V" with the three lines through it is the correct symbol. In the Project Blue Book files, there is a teletype message that is located with a number of newspaper clippings that does refer to the inverted "V," but that teletype message seems to be referring to the newspaper clippings rather than any of the testimony given by Zamora. That is not part of the Air Force investigation.

- In those "unofficial" Blue Book files saved by Carmon Marano and ultimately obtained by Rob Mercer, there was the cursive note that reported the inverted "V" with three lines through it. There is a second card with the same information on it that is a hand-printed version of the first note. Both seem to be derivative of the newspaper articles rather than information gathered from Zamora or that were part of the official Blue Book file.

- In his book *Socorro "Saucer" in a Pentagon Pantry*, Ray Stanford reverses himself, now claiming that the inverted "V" with the three lines is the correct one and the other symbol with the arc over the arrowhead is fake. In other words, Stanford has endorsed both the symbols at different times as being correct. In today's world, he insists that the inverted "V" is the correct one and cannot explain why he claimed just the opposite in his letter to Richard Hall.

- Stanford interviewed Mike Martinez on tape and it seems that Martinez is saying that the inverted "V" is the one that Zamora reported.

- Finally, Hynek, in his September 7, 1964, letter drew the inverted "V" but with one line above it and two lines inside the legs of the "V." Those lines didn't touch the legs.

A variety of other symbols resemble, to a degree, those discussed here, ranging from a rectangle set vertically with an arc for the top and an arrow in the center to others that bear little real resemblance to anything that Zamora might have said. Given that these have so little or no actual supporting evidence, they can be eliminated from the discussion.

The best evidence is for one of the two symbols most often associated with the case. The inverted "V" did get some play in the newspapers, and there are those today who believe it is the correct symbol. But it doesn't appear in the official Blue Book records at any point other than a passing reference, most of those in newspaper clippings that are part of the file. It is not represented in any of the reports prepared by the Lorenzens and doesn't seem to be the one that Zamora himself endorsed. It appears in the newspapers of the time, which suggests that this is the faked image released publicly for the purpose of weeding out those copycats who might claim to have seen the craft. There is no real reason to accept this as the real symbol. It is a dead end.

The preponderance of the evidence points to the symbol with the arc over the arrowhead. It is the one most often described, but it is also the one that seemed to come directly from Zamora. He told both Holder and Byrnes about it, he told Baca Senior about it, and Baca Junior created his illustration from that information. It is the symbol on the two drawings made the night of the landing, one of them within minutes of the craft departing. These two drawings are the only ones that Zamora signed, and, had they been of the faked symbols, there would have been no reason to keep them as part of the Blue Book file. In fact, given that access to the file was restricted in 1964, there is little reason to suspect this is not the correct symbol.

If we were in a court arguing the case, the weight of the evidence would fall on the symbol with the arc over the arrowhead for three very good reasons. That symbol is the only one that has Zamora's signature attached to it, not once, but twice. When Zamora was asked by the city attorney to provide information about the sighting, he worked with Baca's father and indirectly with Rick to produce a good illustration. On the craft that Baca drew, that was the symbol put on by Zamora's instruction. Also, the only symbol consistently mentioned in the Blue Book files is the arc over the arrowhead. The reports contain it, and even those written by other officers only marginally involved contain it. Finally, Hynek's interview with Isabel Davis seems to confirm it.

We have reached the point here that tells us which symbol is correct. We have been able to solve this minor aspect of the case and can say with confidence that the correct symbol is the one endorsed repeatedly by Zamora.

Chapter 10:

Socorro as a Hoax

t wasn't all that long after the Socorro case was announced to the world that the suggestion that it might have been a hoax was made as a possible explanation. Philip Klass, whose self-appointed mission was to prove that there were no alien visitations and anything that suggested otherwise is in error, might have been among the first to publicly suggest hoax and who actually offered some evidence to support his belief.

Klass himself visited Socorro and talked with many of the people who lived there. In his book, *UFOs Explained*, Klass wrote:

> During Hynek's second visit he talked to one local resident who suggested the case might be a hoax. The man was Mr.

Felix Phillips, whose house is located only one thousand feet south of the spot where the UFO allegedly landed. Phillips said that he and his wife had been home at the time of the reported incident, and that several windows and doors had been open – yet neither of them had heard the loud roar that Zamora reported during the UFO landing and later during takeoff. This was curious because Zamora's speeding car was four thousand feet away from the site and *the Phillips home was only one-quarter this distance* [emphasis in original]."[1]

Klass went on to write that Hynek had briefly mentioned the man's suspicions but he had strongly rejected the idea of a hoax. Hynek's interview, which is available in the Project Blue Book files, said, "Although I made a distinct attempt to find a chink in [Zamora's name had been redacted] armor, I simply couldn't find anyone, with the possible exception of a [Felix Phillips, name redacted] who has a house fairly near the site of the original landing, who did anything by uphold [Zamora's] character and reliability, and I again talked with people who had known him since childhood."[2]

This suggests a contradiction in the case that might be relevant. If Phillips was accurately relating his observations, then there was a major problem with the story told by Zamora. Klass would return to this information long after his book was published. Klass, in an online interview conducted by Gary Posner, a friend of Klass and you might say the copy editor of Klass's *SUN* newsletter, told Posner, "When I interviewed a man who lived right near the landing site, and had been working in his garden when the UFO supposedly blasted off, he told me that he hadn't heard a thing, and that when he visited the site soon afterwards he saw no physical evidence to support Zamora's story and suspected it was a hoax."[3]

But there are things in Phillips's testimony that simply do not make sense no matter what you think of the Zamora tale. It seems that Klass underestimated the distance from the landing site to Phillips's house. It was closer to a mile from the site and with the wind blowing in the wrong direction, Phillips might not have heard anything even if he was standing in his garden rather than sitting in his house as he had originally said. Remember that there were others living in that area who had called the police department to report they had heard or seen something in the sky. Holder mentioned it in his report written on the night of the sighting and, though we don't have the names of the witnesses, we do have the documentation in the form of that report. It wasn't evidence added later but something mentioned on the evening of April 24.[4]

Worse still, for the credibility of Phillips, and information that Klass mentioned in his interview with Posner, Phillips had visited the site that evening and saw nothing there. The problem is that people were on the site from the moment that Zamora saw the blue flame in the sky. Zamora might have been 4,000 feet from the landing site when he first heard the roar, but he drove in that direction. When the craft took off, Zamora, who had been within only a few yards of the craft but had retreated to what he thought of as a safe distance, heard the roar again.

Sergeant Chavez, Zamora's friend and a state police officer, arrived within a minute or two of the craft taking off. From that point on, until dark an hour or so later, there were people at the site, including Holder, Byrnes, other police officers, and finally soldiers from White Sands who Holder had ordered to the site to guard it.[5] The question becomes: Why didn't Phillips see those people?

Again, the documentation available from multiple sources, and from those who were on the site within minutes of the craft's departure, suggests that Phillips should have seen activity there. These details were not added later, but rather amount to information that was printed in newspapers and in the various reports written by various military, law enforcement, and civilian people who were in or around the police station that night. The Lorenzens published similar information in their May 1964 *A.P.R.O. Bulletin* to their membership.

As noted, Klass said in the Posner interview that Phillips had been outside at the time the UFO lifted off. This is a very damaging statement, if true. Had he been outside, even if the wind was blowing in the wrong direction, he should have heard something. That he reported he didn't seems odd, given the testimony of Zamora and those reports called into the police station.

Ben Moss and Tony Angiola, who started investigating the case in 2014, said that they had found "audio" witnesses to the case. That is, they had learned that a number of people had heard the object though they might not have seen anything themselves. This strengthens the case, but only slightly. Those people are unavailable to discuss what they might have heard given that the report is more than a half century old.

Stanford, in his book and as mentioned, reported that while he was in Socorro investigating the case, he met with radio station reporter Walter Shrode for dinner. When they arrived at the restaurant, Shrode introduced him to two women who lived on the south side of Socorro. They told Stanford that he could believe what Zamora had said because they had heard the craft. Stanford naturally asked if they had seen it, too, but they had not. They only heard it as it passed over their houses. In fact, according to the two women, some of the neighbors had heard it as well.

One of the women mentioned they had heard it twice, and Stanford assumed that it had flown over twice. One of the women said they had heard it when it landed and later when it took off.

This was important information that hadn't been mentioned at the time and first appeared in Stanford's 1976 book. As near as I could tell, no one had followed up on it. Given that, I asked Stanford if he had the names of the women. It seemed that information like this, especially if it came from actual witnesses, would be valuable. Stanford didn't have the names and told me that they had been older women in 1964 and that they had probably died since then. My thinking was that it was possible that some of the other neighbors, especially if they had been teenagers in 1964, might still be located. All I really needed was an address or two, but information to reduce the search parameters just didn't exist and, given that it was more than 50 years later, such information might not be very useful.

Looking at all this with a somewhat dispassionate eye, it seems to be a wash. Phillips, who is identified and who claimed it was a hoax, wasn't actually in a good position to see or hear anything. He might have been in his house, he might have been in his garden, and he might have walked up to the landing site, but he didn't see anything. There were officials on the scene from the moment that Zamora arrived until well after dark. Phillips's information doesn't have a very high reliability rating given what is available in the Blue Book files and in the reports from the newspapers and the various UFO group publications.

Unfortunately, the same can be said for most of the other witnesses identified. Holder mentioned them in his report that evening, but he provided no names and apparently never bothered to learn their names if that was even possible. At least the existence of these witnesses was documented in Holder's report written, so they are of a little more value than Phillips.

Stanford's two female witnesses who heard the craft don't provide much more in the way of evidence. They heard a roar, twice, and assumed it had something to do with the landing, but we don't know who they are. In that respect, they are less valuable than Phillips, even with his changing story and location.

But Klass and the skeptics weren't finished with the hoax idea. Klass, in Socorro about a year later and asking questions, seemed to find an undercurrent of disbelief and a hint of a hoax. A few of the locals told him to nose around a little, which he did. And he came up with another hoax theory.

It Was to Create a Tourist Attraction

Klass, while he was in Socorro, had noticed that the scientists at the New Mexico Institute of Mining and Technology seemed to be underwhelmed by the idea that an alien spacecraft had landed in their town. As Klass wrote, "If the story was true, the most

exciting scientific event of all time—a visit from an extraterrestrial spaceship—had occurred almost within sight of the institute.
How could these scientists be so uninterested?"[6]

When he asked about this perceived problem, pressing one
man for an explanation, he was told to "nose around." Klass reported that he was told that Socorro had but one industry: the
institute. They needed something to draw people to the area because the town was drying up. The interstate highway made it
too simple to get from El Paso to Albuquerque so that people
just flew by, maybe stopping for gas or a fast meal but rarely stay-
ing overnight, and there was certainly nothing interesting to see.
Eventually the Very Large Array Radio Telescope facility would
be built out on the Plains of San Agustin, but that was years in the
future.

According to Klass, that night he found an interesting article
in the newspaper. It was the suggestion that one of the best ways
for a community to boost itself was to attract industry, and the
way to do that was to attract tourists. Employers and employees
liked to live in communities that were interesting, the same sort of
thing that appeals to tourists.

A year after the sighting—April 24, 1965—the *El Paso Times*
reported that Socorro town officials were considering using the
sighting as a tourist attraction. The story, written by Jake Booher,
Jr., said that the road to the site, which was nearly impassible, had
been graded and that posters were being displayed by the Socorro
Chamber of Commerce, suggesting an attempt to capitalize on
the sighting.

Of course, no one had been aware of such plans prior to
Zamora's sighting, but that didn't prevent some speculation that
has been repeated by both skeptics and some of the most respected
UFO researchers. Klass noted that the landing site was "especially
convenient—almost midway between the two highways to bring
tourists through Socorro—so it was relatively easy and inexpen-
sive for city officials to provide an improved road that connected
the site to the two highways."[7]

According to Klass, the property where the UFO landed had been "worthless scrub land," but if the site became a tourist attraction, there would be a need for refreshment stands and maybe a motel and other such conveniences for tourists who might want to spend the night next to the place a spaceship landed.[8] There was a happy coincidence as well: The land was owned by the mayor, who happened to be Zamora's superior. The mayor was also the town banker, so he wouldn't be unhappy about the influx of tourists and their money.

Klass was speculating that the mayor and Zamora had cooked up the UFO landing as a way of generating tourist interest in the town and then encouraging those tourists to visit the landing site owned by the mayor. The problem with the theory—other than no tourist attraction ever being built—was that, according to the public records, the landing site was owned by the Delia Harris estate and in 1968 was sold to the Richardson family. The mayor never owned it, and there is no evidence that he ever tried to buy it from the estate.[9]

Klass's suggestion was nothing more than his attempt to cloud the case with an irrelevant fact. Because the mayor didn't own the land, there was no reason for him to conspire with Zamora to create a national sensation to bring attention to Socorro and lure tourists in to see where the UFO landed. The sad thing is that this ownership issue has made it into books and articles about the case, and has been used to dismiss it completely. This theory might be worth a footnote but is certainly not evidence of an "official" hoax.

It Was a Student Hoax?

Dr. Donald Menzel, the Harvard astronomer who wrote a number of books explaining all UFOs as hoaxes, illusions, delusions, misidentifications, and confabulations, was quick to point to students as the culprits in the alleged hoax. On September 10, 1964, Menzel wrote to Hynek, "It certainly sounds to me like a hoax or, perhaps a hallucination." And then in a letter on February 19th,

1965, to Hynek, Menzel and his partner, Lyle Boyd, suggested that high school students who didn't like Zamora, because he issued them speeding tickets, "planned the whole business to 'get' Zamora."[10]

Hynek responded:

Opal Grinder [owner of a gas station on the edge of Socorro] does have a high school student working for him, and I talked with him at length. Teenagers generally hate Zamora's guts, but it was added that they hate all 'fuzz' and that if they wanted to get even with Zamora, they would simply beat him up or do something more direct, like letting the air out of his tires or something with immediate results rather than resort to an involved hoax.[11]

It does seem that such an elaborate hoax would have been beyond the capabilities of high school students, no matter how bright and how clever. It should also be noted that although Hynek was not thinking in terms of high school students, he did ask: "My old friend, Dr. Jack Whotman, President of the New Mexico School of Mines (sic), who said he knew of no geophysical or other types of experiments going on in the area at the time. He, as the rest of the townspeople, were puzzled by the event."[12]

That, of course, was not the end of it, because a new round of investigations suggested students at New Mexico Institute of Mining and Technology were identified as the real perpetrators of the hoax. Tony Bragalia found a letter to Nobel Laureate Linus Pauling dated 1968 saying that the event was a hoax, but it should be noted here that Pauling is only the recipient of the letter, so his name here means very little in this context. In other words, that it was sent to Pauling is of little real note.[13]

The letter, however, was written by Stirling Colgate, a reputable scientist, who was at one time the president of the New Mexico Institute of Mining and Technology (following Whotman in that position) and who said the case is a hoax. We don't know what he really knows about it for certain, because he wasn't there in 1964. He talked of pranks and unidentified students, and even that he knew who the pranksters are, but we have nothing solid to corroborate this allegation. He wouldn't release names.

Bragalia located another source, Dave Collis, who was a freshman in 1965, a year after the landing, who had heard some stories from fellow students. He provided what some have considered new evidence of a hoax. According to Bragalia:

Dave Collis was a freshman at New Mexico Tech in 1965, a year after the Socorro UFO incident. Collis went on to become a published scientist helping to lead the Energetic Materials Research and Testing Center at NM Tech. He is considered a world expert in researching blast effects and explosives. Collis explained that he himself enjoyed planning pranks when he was a student at Tech. In 1965, he and his friends had planned a "paranormal" prank and shared the plan with one of his trusted Professors. The Professor (who had been with Tech for years) told him that NM Tech had a long history of pranking—and that one of them was especially noteworthy. Collis then said that the Professor (whose name he does not remember or does not wish to offer) had "confidentially told me that the UFO sighting by the town cop was a hoax done by Techie students." Collis did not want to press the Professor on who did it—or how. Collis says, "[H]e was telling me this in confidence, so I didn't ask for the details and he didn't offer."

When asked if the Professor could have been making up the hoax story, Collis replied that in the context of his conversation with him—there was no reason for him to lie. The Professor had told him the truth about the hoax, of that he was sure. Collis, when told about Stirling Colgate's confirmation that it was a hoax said, "Colgate is a brilliant man and he was a great College President. From what I was told by my Professor, it was a hoax. And if Colgate also says it was a hoax, it was." Collis (who is a pyrotechnics expert and often directed NM Tech's July 4 Fireworks) said that it always has surprised him that people didn't seem to realize just how "terrestrial" the reported Zamora UFO seemed to be in the first place.[14]

Finally, there are names attached to people who supposedly had some inside knowledge, but who weren't involved themselves and weren't part of the prank. They had heard about it from someone else, who still isn't named but was there who believed it to be a hoax with no reason to lie, according to them. We then go back to Colgate who reaffirmed that it was a hoax, but again, it is from others that he heard this, and he supplies no names of the perpetrators. More importantly, there are no details on how they pulled this off.

Collis had an explanation for the hoax: the one that had been floated decades earlier. Collis said that Lonnie Zamora had a reputation for "hounding" the Techie students rather than high school students during that time (1964). The students and the Socorro police did not have a particularly good relationship then. Collis said that there was "a lot of friction" between what were felt to be "elitist and educated Techies" versus the "under-educated and simpler town folk." Zamora harassed the students for seemingly no reason, and at every possible opportunity. Many of the college kids just did not like him. What better way to "get back" at Zamora than for them to fool a fool?

In that same posting, Bragalia pointed out that Colgate had written in a letter, dated 1968, that the whole thing was a hoax created by the students. The date here is important because in a letter dated September 10, 1964, by Donald Menzel and sent to Hynek, Menzel wrote, "It certainly sounds to me like a hoax or, perhaps, some sort of hallucination." This is four years before the Colgate response and we should note that Menzel had not set foot in Socorro, not talked to a single witness and apparently gathered all his information from the newspaper reports with some possible information supplied by those at Project Blue Book. Colgate, on the other hand, was right there in Socorro, so Colgate wins on that point.

Hynek, however, wrote back to Menzel and said, "With respect to the Socorro case, I wish I could substantiate the idea that it was a hoax or a hallucination. Unfortunately, I cannot."[15]

Menzel and Hynek exchanged a number of other letters over the next several months and finally, on April 29, 1965—three years before Colgate communicated his thoughts on the matter to Pauling—Hynek wrote a six-page letter outlining his take on the Socorro landing. He also said that he had discussed the case with Major Hector Quintanilla, the then chief of Project Blue Book, and said that "he and I are in agreement on what follows."[16]

Since the story appeared, Tony Bragalia and I have engaged in a very cordial email exchange about the case.[17] He's convinced that Colgate is telling the truth and that Colgate knows the truth. I pointed out that Hynek's investigation in Socorro was well publicized and that I found it interesting that Colgate, if he knew it was a hoax, had not suggested this to Hynek, which clearly, he had not.

Bragalia wrote to me:

Colgate said that the perpetrators did not want their cover blown. Perhaps Hynek did not get to the right people. More likely the right people simply did not want to talk. As Klass said, the NM scientists were strangely silent about the whole matter, why? Well, they didn't want to involve the school, or implicate any of the students, that is why. And the students themselves were certainly not going to implicate themselves!

I suppose that makes some sense, but the real problem here is that Hynek's investigation was official and taxpayer money was being spent in his attempt to find a solution. As I have said, and as

Hynek wrote, they were looking for any solution, and even a hint of a hoax would have been enough to push this from the unidentified category.

Bragalia wrote back:

> Perhaps Colgate did not learn the truth about the hoax until after the USAF investigation. I think that this is likely. Maybe he learned of the details only some years later and saw no reason to bring up the whole thing again. Perhaps sometime after the event in the mid or late 60s—someone told him the whole story. By 1970 Colgate had returned to Los Alamos. It could even be that he learned the full story many, many years later when he and his student friend were by then old me. But the point is...he says that it was the hoax with the certainty of a scientist.

Although that might be the truth, we don't know that it is. We only know that Colgate said that it was a hoax and that Bragalia believed that it is the truth. I still have trouble accepting the fact that Colgate, as the ranking member of the faculty, could have learned this vital information and not communicated it to Hynek at some point but only sent it off to Linus Pauling some four years later.

It is important to note here that these are documents found in the Project Blue Book files, and, given the timing (the mid-1960s), those writing the various reports and analyses probably believed that the information would not end up in private hands. In other words, they were writing for a very limited audience and didn't expect the civilian UFO world to ever see these letters. In that respect, that were probably very candid.

On the second page of his long explanation, Hynek wrote:

> The hoax hypothesis is, of course, one that suggests itself immediately. It is Quintanilla's and my opinion that both

Chavez and FBI agent Byrnes must have been in on the hoax if we adopt the hoax hypothesis. They testified that there were no tracks in the immediate neighborhood and so that the hoaxsters must themselves have arrived and left by balloon! Had it been a hoax, certainly some paraphernalia should have been left around if the pranksters beat a hasty retreat.[18]

That analysis makes some sense, but we also have to wonder: How many times have we heard similar statements only to learn that a hoax had been perpetrated? There should have been some evidence—but that there wasn't doesn't tell us that it was not a hoax, only that they found no evidence of it. Not exactly the same thing.

The only part that is impressive are the opinions of Sergeant Chavez and FBI agent Byrnes. There were others who drove to the landing site right away and who were later interviewed by Coral and Jim Lorenzen, Ray Stanford, and, of course, J. Allen Hynek. To make the hoax viable, they all had to be in on it at some point or at some level and, of course, the FBI wouldn't engage in a dirty trick of this nature. There is nothing to be gained by either the Army or the FBI by participation.

Hynek finally does suggest the real problem with the hoax idea. He wrote, "If the hoax comes off well, perpetrators like to gloat abit (sic), and there would have been no point in getting even with Zamora if they couldn't have gotten some kudos for it.[19]

Or, they would have exposed the hoax after they learned of Zamora's reaction to the sighting and his sudden world fame. What better way to get even than to point out he was the victim of a hoax and overreacted in a very unprofessional manner? What better way to make him look bad than by showing how he had been fooled by their hoax?

Hynek finally wrote, "Both Quintanilla and I find it impossible to dismiss it as a hoax unless we have some evidence that there was a hoax."[20] Note here that they were looking for evidence of a hoax within days of the sighting and that they found none.

Even those who came at this from the skeptical side of the house have rejected the student hoax idea. In an article for *Skeptical Inquirer*, and later posted to "New Mexicans for Science and Reason," David E. Thomas wrote, "Yet another hypothesis is that physics students with a little too much extra time played a trick on the town, but that rumor doesn't have much credible support."

This does two things for any analysis. It again points out that this hoax idea has been floating around for decades because the *Skeptical Inquirer* article is from the July 2001 issue and the Internet posting from May 2006. It also suggests that the idea doesn't have much support even with the skeptics who often embrace any explanation to avoid the idea that the case has no terrestrial solution. Maybe the hoax was the students taking credit for the landing but had nothing to do with it.

The Skeptics Have an (Almost) New Explanation

David E. Thomas, a member of the New Mexicans for Science and Reason (NMSR), proposed, first in an article in the *Skeptical Inquirer* and later on the NMSR website, an explanation for the Socorro UFO. He outlined the various explanations, including one that suggested there was a craft: It was a spaceship, sort of, but it came from White Sands rather than outer space.[21]

Thomas wrote that Charles Moore, who gained fame with his claim to have launched the balloon array that was mistaken for the Roswell UFO debris, learned from a colleague, Captain James McAndrew, who was working on the Air Force investigation of Roswell in 1994, that there were some special tests being conducted at White Sands involving a Lunar Surveyor and helicopters. The Lunar Surveyor was a three-legged vehicle, unmanned, which was designed to learn about the Moon's surface before the astronauts were sent there on the Apollo missions.

McAndrew found a log, the "Daily Range Schedule for Friday, 24 April 1964," that confirmed the tests. It showed that the Surveyor and a helicopter were being used from 0745 to 1100 on that morning. Thomas wrote, "The timing isn't right for the UFO sightings—the range log calls from morning tests and the sightings occurred in later afternoon—but then things don't always go 'according to plan.' And many tests that have defied completion by morning have been known to somehow get finished in the afternoon."[22]

There were other reasons to suspect the test flight, according to Thomas. The Surveyor's legs slanted in much the same way that Zamora had suggested, and the helicopter carrying the Surveyor would have been a strange thing to see. The Surveyor had a mechanical scoop with a shape that seemed to match the marks on the ground reported by Zamora and many of those who arrived in the minutes and in some cases days after the landing.

The description of the craft, which was aluminum-white, matches the description given by Zamora and the helicopter would have carried a pilot and an engineer who would have been wearing white coveralls (though I wonder why the pilot wouldn't have been wearing a gray flight suit, which was standard issue then).

More importantly, Thomas mentioned that many people in the Socorro area believed that what Zamora had seen was a secret government craft, and officers at Blue Book allegedly pinned it down to a "tenant operation" being carried out at Holloman Air Force Base in Alamogordo that does share testing grounds with White Sands.

Does this explain the Zamora sighting better than a student hoax, some sort of balloon, or even alien visitation?

Actually, no. One of the first problems is that Hector Quintanilla, who was in charge at Blue Book, followed that lead. In his unpublished manuscript, he described his investigation into the landing. He wrote that he was determined to solve the case and decided that he had to talk with the base commander at Holloman, Colonel Garman. According to Quintanilla, Garman told him that he (Quintanilla) could go anywhere and visit any activity on the base that interested him. Quintanilla said that he spent four days talking to everyone he could find and spent time with the down range controllers at White Sands. Quintanilla wrote, "I left Holloman dejected and convinced that the answer to Zamora's experience did not originate and terminate at that base."[23]

But that might not have covered the Lunar Lander. He knew that some of the research had been carried out at Wright-Patterson Air Force Base, so when he reached there, he asked to be briefed on those projects. He learned that it wasn't operational in 1964. That ruled it out, but the Lunar Lander isn't quite the same thing as the Lunar Surveyor. Is that ruled out as well?

The log published by Thomas showed some sort of test on April 24th that was carried out at White Sands. The trouble here is Holder. He was the commander of the Stallion Station at White Sands and his duty location—meaning where he actually worked— was closer to Socorro than it was to the White Sands Missile Range main complex, which is near Alamogordo. Had the answer been that simple, Holder would have known about a test that had left the range for whatever reason, or he could have learned that with a few telephone calls; that would have been in his report written early on the morning of April 25 after his interview with Zamora, but nothing like that is mentioned. Holder is as puzzled as the rest of them.

Skeptics will say that Occam's razor eliminates alien visitation because any explanation that requires the invention of interstellar flight is not a simple explanation. The terrestrial answers are simpler because there isn't that requirement. But Occam's razor also mentions something about covering all the facts, not just those that are convenient for an explanation. Quintanilla, after all the work he had done, all the explanations he had tried, and all the experimental aircraft and space craft he reviewed, and after all the letters he had written to various governmental agencies and defense contractors who might have had something going on, came up empty.

Quintanilla wrote:

I labeled the case "Unidentified" and the UFO buffs and hobby clubs had themselves a field day.... Although I labeled the case "Unidentified" I've never been satisfied with that classification. I've always felt that too many essential elements of the case were missing. These are the intangible elements which are impossible to check, so the solution to this case could very well be lying dormant in Lonnie Zamora's head.[24]

Chapter 11:

Other Landings

Though there are catalogs of UFO landing trace cases, a study of those reports shows that frequently there is no UFO associated with the landing. Farmers in fields, hikers, and even UFO investigators find circular patterns left behind. The idea that a UFO was responsible is often conjecture based on other sightings in the area, the shape of the landing trace, and sometimes the imagination of those who found it.

In Iowa in 1973 a series of landing reports was made. As if to prove the point, Howard Groves thought that lightning had struck when he found a burned area nearly 40 feet across in his soybean field. In the center was a small crater, about 2 feet in diameter, that was surrounded by four smaller holes. To Groves, it looked as if something had taken off in a burst of flame. Unsure what to do, or what he had found, he went home and called the Wright County Sheriff, Robert Shaw, in Clarion, Iowa.[1]

Shaw had been involved with UFO sightings and investigations the year before, so he was interested in what Groves had found. He drove out and, with Groves, carefully inspected the burn, the holes, and the surrounding area. Groves said, "Well, the other night there was something strange. My wife and I had gone to a ball game and when we got home our dog [Ginger] ran into the house. He wouldn't come out. I've never seen him so scared before."[2]

The beans around the small crater for about 20 feet in all directions had wilted as if exposed to an intense heat. They were beginning to crumble. The ground looked like baked clay. Shaw asked a few more questions, took some pictures, and then returned to his office to add the new information to his growing UFO file.

The Wright County Farm Agent also made a visit. He brought a Geiger counter, but there was nothing other than normal background radiation. Soil samples, however, showed that the phosphorus had been burned from the ground near the crater. He had no explanation for that, and he didn't even try to explain the crater.

It was about three weeks after Groves had made the discovery that I had a chance to talk to both the sheriff and Groves. I collected soil samples, which included a gray dust that turned out to be the remains of organic material after exposure to intense heat.

Groves said that he had applied a blowtorch to one of the soybean plants and it had taken 10 minutes to create a similar effect. He couldn't understand how such a large area had been burned. He said, "Whatever it was, it sure must have been hot."[3]

The news media learned of the landing, or possible landing, and reported in the days that followed. Dozens of people came to the Groves farm to look at the alleged UFO landing site. One of them, Don Slaikeu, from Goldfield, Iowa, said that a UFO had landed on his farm about a year earlier.

Slaikeu said that the burn looked like what he had found, but then added an important point: "[A] neighbor saw the thing land." It had lit up his house with a very bright light. Slaikeu found the burn two days later.[4]

In fact, in July 1972, there were at least five landings in Iowa. Near Laurens, the wife of a farmer, who didn't want to be identified, said that she had been surprised by a loud bang. At that point the lights went out and the phone jumped from the wall. The room filled with a bright, and what she said "was a horrible glow for several minutes."[5] The next day her husband found a burned depression in his soybeans.

Near Story City, Iowa, a smaller version of the Laurens burn had been found. A week later, one of the neighbors said that she knew what had happened. She had seen the thing land. According to what she said, "I was awakened by a loud crash. I wanted to see what had happened but couldn't move. My whole body tingled with electricity.... Later, I managed to get out of bed but there was nothing to see. The next day, I felt fine."[6]

Though the woman didn't wish to be identified, her house was a mere 250 yards from the soybean field where Mervin Teig found a burned area. In the burned area, the soybeans were dead and in the center of the burn were two small holes. The ground contained the same gray dust—that is, the burned organic matter that was found on the other Iowa sites.[7]

Teig submitted some of the gray dust for further analysis. It was determined that it was not the result of a lightning strike or a chemical spill. Spectroscopic analysis suggested that the soil inside the burn was no different than the control samples from outside. The difference was that the soil inside the burn area had been subjected to extremely high heat, turning the organic material to ash.[8]

Another of those who visited Teig was Leslie Polling, who had read about the landing in the newspaper. Polling said that he had found a depression on his farm but it was larger than that found by Teig and on one side of the depression the dirt had been thrown out as if from a rocket blast that had been angled upward. He found the same gray ash, and he kept a big clod of the dirt covered with plastic in his garage.

Polling said that he had seen some strange things on his farm before he found the burn. He said that one night he had been in the kitchen when a "sheet of light" had illuminated the room. There was a loud crack and several windows in the house broke. He said that he didn't think it was lightning because lightning had struck close to the house before and hadn't sounded like that.[9]

The trouble with all these landing reports was that no craft was seen in relation to them. There were some anomalous lights and phenomena but no structured craft such as that reported by Zamora.

There was another Iowa case that did contain a report of a craft. The family involved then didn't want to be involved with UFO reports. Three people living in Waverly, Iowa, said they had seen a large, disc-shaped craft late one afternoon. A flash of bright light caught the eye of one of the men and overhead they saw the disc descending toward a hilltop not far away. Seconds later the craft disappeared behind the hill.

One of the men decided to investigate. He leaped from the porch and sprinted across an open field. Before he had run too far, he heard a roar and looked up in time to see the UFO shoot up, into the sky.

He didn't stop, but continued to the hilltop. Below him, in a rock quarry, he could see a large burned area. It was circular, 20 feet in diameter, and all the vegetation inside the burn had been destroyed.

The witnesses did call the police, but the reaction was not what they had expected, though others have seemed to expect just that reaction. Police laughed at the report and accused them all of drinking heavily. They agreed to talk with me only after a promise to not mention their names, which, in the world today seems to uncut the veracity of the tale. It can't be independently verified.[10]

That is not the case in a report from Van Horn, Iowa, on July 13, 1969. Pat Barr, who was 15 at the time, was getting ready for bed with her older cousin, Kathy Mahr, when they heard a roar like a low-flying jet. Outside the window was an object that looked like the classic saucer with two sections of lights on it. Barr said that she thought it was spinning and after she couldn't see the craft she could still see two glowing red lights that had a triangle shape.[11]

The object had hovered over a field to the north of the house. Then it just disappeared. They couldn't see which way it went. It just seemed to fade from sight, with the exception of those two red lights that eventually faded out as well.

The next morning, they told Pat's father, Warren Barr, what they had seen, but he just laughed at them. But he stopped laughing as he went about his chores on the farm. He found a 40-foot circle had been burned into the bean field. As he would tell reporters, the beans had been healthy the day before. He said that it looked as if they had been exposed to extreme heat, but there was no sign of a flame.

Although they wished to keep the story quiet, as often happens, some of it leaked, and a man who worked at a St. Paul television station overheard a conversation about the UFO. A team from the station headed to Iowa, and on August 6, 1969, the *Cedar Rapids Gazette* carried the story.

There was discussion about the circle being the result of a lightning strike, but Vivian Jennings, the Cedar Rapids crop specialist, said that the circular area was barren but the rest of the field was unaffected."[12]

Brad Steiger took an interest in the case and contacted one of his associates, Glenn McWane, to investigate. He took soil samples and provided Steiger with a copy of the analysis completed by a contact at the University of Iowa Medical Department. It said:

My contact's findings were a slightly higher than normal radiation yield. In addition, from the grass enclosed with the sample he found that the strontium 90 was also just a little higher than normal.

On reminding my contact that the alleged landing occurred on July 13 and that my samples were taken on August 11, he went on to state that the count must have been higher, because the amount of rain that had fallen in the area between the time of the sighting and the time that the samples had been obtained...would have diluted the count.

My contact has taken into consideration the amount of fallout considered normal for this area and any nuclear testing that might have been done at this time. My contact is among those employed to keep a close check on the amount of radiation in the Iowa air and soil, and he is always informed on how much fallout is absorbed by plants and how much is absorbed by cows eating grass and how much is consequently given out in milk.[13]

Interestingly, Steiger mentioned that within a month of McWane's investigation he had received a letter from an employee of an Iowa power and light company who had found a series of "burnt circles" near powerlines in northeastern Iowa. By coincidence, I had served in Vietnam with Pat Barr's brother, and when I moved to Iowa and learned of the sighting I visited Warren Barr. He said that he too had heard from a family in northeastern Iowa who told him of the circles, but they didn't want to have reporters or UFO investigators descending on them. He shared the contact information with me, and I had a chance to talk to them as well.

McWane, according to Steiger, had also seen what he thought of as landing depressions. McWane was told that strange things had been going on for a long time. It was the same thing that I was told when I talked to the family. Not only had they seen strange things, but they had taken photographs. The problem was that the photos were streaks of light against a dark background. It wouldn't have taken much in the way of sophistication to fake the pictures, though it didn't seem that was the case.[14]

These landings were a frequent occurrence, but no one else in the area reported the same thing. Or it might be suggested that no one else wanted to admit to seeing UFOs. For me, the investigation didn't go very far, and, although I did try to spot the UFOs, I never had any success.

The Opposite of the Iowa Landings

Though it seemed that landing traces were found but that there was very little that suggested anyone had seen an object to cause those traces, it would be interesting to look at another case reported on January 11, 1961, near Benjamin, Texas, which is located in the panhandle, not all that far from Wichita Falls. W.K. Rutledge, an attorney who was flying a private plane, and George Thomas, his passenger, were en route to Abilene, Texas, from Tulsa, Oklahoma, when they spotted a brightly glowing, red object at about 8,000 feet, that Rutledge would later say, "[l]it up the plane."[15]

Rutledge said that he had changed course to follow the light and contacted the control tower at Shepard Air Force Base, alerting them to the chase. They followed it as it moved around, seen by witnesses on the ground including Mrs. Homer T. Melton, who was the police radio dispatcher and married to the Knox County sheriff. She said that she first heard about the object on the radio and went outside to see for herself. She said that it was red and larger than Venus.

Near Benjamin, the object began to lose altitude and seemed to glide toward the ground, landing about 4 or 5 miles southwest of town in a heavily wooded area. Rutledge began circling the area, attempting to guide Melton, one of his deputies, the police chief, Joe Massey of Munday, and another chief from Knox City to the landing site.

According to an article in the *Wichita Falls Times*, one of the ground searchers, Sheriff's Deputy Stone, had driven to within a hundred yards or so of the object, but Rutledge couldn't direct him any closer. Rutledge had to break off the communications because he was low on fuel and had to land. While he had been circling, the object had ceased to glow and, when Stone had blinked his lights, the glow disappeared completely.

The next morning, according to Richard Hall, writing in his *The UFO Evidence*, the search began again, this time with 20 high school boys and others who lived in the area. The hunt continued until about three in the afternoon.

Hall wrote, "Since there was no convenient airport, Rutledge and Thomas landed on the highway near Benjamin. When they got into town they were immediately met by USAF Lieutenant [Charles] McClure and a Sergeant...." According to Hall, "The Air Force officer's opening implications that the object might have been a balloon or a meteorite were quickly shortcut by Rutledge's firm statement: 'What I saw last night was certainly not a meteorite or a weather balloon.'"[16]

McClure expressed an interest in finding the landing site, so Rutledge and Thomas took him back to his parked aircraft. The sheriff stopped the traffic and they took off. They made three or four passes over the area, but, when they saw nothing, they left. McClure didn't seem interested in joining the ground search that was going on. Later, Rutledge and others were seen in a local restaurant and it appeared that he was filling out the Air Force "ATIC Form 164" used to report a UFO sighting.

Cliff Clines, who was a news editor for the morning edition of the newspaper, was interviewed by Coral Lorenzen. He told her that early on January 11, the witnesses talked about what they had seen and done. After McClure arrived, Rutledge seemed hesitant to talk and his answers were vague.[17]

McClure didn't talk to any of the law enforcement officers, including the police dispatcher who had seen the object herself. Massey said that he and a city alderman had seen a bright light take off like a rocket to about 300 or 400 feet.

In a report to the ATIC at Wright-Patterson Air Force Base on January 18, 1961, McClure wrote:

Reference my message of 13 January TA1702A concerning 10 January sighting. Many ground sightings correlate highly in description and path of the object sighted by Mr. Rutledge and Mr. Thomas [names redacted in original] in the aircraft... but, since these reports were received by the offices of local news media, the preparing officer [McClure] was able to obtain only two witnesses' names. The testimony obtained from [name redacted but is most probably Rutledge] who is considered reliable, verifies unquestionably the description and the path of the object sighted from the aircraft.... The cause and identity of this object remains undeterminable.[18]

Although the Air Force had redacted the names on the form filled out by Rutledge, at the top of the first page someone had written "Pilot." That identified which of the forms in the file Rutledge had filled out. From that, we learn that Rutledge held a private pilot license, that he had four and a half years of military service during World War II, and that he had been a major at the time of his separation.

There is another of the Air Force forms in the file with the case, this one filled out by an observer on the ground. It is clear from the form that this relates to the sighting by Rutledge and Thomas, but the names of the witnesses have been redacted. According to the document:

My wife and I were driving west on the Seymour Highway and were approximately one mile west of the city where we first sighted the object.

At first glance it appeared to be an unusually bright star but a second look quickly convinced us that this object was far too brilliant, and too close at hand to be a star—also quickly became evidence that the object was moving toward the southwest....

At this point we drove off the highway and stopped to view the object better. This was the closest I believe we came to it...the object appeared to be hovering directly above the TV towers and at this point the object appeared to be no more than 1500 feet at the most in altitude and appeared to be no more than 1000 feet or so ahead of us....

The object then began to move again in a southwesterly direction and we followed it proceeding on out the highway another mile or so at which point the object crossed the highway on its southwesterly course.

We then turned almost due south...and observed the object continuing on south west and to our right. We arrived at our home and went in to the back yard and continued to observe the object.... I stayed in the back yard or in the back door of my home and my wife got into the car and drove out...in a westerly direction...to see if she could see any thing (sic) further. *We both observed an airplane following the object, some distance behind it* [author's emphasis]. We saw the blinking wing and tail light of the plane very clearly, and could see the object ahead of the plane and somewhat more south west also very clearly although gradually diminishing in light intensity. At the very last, before the object disappeared the light gave off appeared to grow somewhat more reddish in color—then it disappeared from view. We could not tell for sure whether it had "landed" or had disappeared over the horizon.[19]

Although McClure seemed somewhat puzzled by the sighting, and there was a ground observation that suggested the witnesses had seen, not only the UFO, but the aircraft chasing it, the final Air Force evaluation was that they had probably seen Venus. In the comments section of the project card, it was noted, "The planet

[Venus] was just setting and it is concluded that the atmospheric refraction was principal cause of the misidentification. The description of the object and its motions are those which would be associated with astronomical objt (sic) subjected to the effects of atmospheric refraction."[20]

The real point is that there had been no burned areas or circles of compressed ground, but there were people who saw the object in the sky and watched as it approached the ground. Rutledge and Thomas, in the aircraft, circled the landing area for 20 minutes or so before they were forced to leave due to fuel consumption. Others on the ground reported the same object and, though it can be argued that those witnesses were influenced by the newspaper reports, it can also be said that they accurately reported what they had seen. It is an interesting case because of the landing, the witnesses in the air, and those on the ground.

Another Witnessed Landing

The Project Blue Book narrative about the sighting begins with a telephone call from Clifford Melroe in Gwinner, North Dakota, alerting the officers of the 119th Combat Support Squadron that Randy Rotenberger, the 11-year-old son of Emmanuel Rotenberger, had seen a strange object on September 13, 1966. It had landed in a plowed field near the house and had left impressions in the soft ground. Melroe suggested that someone from the Air Force should take a look at the impressions to explain them.[21]

The Air Force, which is to say the Air Guard in the area, took the report seriously and responded with several high-ranking officers, including Brigadier General Homer G. Goebel, Lieutenant Colonel Thomas E. Marking, and Captain Edward A. Skroch. They learned that Randy had been alone, outside the house waiting for the school bus, when he spotted a metallic object that was shaped like two bowls pressed together rim to rim with two red lights, two white lights, and single, green one around the middle. It landed in a plowed field some 300 yards from the house.

The object landed on three legs, which had feet on the ends that looked like bowls, with the bottom of the bowl sitting on the ground. To Rotenberger, it looked like a camera tripod. There was a transparent bubble on the top of the object but Rotenberger could see nothing moving around inside. He thought it was about 30 feet in diameter and 8 to 10 feet through center at the thickest point.

Frightened by the landed UFO, Rotenberger ran into the house, yelling for his mother. She told him to lock the door. Having done that, he watched the object from a window. After it had been on the ground for about a minute, the UFO lifted off. Rotenberger said there was a blue glow along the bottom and it took off with a roar that was followed by buzzing. His mother heard the roar as the craft lifted off but apparently didn't see it.

Goebel and the other Air Force investigators found the landing impressions in the field and described them as looking as if someone had set a bowling ball on the ground and jumped up and down on it. They also reported that the surrounding area showed no signs of heat and no evidence of a high-velocity wind blast.

The case file contains a report that said, "The symmetrical layout of the depressions is a logical arrangement for a tripod-type landing gear."[22]

It also said, "The absence of vehicular tracks in the field effectively rules out the possibility of the depressions being made by a piece of heavy farm machinery."[23]

Although there was a claim that the depressions were made by a weight of about 1,500 pounds, there was also a note that the estimate is unverified. There is what would be considered a "Memo for the Record," though it is not labeled as such. It reinforces the idea that the estimated weight was probably inaccurate. They didn't get to the field until three days after the sighting and the ground had not been as solidly compressed as had been indicated in other reports.[24]

There are two things that are not explained in the Blue Book file. First, there is a letter from Colonel Louis De Coes to the local power company about a power failure that lasted some four hours. There was no answer to the inquiry in the file.

Second, the official report mentioned that the object had been seen through a rifle's telescopic sight, but there is nothing to suggest that is accurate. In fact, the Air Force form filled out by Rotenberger specially noted that he had not seen the UFO through anything other than window glass after he had returned to the house.

Although there were suggestions throughout the file that some sort of a hoax might have been perpetrated, there is no evidence such was the case. The Air Force investigators wrote that "Although the possibility of a hoax always exists, it is not considered a certainty. The observer obviously lacks observation experience and technical knowledge but he displayed obvious sincerity."[25]

In the end the Air Force was left with no solution. It had originally labeled the case as "Insufficient Data," but that was only because the witness, Rotenberger, hadn't completed the rather long and annoying form. When that was done, and the Air Force had received the information from the North Dakota Air Guard, it labeled the case as "Unidentified."

A Precursor to Delphos

Harold Butcher, who was 16 at the time, said that at about 8:20 p.m. on August 19, 1965, he was operating a milking machine in a dairy barn. He was listening to the radio, which was hanging on the wall when it was filled with static, drowning out the newscast.[26] A tractor that was providing power to the milking machine quit and a bull outside the barn began to bellow. Butcher ran to the window and outside he saw a large, elliptical object, looking like two saucers pasted together rim to rim, was approaching the ground about a quarter mile away.

According to the Project Blue Book files, Butcher said the object was 50 feet long and 20 feet thick. It was shiny like silver, with red-colored streamers along the underside. There was a tail that was from red to yellow. *The A.P.R.O. Bulletin* reported that there was a reddish glow or vapor under the craft.[27]

Butcher said that he heard a steady beep–beep, coming from the craft. It was only on the ground for a few seconds before it shot straight up into the air, disappearing into the clouds, which took on a greenish color, in seconds.

Butcher called to the house to notify his parents. They came out and all of them noticed a strange odor in the air. The Air Force file mentioned that it was like burning gasoline.

Some 30 to 45 minutes later, the object returned. It descended slowly from the clouds toward a wooded area and then rose again, leaving a red trail. The Air Force file seems to indicate that the UFO returned a third time at about 9:00 p.m., again looking as if it was going to land. It rose suddenly to an altitude just below the clouds and then flew away to the south–southwest, emitting a yellow trail.

Butcher's mother then called the state police, who sent troopers out. They, in turn, notified the Air Force, which began an investigation led by Captain James Dorsey, the operations officer of the 4621st AF Group. He was accompanied by four enlisted Air Force technicians. They examined the area where the UFO had hovered, or landed, and found a purplish liquid, singed foliage, and some small, unexplained marks about 2 inches wide and 2 inches apart.[28]

Samples were taken by the Air Force and by NICAP member Jeffrey Gow. NICAP sent the samples to Kawecki Chemical Company, whose president, according to *The UFO Investigator*, was an NICAP advisor, for analysis. Analysis showed that the liquid was made up of "aluminum, iron and silicon. Some phosphorous was found in the weed samples, which the analyst said might cause the phosphine smell, explaining the odd odor."[29]

Air Force analysis seemed to be more specific. In the file it was noted that "[n]o physical evidence of a vehicle or landing was found except an oily substance which was found to be a combination of

Vio strigent (sic) or Gentian Violet plus 3-in-one oil, which is not believed to be connected with this sighting."[30]

Hynek included the case in his book, *The Hynek UFO Report*. He wrote, "There was a strong impulse at Blue Book to regard this case as a hoax, but the evidence pointed in the opposite directions."

In fact, in a synopsis of the case, in the comments section of the Blue Book file, it was reported that:

> The State Police patrolman who interviewed the witnesses said it was his impression that the sighting could be a hoax, but he did not feel that it was, as the people were rural people. Also, the investigating officer and three technicians were convinced that the sighting was not a hoax or fabrication. One technician remained unconvinced....
>
> Although the sequence of events is dubious, the sighting is carried as unidentified by the Air Force since there is no definite concrete explanation.[31]

In the end, the Air Force labeled the case as "Unidentified," though the project card seemed to add a qualification. It said, "Silver object fifty ft long 20 ft thick. Saucer shaped like two plates back to back. Moved in and out of the clouds. Sighting at dusk. Several 15–16 yr old youths made sighting. Sequence of events dubious."[32]

Delphos, Kansas: Another Observed Landing

Few cases have received as much scrutiny as the landing near Delphos, Kansas, that took place on November 2, 1971. Although there was only a single witness to the landing, there were traces left once the craft was gone and the witness's parents saw the lights in the distance, and that elevated the case. It all began at about 7:00 p.m. when Ronald Johnson, 16 at the time, was called to dinner. He didn't arrive right away, as he was completing his chores. Erma and Durel ate and then called Ronald again. He didn't respond to Erma's call.[33]

Ronald Johnson would later tell his parents that, after his mother had called, he had heard a rumbling in the distance and he walked toward the noise. He said that he had seen, hovering just above the ground, in a clump of trees about 75 feet away, a brightly lighted object covered in red, blue, and orange lights. The light was bright, he said, like that of a welder's torch. He watched it for about five minutes before it flashed brightly and caused some temporary sight impairment. After several minutes, Johnson's sight began to return.

He described the craft as about 9 feet in diameter and about 10 feet high, with a dome on top and a bulge around the center. Johnson thought that it looked something like a mushroom.

His mother came out to call him again to dinner, but instead, he called them out of the house. One report said he had run to the house to tell them there was a flying saucer and he could still see it. As the object took off toward the south, it passed over a shed and the rumble became a high-pitched whine. When it was high in the southern sky, after he had alerted his parents, they saw it, too. They just hadn't seen it when it had been close to the ground, and they would later say that they had not heard the rumbling or the high-pitched whine.

With the craft now out of sight, all three of them walked over to where it had been hovering. They found a glowing ring on the ground and saw that some of the trees, close to the ring, were also glowing. They did touch the ground and found that it was not warm but that their fingers became numb, a problem that lasted for about a week. The texture of the soil seemed to be crusty.

With the UFO gone, Johnson and his father climbed into the car to head into Delphos. They thought the newspaper might be interested in the story. Philip Klass, in *UFOs Explained*, reported they had called the editor of the newspaper, Willard Critchfield. In any case, and again according to Klass, Critchfield was on deadline and decided to finish getting the newspaper ready to publish.

Thaddia Smith, a reporter for the local newspaper, and the local sheriff, Ralph Enlow, did visit the farm the next day. Smith wrote, "The circle was still very distinct and plain to see. The soil was dried and crusted. The circle or ring was approximately 8 feet across and outside area were still muddy from recent rains. The area of the ring was dried about a foot across and was very bright in color."[34]

Smith was the one who called the local sheriff, Ralph Enlow, who, with Kansas Highway Patrol Trooper Kenneth Yager and the undersheriff, Harlan Enlow, visited the Johnson farm. Enlow, in his official report, wrote, "Mr. Johnson took us out...where we observed ring shaped somewhat like a doughnut with a hole in the middle. The ring was completely dry.... There were limbs broken from a tree and a dead tree broken off.... There was a slight discoloration on the trees."[35]

Enlow also reported, "We were given a picture taken the previous evening by Mrs. Johnson which showed that the ring glowed in the dark.... The soil sample taken was almost white in color and very dry...the soil was not radioactive."[36]

Enlow's officer report also made another connection with what happened in Socorro. He noted that on 11-03-71 [that is, the day after the sighting by the Johnsons] Mr. Lester Ernsbarger... in Minneapolis, Kansas, advised Deputy Sheriff Leonard Simpson that at approx. 7:30 p.m. 11-02-71 he had observed a bright light descending in the sky in the Delphos area.[37]

About a month after the sighting, Hynek read a newspaper article about the case and called Ted Phillips, who studied landing trace cases and who compiled a catalog of those cases. Phillips visited on December 4, 1971. He discussed the case with the sheriff and was given some soil samples. He then went out to the farm to interview the Johnsons.

Phillips would say that the ring that had been glowing was dry, but the surrounding areas and the inside of the ring were muddy because of local rain. The ring itself was outline by snow, though the snow around it had melted. They scrapped away some of the snow and poured water on it, and the soil in the ring remained dry.

On January 11, 1972, Phillips returned to Delphos. He discussed the possibility of a hoax with both Smith and Sheriff Enlow. Both said that they believed the Johnsons—that the family was respected and that they were truthful. Besides, there was the report from Ernsbarger that provided another witness. The timing of Ernsbarger's report seemed to suggest that he might not have heard the tale prior to coming forward, but there is the possibility of contamination. If Ernsbarger had not heard about the sighting, then his story is further corroboration. The timing is off. When Ernsbarger was apparently seeing the craft descend, according to the timing by the Johnsons, it had been ascending. The discrepancy might not be all that important because the timing, although not exact from either location, might simply be close enough.[38]

On March 12, 1972, the *National Enquirer* announced that it would pay $50,000 to anyone who could provide evidence that proved the Earth was being visited by creatures from another star system. Later still, it announced that it would pay $5,000 to the best UFO case presented that year if no one qualified for the larger reward. The date of the announcement is important to understand the case.[39]

Philip Klass, now alerted to the importance of this case because in May 1972, the *National Enquirer,* having found no single case that was worthy of the top prize, awarded the $5,000 prize to the Johnsons, suggesting it was the best case of the last year, believed that if he could explain this case, then his theory that there was no alien visitation would be validated. In fact, in what is an interesting coincidence, he noted that after he had "explained" the Zamora case that UFO researchers claimed he had picked an easy one. But the truth of the matter is that few researchers accepted his hoax theory as correct. Most rejected it because it was based on a foundation of sand that eroded quickly under any sort of scrutiny.

Some of the objections raised by Klass seem valid on the surface, but many of them were predicated on how he believed the witnesses *should* have acted rather than how they *did* act. For example, he thought that Ronald Johnson should have been more concerned about his eyesight than he was. He believed that the young man should have wanted to see a doctor as quickly as possible but the fact is, his temporary impairment had faded almost immediately and was more akin to blindness caused by a camera's flashbulb than it was something permanent.[40]

The same can be said for the tingling and numbness felt by the older Johnsons. Klass thought that their touching the glowing ring in the minutes after the UFO had departed was the height of foolishness, because they didn't know if the ring was radioactive in some fashion. But that numbness didn't worry either of the Johnsons.

When Durel and Ronald drove into town after the UFO had vanished, Klass thought they should have gone to the doctor rather than the newspaper office. And while there, he thought the editor showed a complete lack of interest in a story of alien creatures landing in rural Kansas.[41]

The trouble is, we don't know how the Johnsons thought and if going to the doctor was routine for them. The numbness was not debilitating and Ronald's blindness had disappeared. Without an immediate need for medical treatment, and with the cost of medical assistance, the thought of a doctor might have not crossed their minds. But the story of the UFO landing was an issue that did.

The other thing is that this was the early 1970s, only a year or two after Edward Condon, the University of Colorado, and the Air Force had declared that there were no UFOs.[42] The newspaper editor, who had probably heard about that and knew that many UFO cases had evaporated under scrutiny, not to mention some of the hoaxes that had floated around, probably believed that his newspaper deadline was more important than an improbable story of alien creatures in a landed UFO. The driving force in a small-town newspaper is not always what others might consider important, and a flying saucer had not made the cut with a deadline looming.

In the late 1960s and into the 1970s, there were many people, mostly teenaged boys, who were launching hot air balloons in an attempt to fool people. These were made of lightweight dry cleaner bags that were nearly transparent and often translucent, obscuring the candles burning inside to give them lift. When the candle burned out it looked as if the UFO had just vanished. In other words, there was no imperative then, just as there is no real imperative now, to report on a flying saucer tale.

Klass had been told by a neighbor that some sort of galvanized watering station for livestock had stood on the landing site. It had been removed at some point, but it might be the source of the strange ring. Klass thought that the sheep, while at the vat, might have urinated, and over the years the accumulation of chemicals from the urine might have created the ring. It would still be visible long after the vat had been removed. In an attempt to confirm his theory, he went to the trouble of tracking down aerial photographs of the land. The Department of Agriculture had periodically taken aerial photographs in an attempt to determine how much land was being farmed. Klass learned that such photographs had been taken in 1965 and 1971. He had blow-ups made and found no evidence of any sort of a structure standing on that particular bit of land. It was a dead end for him, but one that ended the discussion about the galvanized tub that might have been there.[43]

Soil analysis was also possible even decades after the sighting. Phillips had been careful in his collection of the samples. According to an article on the Open Minds website written by Alejandro Rojas, Phyllis Budinger, a retired research scientist for BP/Amoco, had found unusually high concentrations of oxalic acid. Dr. J. Robert Mooney said, "Exhaust from a low temperature ionization or combustion engine (whose fuel source was elemental carbon) could leave a high concentration of acid along with other lower molecular weight acids."[44]

Though all that is interesting, it doesn't completely eliminate the sheep urine as a source of the ring. Oxalic acid is found naturally in a number of plants, and it can lead to kidney stones. According to the Oxalic-Acid Information website:

> The effects of oxalic acid in the human body, when ingested in foods, flow from its ability to combine chemically with certain metals commonly found in—and important to—the human body, such as magnesium and calcium. When oxalic acid combines with such metals, the result is, in chemical terms, a salt; those oxalic-acid + salts are called oxalates. Since oxalic acid is not (so far as known today) a useful nutrient, it is—like all such unneeded components of diet—processed by the body to a convenient form, those oxalates, and that byproduct is then eventually excreted – in this case, in urine.[45]

It might be said that both sides in the discussion have scored points. No evidence on the aerial photographs, which are detailed enough that the vat or trough would have been visible, was found, tending to rule that out. But then, the high degree of oxalic acid might have been from years of a buildup of sheep urine.

Another problem, for Klass at least, was that the Johnsons refused to take lie detector tests. When he got nowhere with that, he suggested hypnotic regression for Ronald, but again the family refused. For Klass, this proved the case was a hoax. The trouble is, of course, that lie detectors are not 100 percent reliable and hypnotic regression is an extremely poor research tool, as we have learned in the last quarter century or so.[46]

The real trouble here is the glowing ring of material that seemed to be a result of the hovering UFO. That was physical evidence that something had been seen, and testing the soil, both of the ring itself and the ground around it, might provide some real proof.

Other analysis that had been carried out by a variety of laboratories of the soil samples didn't seem to do anyone much good. Klass had suggested that his analysis, which was his examination of the photographs of the ring, had not shown evidence of high heat. According to him, "the dried out condition of the soil could not have resulted from the proximity of an extremely hot object because the photo revealed numerous small twigs, some of them within the horseshoe-shaped ring, none of which showed the slightest evidence of heat or burning."[47]

Heat is not the only form of radiation, and tests conducted at Texas A&M University suggested that

[m]icrowaves in the 1,000 to 10,000 megahertz at power densities about 100 watt per centimeter squared, can cause plant symptoms similar to burning and can definitely cause dehydration....

Your description, the "ring" of soil was not only dried, but changed in structure. Changes in soil structure such as you describe would require the application of large amounts of energy. In summary, some of the effects you describe could be attributed to exposure to relatively high power densities of microwaves; others could not. All the biological effects described could conceivably be caused by energy in some portion of the electromagnetic spectrum, but no one area could account for all the effects described.[48]

There are two other points to be made here. First, some believed that the ring was a "Fairy Ring," growth of mushrooms. Such things are not all that uncommon and have been reported in a large number of areas. Analysis of the soil seemed to rule that out to everyone's satisfaction.

Second, Klass suggested that there was a monetary incentive and that the *National Enquirer* prize might have had a role in it. The problem here, however, is that the *National Enquirer* prize was not announced until weeks after the landing. The Johnsons couldn't have known about the plans of a Florida-based publication, so that incentive has been removed as well.[49]

But there is a disturbing aspect to it, according to what Klass wrote. Durel Johnson seemed to think that others were making money off his sighting. He told Klass, "If I don't get anything out of this circle—I mean if I don't get something out of the *National Enquirer*...Ted Phillips is going to get sued."[50]

Klass was suggesting a profit motive for the sighting, though it is equally reasonable that if Johnson thought others were profiting from his son's sighting, he just might be angry about it—angry enough to want to sue people, but that doesn't translate directly into the creation of a hoax for monetary gain. There haven't been many who tried that with success.

In the end, in a final analysis of the case, it seems to come down to which side of the alien visitation argument you occupy. If you believe there has been no alien visitation, then the sighting is explained by the mundane results of the soil analysis and possibly the overactive imagination of a teenaged boy and his parents. If you accept the idea of alien visitation, the evidence isn't so easily dismissed. There was the ring, and the soil did exhibit some unusual properties. There is the additional sighting from Ernsbarger that seems to underscore the sighting and add an element of independent corroboration to it.

~~~

In fact, the same might be said for all the landing trace sightings examined here. Most were reported by young boys who do have a habit of telling tall tales, though that doesn't mean these boys were. There was some physical evidence left behind but none of it so extraordinary that we can make the leap to the extraterrestrial. In many of the Iowa cases, there wasn't a UFO seen in conjunction with a specific sighting, though there had been UFOs reported in the area prior to the discovery of the physical evidence. In others, the UFO was seen and heard prior to the landing trace or the burn marks being found.

In the aggregate, however, we can see the scale tipping toward the extraterrestrial without the case being proven. Would all these people, over all these years, be inventing the same tales for some reason? I learned of the people in northwest Iowa not because of newspaper reports but more by word of mouth. They weren't delighted that I found them, but once inside, they did show me the photographs of the landing traces and objects in the air. Unfortunately, the photographs of the UFOs were little more than streaks of light, and the landing traces had not been properly examined.

And that is the way it is too often. The opportunity to gather solid evidence vanishes over time so that all we have are a few photographs, some soil samples that hint at strangeness but don't actually prove anything, and another lost opportunity. One of the few exceptions to that rule is the Zamora landing. Officials were on the scene literally within minutes, and samples from the landing area were taken quickly. Photographs preserved the landing gear marks. Analysis of much of that was possible.

Chapter 12:
Project Blue Book and Socorro

I t is no secret that in the last years of its existence, Project Blue Book's role had been significantly reduced, and it was little more than a public relations gimmick to fool people into believing the Air Force was investigating flying saucers. The Project Blue Book files contain multiple examples of the war to strip the investigation of its prestige by moving it from the intelligence arena at the Air Technical Intelligence Center into the Office of Public Information, where it would have less prestige. Although that didn't happen, it was one of many plans.[1]

By the mid-1960s, around the time of the Socorro landing, the investigations were haphazard, often conducted by telephone with explanations seemingly plucked from midair. One the best examples of this was a series of sightings made at the Minot Air

Force Base. The sightings took place on October 24, 1968, and were a combination of ground and air observations, radio failure, and radar returns.[2]

The initial sighting began about 30 minutes after midnight when an airman, only identified as Airman Isley in the Blue Book files, saw a bright light east of the base that appeared to be hovering.

At about 2:30 that same morning two others reported seeing bright lights. These included Airman First Class O'Connor and Staff Sergeant Smith. About 38 minutes later—that is, at 3:08—a series of additional sightings began by the various maintenance teams on the base. O'Connor, the maintenance team chief, reported that every member of the team saw an object that was reddish-orange. O'Connor said that it was a large object that was flashing green and white lights. The official report said that the object had passed over them with a roar like that of jet engines.[3]

At 3:29, Staff Sergeant Wagla, Airman First Class Allis, and Airman First Class Deer sighted a UFO. A minute after that, at another location, three others made a similar report.

At this stage, it is unclear if those making the reports had been aware of others making similar reports. If all were men at those various locations and were independently reporting the UFO or UFOs, then a terrestrial explanation becomes much more difficult. However, these various teams would have had radios with them and might have heard others talking about UFOs. It is a question that is never clarified in the official documents.

As all of this was transpiring, the pilots on a B-52 on a training flight reported there was a UFO 24 miles to the northwest. In communication with the tower about that mission, the controller asked the pilots to look out to their one o'clock position to see if there were any orange glows out there.

The pilot responded, "Someone is seeing flying saucers again," which tells us that there had been some discussion about UFOs made at some point. More importantly, it suggests that there had been other reports of the strange lights in the area in the weeks leading up to this.

Not long after that, the controller said that the UFO was being picked up by weather radar. The comment is confusing because it is not clear if that is the name of a radar installation near Minot or weather radar either on the ground or in another airplane. That confusion is contained in the Blue Book file on the case as well.

At 3:58, the pilot had made a request for a TACAN approach and then the radio on the aircraft failed. Two minutes later the radio began working but only periodically. By 4:02 they were able to communicate reliably.

But, they had seen the UFO out the windows of the aircraft, and as the UFO closed on them, the radio trouble began. The UFO was about a mile and a half from the aircraft for a short period of time.

At 4:13, it seems that all those who had been seeing the glowing, orange object had lost sight of it. A few minutes later the controllers told the aircrew that they needed to stop by Base Operations after they landed. The implication was that there would be some sort of debriefing about the UFO sighting.

Those, briefly, are the sightings from Minot on that one occasion: multiple witness in multiple locations, including radar confirmation, and an aircraft that experienced radio failure. And, 14 people in other locations had also made similar sightings. It wasn't just the Air Force people seeing the flying saucers, but civilians as well.

The next day, Project Blue Book became involved. Lieutenant Carmon Marano began to receive telephone calls and wrote a Memo for the Record about those calls. He learned that the commander at Minot Air Force Base and Major General Nichols at 15th Air Force Headquarters were interested in the sightings. With a general involved, others began to take the sightings more seriously.[4]

On October 30, Hector Quintanilla was asked by a colonel at SAC Headquarters in Omaha if he had sent anyone to Minot to investigate but Quintanilla said, according to the Memo for the Record, "We did not send anyone up because I only have four people on my staff."

The investigation staggered along. According to a Memo for the Record, "Colonel Werlich, the Minot officer in charge of the investigation, said that he had the people fill out the AF Form 117.... I monitored them while they filled them out."

Later in that same memo, Marano wrote, "The one we are mainly interested in is the one that cannot be identified. The one of radar and the aircraft correlated pretty well."

The Air Force eventually handed down an explanation for the sightings. It identified the ground/visual sightings as "Probable (Aircraft) (B-52)." Second, it noted "Probably Astro (Sirius)." For the radar sighting it suggested Possible (PLASMA) and finally the Air/Visual as "Possible (PLASMA)."[5]

On the project card, there were additional comments. The ground visual sightings appear to be of the star Sirius and the B-52 that was flying the area. The B-52 radar contact and the temporary loss of UHF transmission could be attributed to plasma, similar to ball lightning. The air-visual from the B-52 could be the star Vega, which was on the horizon at the time, or it could be a light on the ground, or possibly a plasma.

What the Air Force was suggesting was that its personnel were unable to identify a B-52 when they saw it at night and that they were fooled by bright stars. But where it slipped off the rails was in suggesting that a plasma was responsible for some of these sightings.

This plasma theory was one that had been floated by Phil Klass in the mid-1960s as an explanation for other sightings. He seemed to believe that these plasmas, which are basically ionized air, would glow, especially near high power lines, and would take on a circular or disc shape as they spun.[6]

This, to me, didn't seem quite right, and I called a friend who taught physics at the university level. I didn't quite understand what he was saying until I realized that, though the ionized air could exist, it wouldn't glow. It would be like looking through glass—frosty glass to be sure, but glass. There had to be some other mechanism to cause it to glow, and in the sightings in and around Minot, there simply wasn't anything to make that happen.

In other words, the plasma answer simply did not work for some of the sightings. No evidence of these plasmas, glowing or otherwise, had been provided. Although it is conceivable that some of the airmen at Minot had been fooled by the bright stars, it seems unlikely that so many could have been.

The trouble here is that during that time (October 1968), the Air Force had commissioned the University of Colorado to investigate UFOs. Dr. Edward U. Condon was the man in charge, and it is clear from the documentation that the real purpose was to end Project Blue Book. The Air Force wanted Condon to say some good things about the Air Force investigation, determine that there was no threat to national security, and recommend that Project Blue Book be closed.

This wasn't the first time that this had been attempted. The closure and dissatisfaction with it goes back nearly to its inception.

A Very Brief History of the UFO Projects

Although it can be argued that the military interest in UFOs began in 1946 with the investigation of the Scandinavian Ghost Rockets, it did not begin officially until 1948. At the end of 1946, Colonel Howard McCoy was tasked with an unofficial investigation of the reports of things in the sky. He and another officer commandeered an office at Wright Field, locked the doors, and quietly began studying the reports they were receiving. But before they reached the point of finding a solution, that unofficial investigation became official with the publicity surrounding the Kenneth Arnold sighting. Once the newspapers began publishing stories about the flying saucers and the flying discs, the Army Air Forces—which is to say those at the Air Materiel Command at Wright Field in Dayton, Ohio—moved from the locked office that

. . . .

few could enter into larger quarters with a larger staff and a real interest in what was happening around the country.[7]

During summer 1947, Brigadier General George Schulgen, working with Lieutenant Colonel George Garrett and tasked with investigation into the strange aerial phenomena, sent an estimate of the situation forward to General Nathan F. Twining, listing 18 flying disc reports and requesting specific analysis of that information. History seemed to suggest that Schulgen and Garrett would be told that the flying discs were actually a highly classified U.S. government project and not to worry about them. Instead Twining answered in September 1947 that the phenomena was something real and should be investigated. He wanted a project, with a relatively high priority, to be created for that investigation.[8]

This was a transition period for the Army Air Forces. It was being separated into a new service just called the United States Air Force. During this period of transition, there were many changes, but while that was going on, some top officers at Wright Field were working to design the first of the UFO investigations. The name of this project was Sign, which was classified. The newspapers and the public was told that it was called Project Saucer.[9]

Although it was taken seriously at first, within months the prestige had eroded, and the final collapse came with an Estimate of the Situation. This was an intelligence concept in which the information was gathered, evidence presented, and conclusions drawn. According to Captain Edward Ruppelt, who would one day lead Project Blue Book, the estimate was relayed up the chain of command to General Twining. The conclusion was that the flying saucers were interplanetary craft.

Twining, according to Ruppelt, was not impressed with the evidence presented and rejected the estimate. To make it worse, nearly everyone associated with the project was fired. Those on the outside of the project, but who had seen the results of displeasing the general, were quick to adopt an attitude that suggested they didn't believe the flying saucers were alien craft, either. The irony here is that Twining had initiated the project and then, about a year later, had wrecked it.[10]

Sign limped along; nothing was being accomplished but no one really cared. Then, according to some, the name, which had been classified, was compromised. With that, Sign issued a final report and the Air Force announced the end of Sign, which suggested the end of the UFO investigations.

But that didn't mean the Air Force had quit investigating UFOs. The name was changed to Grudge, and the Air Force continued on. But without the command emphasis that had been in place for the beginning of the Project Sign, no one cared much about it. Nothing was being done other than a gathering of reports.

Then one of the generals who had been interested in UFOs asked what was happening with the investigation. Unhappy with the response, he placed command emphasis on it and brought in Ed Ruppelt to run it. Ruppelt had been a bombardier during World War II and was apparently called back to active duty during the Korean War. Rather than getting combat assignment, he was tasked with rebuilding the UFO program.[11] That might have had something to do with his degree in aeronautical engineering rather than his training as a bombardier.

Once again, there was a real interest in learning just what the flying saucers were. For about 18 months in the early 1950s, the investigation attempted to find answers and treated the subject with a degree of respect. During that time, another huge report was prepared about the UFOs. It was then announced that Grudge had been closed, but, in reality, it was just another name change. The investigation continued as Project Blue Book.

In 1953, after a panel chaired by Dr. H.P. Robertson concluded that the problem wasn't alien spacecraft but misidentifications, delusions, and hoaxes, Blue Book again fell into disfavor. There was no reason to continue to study them, though a program of education was suggested to strip flying saucers of their mystery, and an effort was made to debunk them so the public would lose interest in them. Ruppelt, who had left the project for some months, was brought back for a short time and then was replaced again. A new officer who was rabidly anti-saucer was appointed to lead Blue Book, and the tone of the investigation changed with the change. Sightings were to be identified. An "Unidentified" label was unacceptable.[12]

For most of the next decade and a half, the official UFO investigation was guided by the concept that there were no extraterrestrial craft and any case that suggested otherwise was somehow flawed. The numbers of new cases that were labeled as "Unidentified" plummeted. Another category, "Insufficient Data for a Scientific Analysis," skyrocketed. Though those cases remained unexplained, they weren't grouped into that all important "Unidentified" category.[13]

While the Air Force was trying to find a university that would conduct an "independent" investigation that would meet its requirements, there were sighting reports being made, some with interaction with the environment leaving behind a variety of evidence that was always questioned in some fashion. Some of these cases would be labeled as "Unidentified," but most of them received little or no public attention and the interest in UFOs ebbed and flowed.

But at the same time, according to the NICAP's *The U.F.O Investigator* for March 1965, the Air Force had tried to intimidate UFO witnesses, suggesting that various unpleasant things would happen to them as a result of seeing a flying saucer. NICAP reported that on January 12, 1965, a witness, identified only as an officer for a federal law enforcement agency, was driving toward Blaine Air Force Base when a disc, some 30 feet in diameter swooped down at him but then shot upward. The witness leaped from his car and saw the object hovering overhead only 50 feet away. He thought it was going to collide with his car. He said that it was omitting a bright white light with a black spot in the middle.

While it hovered overhead he heard nothing but then, as it shot up into the clouds, there was the sound of rushing air. It moved horizontally for about a quarter mile before disappearing into the clouds.

He wasn't the only one to see the UFO. Others in the area reported that a UFO had landed, though given the circumstances and the object's low approach, they had probably seen the same thing. The law enforcement officer reported the sighting and was told by the Air Force not to talk about it, especially not to the newspapers. This, the Air Force claimed, was for his own good, which is reminiscent of what was told to Zamora in New Mexico. Because he wasn't in the Air Force, and with the permission of his superiors at his law enforcement agency, he told NICAP about it on the condition they would not release his name.

In that same issue, NICAP reported that George W. Monk, Jr., who had been a radar operator in the Air Force and who was a private pilot, said that while operating the radar he spotted an object moving west to east. He said that it was flying at 2,600 miles an hour at 60,000 feet. He said that they didn't scramble any fighters because they couldn't have caught the UFO anyway. Monk said, "We in the operator's room were told not to mention the incident to anyone. No reason given."[14]

Without a date on the sighting, I wondered if what they had seen might not have been a flight of an SR-71 Blackbird. This aircraft, whose performance characteristics are still hard to find, had the altitude capability and the speed to have been the object seen by radar, which would have been a very good reason for the Air Force to tell Monk and the others not to talk about it. This is, of course, speculation on my part.

But that's not the only example cited by NICAP. In the same issue of their *The U.F.O. Investigator*, they report that a former Navy fighter pilot, who had logged more than six thousand hours of flight time, provided information on his sighting of August 13, 1959.[15]

The pilot told researchers that he had been flying from Hobbs, New Mexico, to Albuquerque when his electric compass began to spin wildly. He looked at the magnetic compass and, according to him, it was spinning so wildly that he couldn't read it.

In seconds, he spotted three oval-shaped objects in an echelon formation pass in front of his aircraft. He said they were gray and looked like two bowls glued rim to rim but with the bottoms rounded rather than flat. He thought they were about 8 feet in diameter but also said they might have been larger. The only other thing he noticed was that they left a short, wispy trail.

They circled the aircraft two or three times and then passed to the rear. When the objects flew away, the electric compass settled to its original readings and the magnetic compass stopped spinning as well.

When he arrived in Albuquerque, landing at Kirtland Air Force Base, he was taken to an office and "interrogated for about two hours" by an Air Force major who was apparently the UFO officer for the base.

He wasn't told, specifically, not to talk about the sighting, and he said that he was given a warning: If he had any unusual illnesses in the next six months, get to an Air Force hospital as quickly as he could. They would take care of him there. He said that he relaxed once the six months had passed.[16]

During that time—the late 1950s through the mid-1960s—the Air Force was denying that UFOs existed but were classifying the reports that had no good explanation. Even if it didn't tell witnesses not to talk to keep them silent, it was attacking their credibility to reduce the importance of their sightings or to convince others not to listen. In one case, several witnesses, including members of the Army Security Agency, reported to NICAP that 12 to 15 oval-shaped objects were seen near the capital, chased by two fighters in early 1965. One of those men, Paul Dickey, identified as their spokesman, had six years in Naval Intelligence and had a degree in electrical engineering.

The Air Force response? "There was no such incident. It just didn't happen."[17]

That attitude and Air Force Regulations prevented many witnesses from talking about their sightings, and the more interesting the sightings, the more pressure was applied. It might be said that the Air Force was doing one of its jobs with the suppression of UFO data.

Air Force Regulations

Nothing is done in the military without a regulation to control it. High-ranking commanders often say that regulations are for the guidance of the commander; others suggest that they be followed carefully without deviation. Over the course of history, the Air Force issued two regulations about UFOs. One simply upgraded and revised the early versions, but both did the same thing: kept military witnesses and military investigators from talking about certain UFO sightings.

Originally, the Air Force operated under AFR (Air Force Regulation) 200-2. In the 1960s, the regulation was revised and renumbered. It became AFR 87-17. Both regulations covered the reporting requirements—that is, what was seen by whom, along with the definitions used in the regulation such as UFOB (Unidentified Flying Object), who held the responsibility for reporting and investigation of the sightings, and finally, what facts were releasable to the general public.

Air Force Regulation, or rather one of the copies now available online, was published on August 12, 1954. Paragraph nine, Releasable Facts, laid out who had what authority. It said:

Headquarters USAF will release summaries of evaluated data which will inform the public on this subject. In response to local inquiries, it is permissible to in form (sic) news media representatives on UFOB's when the object is positively identified as a familiar object (see paragraph 2b), except that the following types of data warrants protection and should not be revealed: Names of principles (sic), intercept and investigation procedures, and classified radar data. For those objects which are not explainable, only the fact that ATIC will analyze the data is worthy of release, due to the many unknowns involved.[18]

Although not spelled out exactly, the intention is clear: If there is a solution for a sighting, one that is readily available and acceptable, then the information can be released to the news media. If, however, there is no solution—meaning it was "Unidentified"— then the news media is only told that a higher-level organization is now responsible for analyzing the data. In other words, though not saying so expressly, the unidentified sightings are classified while those that are not, are unclassified.

Air Force Regulation 87-17, dated September 19, 1966, replaced the earlier regulation and the tone of its "Releasable Information" was more detailed. Some of it details instructions when dealing with Congress or other high-level officials. Information is now released by SAF-OI (Secretary of the Air Force, Office of Information) rather than the Air Technical Intelligence Center, which was much more prestigious. Releasing the information through the Office of Information instead of an intelligence function suggested that it wasn't worth the time and energy of intelligence officers to investigate. In other words, UFOs just weren't very important.

The regulation ordered SAF-OI to "respond to correspondence from individuals requesting information on UFO programs and evaluations of sightings." But what is interesting, at least in this context, is the paragraph label "Exceptions." It says:

In response to local inquiries regarding UFOs reported in the vicinity of an Air Force Base, the base commander may release information to the news media or public after the sighting has been positively identified. If the stimulus for the sighting is difficult to identify at the base level, the commander may state that the sighting is under investigation and conclusions will be released by SAF-OI after the investigation is completed. The commander may also state that the Air Force will review and analyze the results of the investigation. Any further inquiries will be directed to SAF-OI.

In other words, the buck is passed up the chain of command—not to any of the intelligence functions but to the public affairs people. It is a way of stalling the inquiries, a way to avoid answering the questions and a way of burying the UFO information under a mound of paper. And finally, if an answer is received, it is of little real value because the officer answering the question might not have all the facts.

Below is an example of this found in the Project Blue Book files. A civilian was interested in the story of a UFO crash near Las Vegas on April 18, 1962. The query had to do with jet interceptors being scrambled from of the Air Force bases in the area. On September 21, 1962, Major C.R. Hart of the Public Information Office (SAF-OI) responded by writing:

> The official records of the Air Force list the 18 April 1962 Nevada sighting to which you refer as "unidentified, insufficient data." There is an additional note to the effect that "the reported track is characteristic of that registered by a U-2 or a high balloon but there is insufficient data to fully support such an evaluation." The phenomena reported was not intercepted or fired upon.[19]

However, the Blue Book files clearly show that an intercept was attempted. The conclusion to be drawn here is that Hart did not have access to the Blue Book files, or he did not have access to all of them. His answer was probably accurate as far as he knew it, but it was not the reality of the situation.

This, however, was probably the theory behind the regulation. SAF-OI could honestly answer the question because, as far as they knew, it was the truth. At that time, no one expected the Blue Book files to be opened to the general public for close scrutiny, though most of the cases were not classified. They did not expect them to be declassified and sent to the National Archives, where the public could review them, and certainly never envisioned the Internet, which put all the documents online for all to see with a couple of clicks of the mouse.

The End of Blue Book

Not all that long ago, I had the opportunity to speak with one of the officers who had been at Project Blue Book at the end. What he said was surprising because of the somewhat cavalier way the information was treated at the end. Lieutenant Carmon Marano, who had written those memos for the record about the Minot UFO sightings, was the guest on the radio show *A Different Perspective* on the X-Zone Broadcast Network.[20]

When asked what he had thought of the Minot case, he said that he found it confusing and that there were so many people involved both on the ground and in the air. One of the things he remembered was that the ground had been foggy, which might have made it difficult for the witnesses to confuse stars with UFOs. He also said that there had been a temperature inversion that night, and that can cause light to bend so that objects beyond the horizon that would have been impossible to see under normal conditions would be visible.

We never did clear up the confusion about the radars. According to Marano, the B-52 had a weather radar in the nose and a fire control system radar in the rear that aimed and fired the air defense cannons. He thought that the mention of Weathers Radar might have been a mistake about the weather radar. This was a point that was never cleared up by the official investigation and was a point that probably should have been resolved in the 1960s.

The other point that he made was that he hadn't gone to Minot, but had been talking to the people there on the telephone. The case, when it first was reported to Blue Book, was classified, which was in keeping with the instructions about unidentified cases. According to Marano, Quintanilla handled the evaluation that did slide off into a fantasy about atmospheric ionization.

While Marano was at Blue Book, the University of Colorado was also doing its study for the Air Force. He said that there had been "a lot of sightings reported to the Air Force that never made it to Blue Book" and added that those reported to other Air Force bases might have never been forwarded to them.[21] That was left to the discretion of the officer who investigated. He or she might decide there was a solution, that it wasn't all that spectacular, or that it didn't have enough information for any sort of a scientific analysis so there was no point in passing the information on to Blue Book.

He made another point that was interesting and something that I had suspected for a very long time: He said they "weren't allowed to investigate unless they [UFOs] were officially reported to the Air Force.... We investigated if they were directly reported to us and had completed the form [Air Force Form 117]."[22]

He said, "Once Dr. Condon issued his report and then the Air Force decided to close us down, it took several weeks, at least, to pack up all the files." They then shipped them off to Maxwell Air Force, which was the home of the Air Force archives. Though Marano didn't say it, those files were eventually sent to the National Archives in Washington, D.C.[23]

One of the points of controversy that surrounded the Socorro landing was that Marano had a thick file of material that eventually ended up in the hands of veteran UFO researcher Rob Mercer. I asked about that file and Marano said, "It had never been part of the official case files. I had inherited the desk and the materials from the guy who had the desk before me and he inherited from the guy before him.... So, I had all this stuff in my desk and I had my choice basically I could throw it away or I could pack it up and keep it."[24]

He said that he had intended to read through it at some point but never did. He said that when he arrived at Blue Book he had a mild interest in the extraterrestrial but it wasn't anything overpowering. When Mercer tracked him down, Marano just said he would send it on to Mercer. That material had never been part of the official file on Socorro, but it was all based on the material in the official file and the various newspaper and magazine articles about it that were published in the years that followed.[25]

The purpose of those unofficial files, or at least part of them, was for the benefit of the press. Marano said that very little of the Blue Book material was classified. The unclassified files were open to the public and a number of reporters went through them. Marano said that he had created a binder that had some of the more interesting material, including photographs, it in. If a reporter had a question about a specific case, they would pull the whole file for him or her.

The impact of the discussion, then, was the information about the Socorro case file that Marano had saved was that it was not part of the official documentation of the case. The one major problem that came from that file was the suggestion that the real symbol seen by Zamora was an inverted "V" with three bars through it. The two handwritten cards that had that symbol on it were not in the official file. The symbol in the official file was the one that had the arc over the top and the arrow pointing up into it. This was the symbol that Zamora told the first investigators that he had seen, it was the one that he had drawn within minutes of the craft lifting off, it was the one that he drew later and signed for Captain Holder and FBI agent Byrnes, and it was the one that was drawn on the illustration of the craft that Rick Baca drew.

If nothing else, Marano was able to clear up the difference between what was in the official file and what was in that other unofficial one. (The complete analysis of the symbol in its various incarnations can be found in Chapter 11.)

Chapter 13:
Physical Evidence

With most UFO sightings, you are left with only the witness testimony, and, if you are lucky, the witnesses don't know one another so that one can then provide corroboration for the other. Sometimes there are photographs that can be analyzed, and sometimes there are radar contacts with photographs of the radar scopes. And sometimes there are physical traces left behind when the craft takes off. This provides something real and tangible that can be measured and sometimes with residue that can be taken into the laboratory and analyzed.

With the Socorro landing, there was additional physical evidence to be found on the ground. Once the object had taken off, Zamora walked a short distance into the arroyo where the craft had been sitting. According to Ray Stanford, "It seems to have both excited and frightened Zamora a little when he saw that the bushes were smoldering and smoking in several places."[1] That was the first indication for Zamora that there would be some sort of physical evidence of the UFO landing.

FOREIGN TECHNOLOGY DIVISION, AFSC   UNCLASSIFIED

UNCLASSIFIED

The landing site on the south side of Socorro, taken within hours of the landing. Photo courtesy of the U.S. Air Force.

After Chavez arrived on the scene the two of them walked to the edge of the arroyo. Coral Lorenzen wrote, "[They] looked at the ground where the object had landed. It was still smoking. Several clumps of range grass were burned, as well as a stubby mesquite bush."[2]

This information was also part of the Project Blue Book file on the case. In an unsigned document titled "Narrative of Socorro, New Mexico Sighting, 24 April 1964," the unidentified writer noted, "Sgt Chavez was skeptical of the situation and proceeded to where Zamora had observed the object. Here he found the marks and burns. Smoke appeared to be coming from a bush which was burned but no flame or coals were visible. Sgt Chavez broke a limb from the bush and it was cold to the touch."[3]

That wasn't, of course, the only physical evidence. On the landing site, they found four impressions in the dirt and sand. Lorenzen wrote, "There were four 8 X 12–inch wedge-shaped depressions, 3 to 4 inches deep arranged in an uneven rectangle. There were also four circular depressions about 4½ inches in diameter and approximately 3 inches deep not far from one point of the large indentations."[4]

Ray Stanford gives the credit for the discovery of the impression to Chavez. Chavez, down on the landing site, found a quadrangle apparently made by the landing gear that Zamora had seen. According to Stanford, these were made by something of great weight.[5]

Within hours of the sighting, Holder and Byrnes were on the landing site. They had interviewed Zamora and then, riding in the same car, headed out. According to Holder's report in the Blue Book files, "Enroute (Mr. Byrnes and I went in the same vehicle) we stopped by the residence of Sgt. Castle, NCOIC [Non-Commissioned Officer In Charge] SRC M.P., who then accompanied us to the site and assisted in taking the enclosed measurements and observations. Present when we arrived were Officer [name redacted], Officers Melvin Ratzlaff, Bill Pyland, all of the Socorro Police Department, who assisted in making the measurements."[6] Hynek would later report that Holder "had done a good job procuring measurements and other data before the coming of the crowd of curiosity seekers."[7]

Lorenzen reported, "Holder and the FBI man [Byrnes] came out to the site, took measurements, and the FBI man piled rocks around the indentations to preserve them."[8]

Included in the Blue Book file was a diagram that suggested something of a trapezoid area, with the four depressions at the four corners. Also noted was an area that was described as footprints, but these are the circular depressions that Coral Lorenzen had mentioned. Some believed these might represent holes made by some sort of ladder that allowed the two beings to exit and then reenter the craft.

J. Allen Hynek was on the scene within a few days of the sighting. In his report back to Blue Book, he said little about the landing traces, other than that Holder and Byrnes had thought the markings were fresh. Moody reinforced this in his report, writing, "Further he [Chavez] stated that the marks were definitely 'fresh', and the dirt showed evidence of 'dew' or moisture."[9] This all suggests that they were made by the craft. He didn't provide a description of them, but then other documents in the files did.

In another of the reports in the Blue Book files, one that was also probably prepared by Sergeant David Moody of the Blue Book staff, who happened to be in Albuquerque at the time, there is a little more about these impressions. He wrote, "There was no evidence of markings of any sort in the area other than the shallow depressions at the location where Mr (sic) Zamora reported the sighting."[10]

At the time of the first search, a sweep was made to determine if there was any excess radiation in that area. Nothing was found to suggest that there was a higher than normal level of background radiation on the site. Zamora, and those who arrived shortly after the craft had departed, never exhibited any signs of a sunburn or sickness due to radiation.

According to Hynek, in a report about his trip made in March 1965, he was interviewing Socorro residents and the topic of a movie came up. This film was supposedly being made by Empire Studios about UFO sightings and the Socorro landing was one of them. Hynek wrote, "One rather interesting item is that the burning bush has recently exuded some sap, and one of the movie people took this to Los Angeles to have it analyzed and found it radioactive!"[11]

The next day, before all the tourists arrived, and all the other UFO investigators arrived, photographs of the site were taken. These included pictures of the landing impressions and the partially burned bush. The photographs were attached to the Blue Book file of the case.

Soil and Other Samples

Given that there were both law enforcement and government officials on the scene within a few hours of the report, and given that the witness (Zamora) could take them to the exact location, soil samples, fragments of the burned bush, and several samples of metal that might have come from the landing gear were taken. Some of this would erupt into controversy with the private UFO investigator and one of the national, civilian UFO organizations involved.

The Blue Book files contain notes made about a telephone call between Captain Theodore W. Cuny of the 1005th Special Investigation Group in Washington and Major K.S. Sameshima. That information apparently was communicated to Cuny by Lieutenant Colonel King of the Counter Intelligence Division, who, in turn had read about it in an Albuquerque newspaper. One of the interesting things about it was this:

> Upon being informed of this, the Army (a Captain R T Holder of White Sands) roped off the area. Also the FBI at Albuquerque proceed to the area, and allegedly confirmed that "something" had been there. They reportedly found 4"x5" impressions in the ground somewhat like the stand legs; the impressions appeared burned. The newspaper stated that the Army took soil samples.[12]

These samples, according to the information available, were given to Hynek when he arrived late on Tuesday (April 28). This seems to explain why Hynek wasn't prepared to collect samples himself when he was there. He had the samples taken that first night by Holder before the site had been compromised by others including tourists and curiosity seekers.

Ray Stanford reported that when he arrived at the landing site on Wednesday, Hynek was already there with a number of others. They inspected the scene, which had been visited by many people in the days after the story made the news. Stanford began to take soil samples, and according to him Hynek asked for some of the small vials so that he could take samples as well.[13] These would have been in addition to those that Harder had collected and given to him earlier.

According to the Blue Book files, "Laboratory analysis of soil samples disclosed no foreign material.... Laboratory analysis of the burned bush showed no chemicals which would indicate a type of propellant."[14] That was just a fancy way of saying they found no evidence of gasoline, lighter fluid, or any other chemical that could have been used to set the bush on fire. That ruled out one of the elements of the hoax.

Blue Book also contains an Evaluation Report dated May 19, 1964, that amplified this information. The report said, "Spectroscopic analysis indicated the gross composition to the same for all samples.... There is apparently no significant differences in elemental composition between different samples."[15]

Hynek also wrote, "They [NICAP and APRO] will probably say that the burns are 'plasmaburns' [sic] which can scorch locally, I understand."[16] I have found nothing to suggest that either organization ever made such a claim.

That wasn't all that had been found. Sand that had apparently been subjected to high heat, that is vitrified, was reported on the site. Dr. James McDonald, a University of Arizona physicist, wrote to Dick Hall, then of NICAP:

> Briefly, a woman who is now a radiological chemist with the Public Health Service in Las Vegas [Nevada] was involved in some specific analyses of the materials collected at the Socorro site, and when she was there, the morning after, she claims that there was a patch of melted and resolidi-fied (sic) sand right under the landing area. I have talked to her both by telephone and in person here in Tucson recently.... I must say, it's very hard to imagine how such material could have been there not only on the evening of

the 24th but still there on the morning of the 25th without it[s] ever having been reported before.... She did the analyses on the plant-fluids exuded from stems of greasewood and mesquite that had been scorched. She said there were a few organic materials they couldn't identify, but most of the stuff that had come out through the cracks and blisters in the stems were just saps from the phloem and xylem. Shortly after she finished the work, Air Force personnel came and took all her notes and materials and told her she wasn't to talk about it anymore.[17]

As Jerry Clark noted, there is no mention of this anywhere else. There is nothing in the Blue Book file about it. None of those who were on the scene that night or the next morning made any mention of it. McDonald did not identify his source on it, but then, the Socorro case involves any number of unidentified sources (which is one of the major problems not only with this case but many UFO cases).

Stanford does, however, point to additional and possibly corroborative information for McDonald's report. According to him, when he was told by a police officer about one of the rocks, an Air Force officer standing near the center of it looked down at what Stanford said was a large rock that had a "bubbly looking" surface. He questioned Zamora about the actual landing site and examined the other rocks in the area, but they didn't look the same. Portions of the rock had a glassy surface, which seems to suggest that high heat had been applied in the area causing some of the sand and silicon material to melt, running together and creating a melted patch to which McDonald had referred.

According to Stanford, "Shortly thereafter the officer stood up and made notes on the location of the vitrified object...and about how it differed from natural rocks in the area."[18]

Stanford reported that he dismissed the story when he first heard it but later, after learning of the McDonald letter, and hearing it from reliable police sources, he believed that this important information had been concealed from the public. He could learn nothing more about this and no evidence of this sort appeared in the Blue Book files.

Metallic Remains

The most controversial aspect of the physical evidence is that found on some of the rocks on the landing site. These small, almost-microscopic fragments were embedded on the rocks where the landing gear had scraped them. They were collected and analyzed; in the end, it was one of those "who do you want to believe?" situations.

The Blue Book files contains no reports on the analysis of any metal fragments. It doesn't seem that any were actually collected by any of the military personnel on the scene or by other official representatives including Byrnes and Hynek.

Stanford seems to indicate the same thing when he was on the site with Hynek, Zamora, and Chavez on the Wednesday after the landing. Stanford, in searching the site, had seen a rock on which one of the object's landing gear had apparently scraped. He tried to ignore it so that others wouldn't realize the significance of it. With the others, he left to attend the press conference that Hynek was going to hold, but the instant it was over, he headed straight back to the landing site.

The rock was still there and Stanford carefully collected it. Stanford's background includes the collection of dinosaur samples, so that he was not unfamiliar with the proper procedures. Before he removed it, he studied it, photographed it, and observed its relation to the other rocks and impressions on the site. He noticed abrasions on the stone that looked to be metallic. These could represent important evidence of what Zamora had seen and what had landed there.

With no real trouble, Stanford was able to get the stone to his car, carefully wrapped in case some of the very small metallic fragments fell away because of the handling. On May 3, 1964, he wrote to Dick Hall and the controversy began. He wrote, "Metal traces on rock... are *very minute* [italics in original], but sufficient for analysis & may give us the *physical evidence* [italics in original] we've been waiting."[19]

Richard Hall, who was directly involved in the attempted analysis of the metal fragments. Copyright CUFOS. Photo by Mark Rodeghier.

But there was a new problem: Stanford, excited about what he had found, showed it to a Phoenix doctor. They had been outside when Stanford showed him the rock. The doctor went inside for a magnifying glass and when he returned, he held out his hand. Without thinking about it, Stanford gave the rock to the doctor and then realized that he (the doctor) put his hand on the spot where the biggest and possibly the best of the metallic slivers were. Upon examination, they realized that the majority of the residue was gone.

They tried to find the slivers using a magnet but they had no luck. Stanford had to write to Hall explaining that he had lost the best of the material. There was some residue left and that small amount might be enough for a meaningful analysis. It least that was what he hoped.

Hall thought that NICAP scientific consultant Walter Webb would have the best luck in getting the small samples analyzed. Stanford disagreed, and this resulted in a number of letters being exchanged until Hall wrote that he had scientists at the Goddard Space Flight Center interested in analyzing the metal fragments.

The details were eventually worked out, and Hall identified his contact as Henry Frankel, a former believer in UFOs but who was then more skeptical. At Goddard, Frankel was shown the rock and, according to Webb, the sight of the rock was discouraging. Frankel, however, wasn't above trying and sent them all to a cafeteria while he made his examination, promising to save half the remaining slivers.

When Frankel didn't return, the group—that is Hall, Stanford, and Webb—went in search of him. Frankel was gone and the lab was empty except for a technician. The rock had been scraped clean, according to Stanford, but the technician claimed that some of the scrapings were still available. Stanford, however, disagreed, said that they were just the "pseudometallic refractions from crystals."[20]

That wasn't the end of it. Frankel did return and said there were be additional tests made. He would have the results on the following Wednesday.

Then the story, according to Stanford, descends into the paranoid. Stanford, with his friend Robert McGarey, a Navy captain, who is identified with a pseudonym, went out to dinner. The captain told them that they were being naïve, suggesting that the government would never allow them to retain any evidence that would prove the extraterrestrial nature of UFOs. He hinted that the government knew that UFOs existed and in this context obviously suggested that they were alien. The captain sort of mocked Stanford by telling him that they had just given away their evidence.

According to Stanford, the captain said:

Those boys at Goddard know that they must report any findings as important as a strange, UFO alloy to the highest authority in NASA. Once that authority receives the news, the president will be informed, for the matter is pertinent to national security and stability.... Frankel may privately tell you of his findings, but when it comes down to brass tacks, they can never verify any important test results, officially.[21]

Stanford then asked, "You mean that the physical evidence of the Socorro UFO is, in effect, lost to the world?" The answer was "absolutely. This shows how little you do-it-yourself revelators of UFO facts really know. You just gave your evidence into the hands of what you apparently consider the enemy."[22]

On Wednesday morning, Stanford called Frankel. Jerry Clark noted that Frankel's comments are in quotation marks even though Stanford had not recorded the conversation. He had taken notes of it. Frankel told Stanford that the particles were not natural. "They were a zinc-iron alloy with other trace elements; based on the extensive charts Goddard possessed, Frankel could state with confidence that the alloy was unlike any known to be manufactured on earth."[23]

To reinforce the point, according to Stanford, Frankel said that he thought this meant that the object seen by Zamora could have been manufactured on another world. This was, of course, an unbelievable conclusion by a scientist at a nationally recognized laboratory. To make it even better, Frankel said that he would pass the information along to Hall.

Hall, being the cautious sort, and afraid of burning important bridges, suggested that Stanford go easy in his discussions with Frankel and those at NASA. He didn't want Frankel pressured. When Stanford called a week later, Frankel wouldn't take that call, or any other calls made over the next several days and then several weeks.[24]

Then, to make it worse, another man, Thomas P. Sciacca, Jr., whom Stanford had met during the visit to Goddard, said that Frankel was no longer involved in the project and that he had been in error with his conclusions. If there were complaints, Sciacca would handle them, but only if they were put into writing.

On September 11, 1964, a formal statement of the analysis was forwarded to Hall. It was meant to end the confusion about their findings and to set the record straight. That information was published by NICAP in their newsletter:

> The shiny substance found on a rock adjacent to one of the imprints left at the Socorro, N.M. landing site has been identified as Silica, according to a report from a top Washington laboratory. Silica is a very common substance (quartz and sand are forms of it). These results threw cold water on the hope that objective physical evidence had been found in the form of metal....
>
> In the previous issue, we reported the finding of the substance by Ray Stanford, NICAP member authorized to investigate this case, as he and the witness Ptn. [Patrolman] Lonnie Zamora, examined the imprint on April 29. Zamora noticed the rock looked like it had been struck by a leg of the UFO. Stanford, realizing the importance of the traces, removed the rock and transported it to NICAP for analysis.[25]

Stanford didn't respond to the information for more than a decade. It was with the publication of *Socorro "Saucer" in a Pentagon Pantry* that Stanford let his thoughts be known. He told the story of his journey from the landing site in Socorro and the recovery of what might have been important physical evidence to the loss of that evidence because of Richard Hall and NICAP. Stanford hadn't wanted to use Goddard but Hall led him there.

Hall responded to Stanford's book and the allegations about Frankel with a scathing review in the *MUFON UFO Journal*. He wrote, in part:

> In a nutshell, I consider Stanford's account of NICAP's part in the Socorro investigation—and particularly his unfounded claims of a secret, positive analysis report on the alleged "metal scrapings of the rock"—to be both highly distorted and a highly subjective version of what transpired....[26]
>
> Neither Dr. Frankel nor anyone else at NASA ever suggested to me that they were leaning toward an extraterrestrial interpretation. In fact, when Dr. Frankel talked to me about tentative findings of a zinc-iron alloy, he said to me that the results suggested a zinc pail....
>
> His [meaning Stanford's] entire case rests on two apparently undocumented and unverifiable phone calls that only he can witness. In addition, no one else involved in the Socorro investigation remembers the startling [and presumably unforgettable] positive NASA analysis report that only Stanford remembers.[27]

Stanford's response was also published in the pages of the *MUFON UFO Journal* as well as his book on the Socorro landing. He pointed out that he had explained, in his book, how the conversations had taken place. He reacted strongly to Hall's somewhat-guarded suggestion that Stanford had not been completely candid in his descriptions of the search for the lab to analyze the fragments and then once position results.

What was overlooked in the exchange was that alleged evidence was handled poorly; that alleged conversations could not be corroborated; that the information from NASA, based on their examination of the material, had a mundane answer; and that hyperbole was sometimes substituted for analysis. In the end, it was clear that even if the material from the rock had been from an alien spacecraft, there was nothing in the analysis to prove that.

The materials were not exotic and they didn't vary from those found on Earth.

There was one point that Stanford made, and it was about the melted sand, the vitrified material that was allegedly recovered. Here, Stanford acknowledges that the source of the McDonald letter was Hall and that should have been noted in the book.

The squabble continued to the point where Hall had said that Stanford had selected the NASA lab and Stanford saying that it was Hall who pushed it on him. In the end, nothing was resolved, and those on the outside could only regret that possible physical evidence that might have answered some of the questions had been lost.

Conclusions

For years I, like so many others, had said that the Socorro UFO landing would have been a great case except that there was a single witness. Only Lonnie Zamora saw and heard the craft. Had there been additional witnesses, coupled with the landing traces found within minutes of the departure of the craft, this would have been a stunning sighting. If only...

The Lone Witness?

When Ben Moss and Tony Angiola appeared on the *A Different Perspective* radio show, they said that three people had seen the object or the flame from the object in the minutes before it landed. I asked for the source of this information, but somehow we got off

239

on another tangent. The answer, however, was in the Project Blue Book files. Captain Harder, in his report written on the night of the sighting, or in the early morning of the next day, reported that three telephone calls had been made to the Socorro police about the object. Apparently, no one ever followed up on it, but the information is there. Without the names and an investigation of it, this isn't much help, but it does suggest something was in the sky and the reports were independent of Zamora and each other.

Ray Stanford reported that in the days or weeks after the sighting, while he was in Socorro, he met two women who described their sighting of the object to him. Stanford apparently never followed up on this but, given a proper interview with them, we have additional information about Zamora's sighting. I talked to Stanford about this, hoping to learn the names, but he didn't remember them. He suggested that they had been older women and that 50 years had passed. I thought that we might learn where they lived in Socorro in 1964 and might be able to find someone who would go on the record. Sure, it would be a long shot, but it might produce some results.

Stanford also reported that every member of the small law enforcement contingency in Socorro had either seen Zamora's craft or one similar to it. According to him, Sergeant Chavez, for example, who arrived within minutes of the craft lifting off, saw that craft in the distance. The Blue Book file, and more importantly, the reports and documents created that night, seem to rule this out. In those first few hours, before some of the treatment of Zamora had been observed, there was no reason for any of those officers to have not shared the information with either Holder or Byrnes, but none did. The record seems clear on this: Chavez didn't see anything, though he might have arrived before the craft had completely disappeared.

Opal Grinder, the gas station operator, told of the Colorado family who stopped at his business shortly after the object landed. They said enough that it is clear that they would have been good witnesses, and because they were not from Socorro, would have added a dimension of independent corroboration. Grinder didn't know who they were and there was no way to track them. It is also disturbing that they never came forward. The story went national almost immediately. In 1964, I lived in Colorado; I know that it was reported in the Denver area. Without them, this story doesn't provide much in the way of evidence.

There were also the two men from Dubuque, Iowa, who said they had seen the object as they passed through Socorro. Here we had their names, and their story appeared in the newspaper within days of the sighting. Although this would be good corroboration for Zamora's sighting, I have little faith in this report.

First, it is an amazing coincidence that they were driving through Socorro at the right time, but their tales just don't add up. They mention in the newspaper article something about a melted pop bottle at the landing site, but this is actually something that is associated with the La Madera sighting reported shortly after Zamora's sighting. Besides, given their location and the fact that they did not go to the landing site, it is impossible for them to have seen melted glass on the site.

Second, Ralph DeGraw interviewed them years after the event and their stories didn't match. Though, after years, you would expect some deviation, there is just too much difference between them. If they witnessed the same thing while in the same car, their stories should have been closer. I discount this tale, though it would be nice if it had been true.

There have been other suggestions of possible corroboration, but none of them have panned out. For this sighting, the best information are the three telephone calls to the police. Without the names or any additional information, this doesn't help all that much. However, it can be said that Zamora wasn't the lone witness. There were others, and the information was supplied on the night of the sighting.

Did Zamora See Occupants?

The simple answer is yes. The problem arose when FBI agent Arthur Byrnes suggested that the mention of creatures would be ridiculed by the media. Although that is a real consideration, especially in 1964, that information did get out. Zamora had mentioned it before Byrnes said anything, and several of the media outlets reported it. Coral Lorenzen, who arrived within 48 hours, knew about them. Zamora admitted that he had seen creatures.

Ben Moss and Tony Angiola suggested that Zamora had only seen the white coveralls and hadn't actually seen a humanoid creature. However, the Blue Book reports, now available to researchers, prove that he was talking about actual beings. They were smaller than average adults, about 5 feet tall, but they were fully formed. The idea that he had only seen coveralls seemed to grow out of an interview that Hynek gave a few days after the sighting. He was attempting to provide some cover for Zamora. All it did was confuse the issue, but Zamora did see alien creatures, or rather humanoid creatures. He did provide descriptions of them.

Physical Evidence?

There was physical evidence. There were impressions made by the landing gear. Those on the site saw the impressions and suggested they had been pressed into the ground rather than dug out. These observations were made by the various law enforcement officials that include the FBI. Holder, as the military representative, said the same thing. The landing gear marks were photographed by several people, including the military representatives, and those photographs are available for examination.

Philip Klass suggested that this evidence was indicative of a hoax. Using a pot scrubber, knitting needles, and a flat map of the landing site, he showed how asymmetrical the landing gear was. Overlooking the fact that an alien race might not have the same ascetics as we do, Klass's example was flawed. The landing area was not flat, and the differences in the terrain explained the reason for the asymmetry of the landing gear. It compensated for the terrain.

Other evidence, the charred remains of a bush and some of the grass, also argued for some sort of extraordinary event. In the various samples taken of the soil and the organic material, no evidence of an accelerant anywhere on the landing site was found. The grass and the bush had not been burned by a petrochemical fuel. There was no real evidence of radiation on the site, which suggested the source of the flame seen by Zamora had not been radioactive. Chavez said that the bush, though still smoking, was cool to the touch. There was no explanation for this observation.

The soil samples taken by so many revealed nothing extraordinary. There was no difference between the samples taken from the ground under where the object had stood and the control samples taken from other locations around the landing site. All this proved was that the craft, whatever it might have been, left no chemical traces of its landing or its takeoff.

The metallic evidence recovered by Stanford was lost through his carelessness and the investigation by NASA. Today it makes no difference whether Stanford had sought out NASA through Dick Hall or Hall had made the suggestion and pushed Stanford into it. The result is the same. According to Stanford, the few traces that had been left for analysis by NASA resulted in a suggestion of something of an alien nature, though that was verbal communication without benefit of a recording. If the official NASA report is to be believed, and Hall, along with NICAP, accepted it as authentic, there was nothing found during the analysis of the samples to take this to the extraterrestrial.

What all this means is simply that even if the craft was alien in nature, it left nothing behind that would allow us to make that leap. The physical evidence, even the landing pad traces and the burned area, could have been created by terrestrial technology. In other words, though all this is interesting, the physical evidence does not move us to extraterrestrial visitation.

The Zamora Symbol

Here is another area in which it seems that Holder and Byrnes can be held responsible for the confusion. Holder suggested that they withhold the information about the symbol so that they might weed out copycats. The Blue Book files have many representations of the symbol, and they all show basically the same design. This is the arc over the arrowhead with a line underneath. Given that the Blue Book files are now available for all to read, and given that several people, including Zamora, signed drawings or reports that contained illustrations in them, it seems difficult to believe that this is now an area of controversy.

Zamora told Holder that after the craft lifted off, he drew the symbol on a scrap of paper. He gave that to Holder after he had signed it, and that scrap was eventually sent to Wright-Patterson and is in the Blue Book files. Zamora also drew for Holder and Byrnes an outline of the ship and the symbol he saw on it. He signed that as well. This illustration is also located in the Blue Book files.

Going through the Blue Book files, there is a report by Major William Connor that contains his illustration of the symbol. It matches that which Zamora drew in the police station that night for Holder and Byrnes. In fact, in the official file, there is no representation of the inverted "V" with the three lines through it. That symbol only appears in newspaper articles from 1964.

Rick Baca, who created a drawing of the craft that Zamora had seen in the days that followed the sighting, said that the arc and arrowhead was the correct symbol. He drew the craft from the descriptions obtain by his father, and when Zamora saw it, he not only said that it looked like what he had seen, but had Baca's father draw the symbol on the side. It matched those that Zamora had drawn himself and then signed on the night of the sighting.

Rick Baca holding a drawing of the UFO as described by Lonnie Zamora in the days that followed the landing. Under Zamora's direction, the color and shape of the symbol were added a few days later. Photo courtesy of Paul Harden.

Even Stanford, in a letter to Dick Hall, verified the arc symbol as opposed to the inverted "V" with the three lines through it. In a letter dated May 5, 1964, Stanford made it clear that the proper symbol was the one that had the arc over the arrowhead and the inverted "V" with the three lines through it was the fake: "[I]f a person(s) claim UFO 'contact' with "A" or [inverted 'V' with the three lines through it] on the side we can suspect a hoax."

There is also a document created by Hynek about the case. One page contains illustrations of the craft, the landing gear pattern, and the symbols. Here there are a variety of those symbols, including the proper arc over arrowhead. The inverted "V" is there as well, but it is labeled as "papers," meaning that this was what had been published in the newspapers.

Where did the other symbol originate? It did appear in some newspapers of the time. They apparently received it from those officials involved with the investigation, which included Holder and Byrnes. There is nothing in any of the files to suggest who came up with the specific drawing, but it is not part of the official Blue Book file.

Rob Mercer was the one who obtained the "unofficial" file from former Blue Book officer Carmon Marano. This file was one that had been assembled by one of the former members of the Blue Book team and contained two cards with the inverted "V" symbol on them. They were actually copies of the same thing, one in a rather sloppy handwriting and the other printed more neatly. Rather than having been gathered from Zamora, it seems, based on the sentence construction, they were taken from newspaper reports. In other words, it was information gathered from newspapers rather than those involved in the sighting and investigation.

Ray Stanford, in his book, seems to have reversed himself. He now suggests that the inverted "V" is the correct symbol and not the arc over the arrowhead. It would seem that we can quote him on which is the correct symbol and make a case for either one, but it also seems that his first information on it—that is the May 1964 letter—is probably the more accurate one.

The preponderance of the evidence tells us which symbol is correct. It is the one drawn and signed by Zamora, it is the one that appears in all the documents in the official Blue Book file, and it is the one that was put on the drawing made by Baca with Zamora adding the symbol later.

The Final Analysis

Here's where we are on this. Had so many people not been pushing so many agendas, and had the media and some of the investigators not treated Zamora with such distain, this case might have been just what Allen Hynek, the Air Force consultant, seemed to fear. In a report on his Socorro trip, he wrote, "No doubt was left in my mind but that NICAP and APRO, and possibly others, would consider this the best authenticated landing sighting on record. They will use it, very likely as a lever for a congressional investigation, and will deride any attempt to 'explain it away' as a balloon, conventional helicopter, etc."[1]

Reading between the lines here, this suggests that Hynek was confounded by the landing, the witnesses, and the evidence. He had no explanation for it and that seemed to have worried him. This was prior to his conversion to the other side of the UFO debate. At this point, he still considered the idea of alien visitation as unlikely.

Hector Quintanilla, at Blue Book, was under pressure to provide an answer. In his unpublished memoir of his activities at Blue Book, he wrote, "I was determined to solve the case and come hell or high water I was going to find the vehicle or stimulus."[2]

He reported that he had authority to review all the classified research programs at Holloman Air Force Base but after four days he found nothing to explain the sighting. He thought about the Lunar Lander, but the briefings he had on that project showed that it was not operational in April 1964.

Eventually he determined that it was time for him to pass judgment on the case. He wrote:

> I labeled the case "Unidentified" and the UFO buffs and hobby clubs had themselves a field day. According to them, here was proof that our beloved planet had been visited by an extraterrestrial vehicle. Although I labeled the case "Unidentified" I've never been satisfied with that classification. I've always felt that too many essential elements of the case were missing. There are the intangible elements which are impossible to check, so the solution to the case could very well be lying dormant in Lonnie Zamora's head.[3]

Again, one of those charged with investigating the case was unable to provide a plausible explanation for it. Instead he insisted that the solution was with Zamora but offered nothing to suggest what that might be, or what essential element the investigators of the case had failed to find.

What this means is that the Air Force through Project Blue Book and through its consultant found nothing to explain what had been seen. They found no secret project located at Holloman that would explain the sighting. Searches of the various defense contractors and other research organizations provided no answer. Documentation of the military activities at Holloman, White Sands, and Kirtland provide no answer. In fact, Quintanilla had queried the White House Command Post and was told that the only thing they had going on were U-2 flights, which obviously wasn't the answer.[4]

Hynek, during his trip to Socorro, had spoken to a colleague, the president of the New Mexico Institute of Mining and Technology, Dr. Jack Whotman, and was told that they had nothing that would have been in the area and that the students were not responsible. It was not a student hoax.

The bottom line on this is that, as in so many other UFO cases, the personalities, the agendas of so many organizations both civilian and government, and feuding has taken precedence over the investigation. It seems, in the very beginning, that the New Mexican law enforcement officers involved, the military officers, and the FBI agent all had a common goal: to figure out what had landed. The area was cordoned off, samples were taken, and Zamora was interviewed by professionals. But almost before the sun was up, the story was out, and everyone else headed to Socorro.

Had the investigation continued in a professional manner, had the news media not jumped into the report, and had some of the civilian researchers stayed out of the way, then we might have some interesting answers. Metallic residue was lost through clumsy handling, soil samples taken by so many revealed nothing extraordinary, and the plants revealed no sign of having been burned by any chemical process.

Today, we know that the case is not single witness, we know that landing traces were left behind, and no Earthly explanation has been offered. We are left with a case that is interesting, has evidence other than witness testimony, and has not been explained. It is, in the truest sense of the word, "Unidentified." We don't know what it was, but we know what it wasn't. And though that does not take us immediately to the extraterrestrial, it gets us very close to it. This is one of the defining cases of UFO history and it deserved better than it got. It is the very definition of Unidentified.

Notes

Introduction

1. To listen to that interview, see *https://youtu.be/xd5ToD13d1E,* or search for Ben Moss and Tony Angiola on *www. kevinrandle.blogspot.com.*

2. Stanford, *Socorro "Saucer."*

3. To listen to that interview, see *https://youtu.be/FIr36JIf48,* or search for Rob Mercer on *www.kevinrandle.blogspot.com.*

4. To listen to that interview, see *https://youtube.com/ watch?v=Wyz0ZAvhv79,* or search for Carmon Marano on *www.kevinrandle.blogspot.com.*

5. After hearing this, I went through the microfilm copy of the Socorro UFO landing case, and then many other files

from that time period, and found they weren't classified at all. Some of the earlier cases were. If there was some sort of national security aspect to the case, then it might be classified, but generally, the cases carried no classified markings.

Chapter 1

1. See Air Force regulations AFR 200-2 (August 1953) and AFR 80-17A (November 1966), and JANAP 146(E), which governs reporting of vital intelligence. UFO sightings fall under it for reporting. The air defense mission for the Air Force fell first under the Air Defense Command and later the Aerospace Defense Command, which was finally deactivated. In 1964, the mission was defense of the continental United States, which by default, gave it the mission of intercepting and identifying any intruders into U.S. airspace. That meant it was required to identify unknown vehicles inside that air space.

2. Randle and Cornett, "How the Air Force Hid," pp. 18–21, 53–54, 56–57.

3. *Mountain Mail* (Magdalena, New Mexico) obituary, November 5, 2009, accessed November 9, 2016.

4. Information supplied by Robert Charles Cornett, who was at the very large array outside of Socorro and who called Zamora, who in turn invited him to the barbeque as long as he didn't mention UFOs.

5. See, for example, Stanford, *Socorro Saucer in a Pentagon Pantry*, pp. 89–94, and Richards, "UFO Witness Sighs," pp. A-1–2.

6. The description of the event is taken from the statement made by Patrolman Lonnie Zamora and found in the Project Blue Book files, available on microfilm roll no. 50, case no. 8766. Portions of the statement can be found in Clark, *UFO Encyclopedia*, pp. 856–858, and Steiger, *Project Blue Book*, pp. 115–121.

7. Steiger, *Project Blue Book*, p. 118; Project Blue Book files, roll no. 50, case no. 8766.

8. Ibid.

9. Ibid.

10. Steiger, *Project Blue Book,* p. 118; Clark, *UFO Encyclopedia,* p. 857; Project Blue Book files, roll no. 50, case no. 8766.

11. Clark, *UFO Encyclopedia,* p. 857; Project Blue Book files, roll no. 50, case no. 8766. There is some question about the author of the statement. It seems to be a combination of Zamora's words and the notes made by one of the interviewing officials in the hours after the sighting.

12. Steiger, *Project Blue Book,* p. 119; Project Blue Book files, roll no. 50, case no. 8766.

13. Steiger, *Project Blue Book,* pp. 118–121; *Clark, UFO Encyclopedia,* pp. 857–858; Project Blue Book files, roll no. 50, case no. 8766. Again, this narrative was written mostly in the first person, but it seems to be a statement taken down by a third party.

14. "UAO Landing," p. 3; Stanford, *Socorro "Saucer,"* pp. 30–33.

15. "UAO Landing," p. 3.

16. "Evidence of UFO," p. 1.

17. Project Blue Book files, roll no. 50, case no. 8766; Stanford, *Socorro "Saucer,"* p. 35.

18. Stanford, *Socorro "Saucer,"* pp. 35–36.

19. "UAO Landing," p. 3.

20. Stanford, *Socorro "Saucer,"* pp. 41–43.

21. "UAO Landing," p. 3.

22. Clark, *UFO Encyclopedia,* p. 860.

23. For a time line of the events, Stanford, *Socorro "Saucer,"* pp, 32–35.

24. "UAO Landing," p. 4; Stanford, *Socorro "Saucer,"* pp. 42–43.

25. "Evidence of UFO," p. 1.

26. Clark, *UFO Encyclopedia,* p. 861.

27. Stanford, *Socorro "Saucer,"* pp. 42–46.

28. Ibid., pp. 46–47.

29. Ibid., pp. 46–48.

30. Ibid.

Chapter 2

1. Project Blue Book files, roll no. 1, case no. 10; Maccabee, "The Arnold Phenomenon"; Long, "Kenneth Arnold Revisited"; Sutherly, "Ken Arnold, pp. 42–43, 62, 64–66.

2. Project Blue Book files, roll no. 1, case no. 10; Clark, *UFO Encyclopedia,* pp. 139–142.

3. Project Blue Book files, roll no. 1, case no. 10.

4. Badufos.blogspot.com/2016/08/Kenneth-arnold-and-pelicans.html, accessed March 26, 2017. The idea that pelicans were responsible for the Arnold sighting was first advanced decades ago.

5. Project Blue Book files, roll no. 1, case no. 34; Ruppelt, *The Report,* p. 32.

6. Various newspapers around the country reported, including the *Phoenix Gazette, Albuquerque Tribune,* and *El Paso Herald–Post.*

7. Project Blue Book files, rolls no. 11, 12, and 13; Ruppelt, *The Report,* pp. 207–227; Randle, *Invasion*; Clark, *UFO Encyclopedia,* pp. 998–1,004; Peeples, *Watch the Skies!,* pp. 62–86.

8. Project Blue Book files, rolls no. 11, 12, and 13.

9. Dewey Fournet, telephone interview with Kevin Randle, July 17, 1995.

10. Ruppelt, *The Report,* pp. 207–227.

11. Dewey Fournet, telephone interview with Kevin Randle, July 17, 1995.

12. Albert Chop, telephone interview with Kevin Randle, August 20, 1995.

13. Ibid.

14. Project Blue Book, roll no. 29, case no. 5120; Clark, *UFO Encyclopedia,* pp. 581–582; Hynek, *The UFO Experience*; Swords and Powell, *UFOs and Government,* pp. 252–255, 263.

15. Project Blue Book files, roll no. 29, case no. 5120.

16. Glenn H. Toy, telephone interview with Kevin Randle, December 11, 2014.

17. Glenn H. Toy, statement in Project Blue Book files, microfilm roll no. 50.

18. Project Blue Book files, microfilm roll no. 50.

19. Glenn H. Toy, telephone interview with Kevin Randle, December 11, 2014.

20. There were, in fact, witnesses at 13 separate locations, and some of those locations had more than a single witness. Pedro Saucedo, for example, was with a pal.

21. "The Levelland Case," p. 1; Lorenzen, *Flying Saucers*, pp. 91–99.

22. Project Blue Book files roll no. 45, case no. 7868; Edwards, "Mystery Blast," pp. 68–72; Stalnaker, "Brilliant Red Explosion," 1962, p. 1; Clark, *UFO Encyclopedia*, pp. 279–281; Holloway, "The Nevada Fireball"; Randle, "The Nevada Fireball."

23. Stalnaker, "Brilliant Red Explosion," p. 1.

24. Ibid.

25. Walter Butt, telephone interview by Kevin Randle, November 1988.

26. Project Blue Book files, roll no. 45, case no. 7868.

27. Ibid.

Chapter 3

1. The sources for this story, including quotations, are Stanford, *Socorro "Saucer,"* pp. 12–17; and Clark, *UFO Encyclopedia*, pp. 859–860.

2. Steiger, *Project Blue Book*, pp. 125–126.

3. In every other instance, Major Connor has been identified as the public relations officer at Kirtland AFB. Though the assignment to UFO investigation was nearly always an additional duty, it is important to note that Connor was a field grade officer and not a newly commissioned second lieutenant. This suggests a high level of interest by the Air Force.

4. Project Blue Book files, roll no. 50, case no. 8766. Letter from Colonel de Jonckheere to Headquarters, USAF

SAFOI [Secretary of the Air Force, Office of Information)
PB, dated May 28, 1964.

5. Project Blue Book files, roll no. 50, case no. 8766, teletype
message marked "routine."

6. Both Ben Moss and Tony Angiola talked about these
other, unidentified witnesses on the radio version of "A
Different Perspective," which can be heard at *https://youtu.
be/xd5ToD13d1E.*

7. Project Blue Book files, roll no. 50, case no. 8766, undated
report signed by Holder but probably written late on April
24th or very early on April 25th.

8. Stanford, *Socorro "Saucer,"* pp. 82–84; Clark, *UFO
Encyclopedia,* p. 860; Ray Stanford, telephone interview by
Kevin Randle, February 23, 2016.

9. Ray Stanford talked about the auditory witnesses on the
radio version of "A Different Perspective," which can be
heard at *www.youtube.com/watch?v=q8QfQ4F_7ww.*

10. Ray Stanford, email to Kevin Randle, November 22, 2016.

11. Stanford, *Socorro "Saucer,"* pp. 83–84.

12. Clark, *UFO Encyclopedia,* pp. 859–860.

13. Ibid.

14. Ray Stanford on the radio version of "A Different
Perspective," which can be heard at *www.youtube.com/
watch?v=q8QfQ4F_7ww.*

15. "UAO Landing," pp. 3–4.

16. Walter Shrode, KSRC radio, Socorro, New Mexico, April
25, 1947, from Wendy Connors audio collection of UFO
related recordings. See also *www.roswellproof.com/Socorro/
Socorro_Zamora_interview.html.*

17. "UAO Landing," pp. 3–4.

18. *Hobbs New Mexico News-Sun,* April 23, 1965.

19. "Two Dubuquers," pp. 1, 2.

20. Hynek, *The Hynek UFO Report,* p. 218; "UAO Landing," pp.
3–4.

21. In later interviews, they would revise this, suggesting that
they were west of town when they spotted the dust and then
the smoke. Had they been east of town, they would have

been heading away from Socorro and the object would
have been behind them.

22. "Two Dubuquers," pp. 1, 2.

23. DeGraw, "Socorro Witness Interviews," pp. 14–15.

24. Ibid., p. 15.

25. Ibid.

Chapter 4

1. Stanford, *Socorro "Saucer,"* pp. 22–24.

2. "UAO Landing," pp. 3–4.

3. Clark, *UFO Encyclopedia,* p. 859.

4. Stanford, *Socorro "Saucer,"* p. 31.

5. "UAO Landing," p. 3.

6. Ibid.

7. Clark, *UFO Encyclopedia,* p. 859; Stanford, *Socorro "Saucer,"*
   pp. 35–38; "UAO Landing," pp. 4–5.

8. Sunset in Socorro on April 24, 1964, was 6:46 p.m.
   Available light would have persisted for about another
   20 minutes but would have been fading fast, especially
   because of the mountains to the west. With the sun setting
   and the light fading rapidly, they had little choice but to
   leave the landing site.

9. Clark, *UFO Encyclopedia,* p. 860.

10. Richard T. Holder signed statement in the Project Blue
    Book files. It is at the point we can begin to straighten out
    some of the trouble with the sequence of events that took
    place after Zamora and Chavez returned to the police
    station.

11. Recording from Wendy Connor's collection of UFO
    interviews. The transcript can be found on Rudiak's
    Roswell Proof website: *www.roswellproof.com/Socorro/Socorro_
    Zamora_interview.html.*

12. Stanford, *Socorro "Saucer,"* pp. 42–43; "UAO Landing," pp.
    3–4.

13. Richard T. Holder signed statement in the Project Blue
    Book files.

14. Ibid. Ray Stanford has a similar notation in his book, though he had inserted Byrnes's name into the statement written by Holder. Also see Stanford, *Socorro "Saucer,"* p. 42.

15. Clark, *UFO Encyclopedia,* p. 861. Based on an interview Clark conducted with Holder in 1995.

16. "UAO Landing," pp. 3–4.

17. Ibid.

18. Ibid.

19. Ibid., pp. 4 – 7.

20. Ibid., p. 7. Although Coral Lorenzen suggested an attempt at censorship, the real reason was more likely an attempt to keep the story on a rational track and a fear that it would be derailed by talk of little green men.

21. Richards, "UFO Witness," pp. A-1–A-2.

22. Ibid., p. 5.

23. Coral Lorenzen reported that while she and her husband were in Socorro, Jim Lorenzen saw Moody standing in a hallway and introduced himself, his last name apparently escaping Moody's attention. Moody, in the discussion with those at the station, mentioned Dan Fry, who had been an electrician at White Sands and who had claimed contact with alien creatures. Moody then said, "[A]nd there is a woman who heads a research organization.... Her name is Coral Lorenzen. She's a nut." See "UAO Landing," p. 4.

24. Clark, *UFO Encyclopedia,* pp. 861–862; "UFO Sighting Re-Enacted."

25. Project Blue Book files, roll no. 50, case no. 8766 (Hynek memo on his trip to New Mexico).

26. Stanford, *Socorro "Saucer,"* pp. 56–58.

27. Clark, *UFO Encyclopedia,* p. 862.

28. Stanford, *Socorro "Saucer,"* pp. 61–63.

29. Ibid., p. 79.

30. Stanford, *Socorro "Saucer,"* pp. 89–90.

31. Richards, "UFO Witness," pp. A-1–A-2.

32. Stanford, *Socorro "Saucer,"* pp. 90–91.

33. Hynek, "Socorro Revisited"; Steiger, *Blue Book,* pp. 121–128.

34. This is actually Felix Phillips, who lived a quarter mile or more from the landing site.

35. Hynek, "Socorro Revisited."

36. Ibid. See also Clark, *UFO Encyclopedia,* p. 864.

37. Ibid.

38. Ben Moss and Tony Angiola, presentation made to the 47th Annual MUFON Symposium, Orlando, Florida, on August 26–27, 2016.

Chapter 5

1. Project Blue Book files, roll 50, case no. 8755; "Mystery Object," p. 1; "'Flying Saucer' Reports"; Clark, *UFO Encyclopedia,* pp. 865–866; Lorenzen, "Incident at La Madera," pp. 4, 6; "Physical Evidence," p 5.

2. Project Blue Book files, roll no. 50, case no. 8755; "The UFO Reporter," summer 1965 (article in Blue Book with no other identification).

3. Lorenzen, "Incident," p. 4.

4. Martin E. Vigil letter to Richard H. Hall, June 9, 1964; "Physical Evidence," p. 5.

5. Lorenzen, "Incident," p. 5.

6. "Edgewood Man."

7. Project Blue Book files, roll 50, case no. 8755.

8. Akers, "Landing Region." One of the most important parts of the article was the mention of the melted soft drink bottle. It would surface in a number of accounts, including one that related specifically to the Socorro landing.

9. Lorenzen, "Incident," p. 5.

10. Thomas, "'Flying Saucers."

11. Project Blue Book files, roll 50, case no. 8755.

12. Clark, *UFO Encyclopedia,* p. 866. "Flying Saucer Puts."

13. Lorenzen, "UAO Landing," pp. 1, 3–4; Project Blue Book files, roll no. 50, case 8755 as "Information Only," from

the FSIC Bulletin, Vol. 2, #1 but the origin tracks back to
Coral Lorenzen.

14. Lorenzen, "UAO Landing," p. 3.

15. Good, *Alien Contact*, pp. 111–114.

16. At one time Norton Air Force Base housed the collection
of still and motion pictures from a variety of Air Force
missions and commands, and these included those that
had been part of Project Blue Book.

17. Emenegger, *UFOs*, pp. 127–129. This information is
apparently part of a dramatization for a documentary
about the Holloman AFB landing that is based on the
April 1964 incident.

18. At this time, Area 51 and Groomlake were not general
knowledge.

19. Good, *Alien Contact*, p. 113.

20. Ibid., pp. 113–114. See also *UFO Cover-Up?* (video tape in
author's files).

21. Ibid.

22. Smothers, "Girl Says"; "Flying Object Expert."

23. Project Blue Book files, roll no. 50, case no. 8755.

24. "Flying Object Expert"; "Couple Reports Sighting"; Project
Blue Book files, roll no. 50, case no. 8755.

25. "'Flying Saucer' Reports"; Project Blue Book files, roll no.
50, case no. 8755.

26. "'Flying Bathtub' Seen."

27. Randle, *The UFO Dossier*, pp.102, 107–113, 133; Lorenzen,
"The Stokes Case," pp. 2, 6.

28. Smothers, "Girl Says."

29. Lorenzen, "The Stull Case," pp. 1–2.

30. Ibid., p. 2.

31. Ibid.

32. Project Blue Book files, roll no. 50, case number 8759.

33. Paskind, "Man Here."

34. Ibid.

35. Project Blue Book files, roll no. 48, case 8398.

36. Ibid.

37. Ibid.

Chapter 6

1. See, for example, Peeples, *Watch the Skies!*, p. 182.

2. This is the spelling that appears in most of the reports, but in the Project Blue Book files his name is spelled Squyers.

3. Project Blue Book files, roll no. 14, case no. 1972.

4. "Flying Saucer Seen Hovering Near Ground Northeast of Frontenac, Radio Man Tells Police; Disappears in Sky." Newspaper clipping from *www.ufologie.patrickgross.org/bb/1972.htm*, accessed December 16, 2016.

5. Hynek, *The Hynek UFO Report*, p. 191.

6. Ibid. See also Project Blue Book files, roll no. 14, case no. 1972.

7. "Flying Saucer Seen Hovering Near Ground Northeast of Frontenac, Radio Man Tells Police; Disappears in Sky." Newspaper clipping from *www.ufologie.patrickgross.org/bb/1972.htm*, accessed December 16, 2016.

8. According to information included in the Project Blue Book Special Report No. #14, "Having an artificial leg, he could not leave the road since the surrounding terrain was rough. However, he was within about 100 yards of it at the point he was standing on the road."

9. See *www.ufocasebook.com/pittsburgkansas1952.html*, accessed December 17, 2016. See also Project Blue Book Special Report #14, Project Blue Book files, roll no. 86; and Steiger, *Project Blue Book*, p. 163.

10. This is a reference to Air Force Regulation 200-2, which covered the reports of UFOs, the investigation of them, and other administrative matters.

11. Hynek, *The Hynek UFO Report*, p. 193.

12. Project Blue Book files, roll no. 60, case 10274.

13. Hewes, "The Oklahoma Humanoid," pp. 12–17.

14. Ibid. See also Clark, *UFO Encyclopedia*, pp. 579–580.

15. Clark, *UFO Encyclopedia,* p. 580; Project Blue Book files, roll no. 60, summary of the case.

16. Crawford, Hewes, and Hewes, *The Intruders.*

17. Hynek, *Hynek UFO Report,* pp. 198–200.

18. Ibid., pp. 193–196.

19. He is frequently identified in various publications as Oscar, as opposed to Oskar.

20. Bloecher, "Herr Linke," p. 6. Krause is identified as a judge in the Project Blue Book report on the case.

21. The Blue Book report misspells the town as Hasselbach, Saxsonia.

22. CIA statement that appears in Hynek, *Hynek UFO Report,* p. 194. For an alternative statement, see Edwards, *Flying Saucers,* pp. 97–98. Edwards's information seemed to come from a newspaper article. The best information is from Bloecher and the *MUFON UFO Journal.*

23. Bloecher, "Herr Linke," p. 6.

24. Ibid., p. 8.

25. Kottmeyer, "Missing Linke." It should also be noted that some had suggested that this ring of fire is similar to the jets on the Spitzbergen crashed saucer reported in 1952. The problem is that it is clear that the Spitzbergen crash is a hoax.

26. Ibid., p. 8.

27. Ibid.

28. *Hynek, The Hynek UFO Report, p. 193.*

Chapter 7

1. Project Blue Book files, roll 15, case no. 2078.

2. Nickell, "The Flatwoods"; Nickell, in Story, *The Encyclopedia,* pp. 194–200.

3. Sanderson, *Uninvited Visitors,* pp. 37–52.

4. Clark, *UFO Encyclopedia,* pp. 409–412; Lorenzen and Lorenzen, *Encounters,* pp. 169–170.

5. Clark, *UFO Encyclopedia,* p. 410.

6. Sanderson, *Uninvited Visitors.*

7. Barker, *They Knew Too Much,* pp. 17–25; Keyhoe, *Flying Saucers.*

8. Snitowski, "The West Virginia," pp. 39–41.

9. Ibid.

10. "More on the 'Green Monster.'"

11. Painter, "What Happened," pp. 28–35.

12. Ibid., p. 32.

13. Clark, *UFO Encyclopedia,* p. 411.

14. Davis and Bloecher, *Close Encounter*; Project Blue Book files, roll no. 24; Clark, *UFO Encyclopedia,* pp. 552–553; Story, *The Encyclopedia,* pp. 293–294; Lorenzen and Lorenzen, *Encounters,* pp. 174–175.

15. Davis and Bloecher, *Close Encounter,* pp. 35–36.

16. "Story of Space-Ship," p. 1.

17. Ibid.

18. Davis and Bloecher, *Close Encounter,* pp. 37–38.

19. Letter dated August 19, 1957, signed by Captain Wallace W. Elwood, Project Blue Book files.

20. Ibid.

21. Carmon Marano, telephone interview with Kevin Randle, November 2, 2016.

22. Letter dated September 17, 1957, signed by Captain Robert J. Hertell, Project Blue Book files.

23. "Story of Space-Ship," p. 1.

24. All quotes in this section from the letter dated September 17, 1957, signed by Captain Robert J. Hertell, Project Blue Book files.

25. "Spacecraft Story," pp. 1, 2.

26. Lorenzen, Coral. "Little, Little Men," p. 8.

27. Ibid.

28. Steiger, *Strangers,* pp. 126–129.

29. Email from Jim Bain to Susan Lubbers, editor of the *Long Prairie Leader,* and confirmed to Kevin Randle by Jim Bain.

Chapter 8

1. Jesse Marcel, Jr. personal interviews by Kevin Randle and Donald Schmitt, August 2, 1989, and August 18, 1990; Marcel and Marcel, *The Roswell Legacy.*

2. The Marcels' illustrations can be found online. See also Pflock, *Roswell,* photo section.

3. See *www.anomalies-unlimited.com/Alien%20Writing/Martian. html,* accessed February 7, 2017.

4. Vallee, *Revelations,* p. 21; Randle, *Crash,* pp. 23–25.

5. Gillmor, *Scientific Study,* p. 391. I will note here that Warren Smith, invited to participate in an investigation by Schirmer, reported that he had found markings on the ground that were allegedly left by the object. No one else reported them, no photographs were taken, and Smith's confession to me that he sometimes invented UFO stories and evidence to help validate a sighting suggest that this was just another of his tales.

6. It must be noted that in 1966 a movie, *Mars Needs Women,* was released in which the "Martians" wore a helmet that had a piece over each ear with an antenna sticking out of it.

7. Clark, *UFO Encyclopedia,* p. 819.

8. Bullard, *UFO Abductions,* p. 250.

9. In a discussion with Coral Lorenzen in the mid-1970s, after an investigation of the Pat Roach abduction in which she reported seeing a Sam Browne belt on the uniform of the alien abductors, Coral told me that this was something that had been reported in other cases, but had not been published as a way of separating the copycats from the true abductees. The problem was that all the researchers were sharing the information with one another, so there was a possibility of cross-contamination. I will note that my investigation suggests that the Roach abduction was the result of an episode of sleep paralysis rather than alien abduction.

10. Lorenzen and Lorenzen, *Encounters,* pp. 61–87, 95–96, 98–99, 155; Lorenzen and Lorenzen, *Flying Saucer Occupants,*

pp. 42–72; Vallee, *Dimensions,* pp. 122–124; Dolan, *UFOs,* pp. 201–202.

11. Coral Lorenzen told me that she had said the hair under the arm was red rather than mention it was red public hair, the implication being that there had been no underarm hair. Lorenzen didn't want to mention public hair in the *APRO Bulletin* but thought the hair color important so she changed the location.

12. Clark, *UFO Encyclopedia,* p. 162.

13. Project Blue Book Files, roll no. 54, case no. 9338.

14. Clark, *UFO Encyclopedia,* p. 164.

15. Ibid.

16. Project Blue Book Files, roll no. 54, case no. 9338.

17. Clark, *UFO Encyclopedia,* p. 166.

18. For a good analysis of the UMMO hoax, see Clark, *UFO Encyclopedia,* pp. 939–942.

19. Project Blue Book files, roll no. 59, case no. 10129; Murphy, "Object"; Wilson, "East of Roswell," pp. 19–23; Kean, "Forty Years," pp. 3–9, 28–31; Gordon, "Kecksburg Crash," pp. 3–5, 9; Young, "The Kecksburg"; Gordon, "The Military," pp. 174–179.

20. Sheaffer, Robert. "Discovery Canada Serves up the Kecksburg Crash Yarn." Badufos.blogspot.com/2014/01/discovery-canada-serves-up-kecksburg.html (accessed April 4, 2017); Printy, Tim. SUNlite 3,6 (November-October 2011): pp. 1, 6 – 44.

21. Pflock, *Roswell,* photo section.

Chapter 9

1. Stanford, *Socorro "Saucer,"* pp. 206–211.

2. Project Blue Book files, roll no. 50, case no. 8766.

3. Ibid.

4. "UAO Landing," p. 3.

5. Rick Baca, who drew the picture, telephone interview with Kevin Randle, March 6, 2017.

6. Project Blue Book files, roll no. 50, case no. 8766.

7. Paul Harden, emails to Kevin Randle dated September 17, 2011; December 2, 2016; December 3, 2016; March 1, 2017; and March 2, 2017.

8. According to Baca, the symbol was added after it appeared in the newspaper. Hynek did suggest that the symbol not be published then, but Harden had been the first to make the suggestion.

9. Rick Baca, telephone interview with Kevin Randle, March 6, 2017.

10. Rich Reynolds, email to Kevin Randle.

11. Ray Stanford, letter to Richard Hall, May 3, 1964.

12. Stanford, *Socorro "Saucer,"* p. 209.

13. See *www.roswellproof.com/Socorro/Socorro.Hynek_interview.html*.

14. *http://theozfiles.blogspot.com/2014/06*, June 4, 2014.

15. Interview with Carmon Marano, October 26, 2016; see *http://kevinrandle.blogspot.com/2016/11/x-zone-broadcast-network-former-blue.html* or *www.youtube.com/watch?=Wyz0Zvhv7g*.

Chapter 10

1. Klass, *UFOs Explained,* p. 108.

2. Project Blue Book files, roll no. 50, case no. 8766.

3. See *www.gpposner.com/Klass_inter.htm*, first accessed September 12, 2011, last accessed February 28, 2017. See also *www.kevinrandle.blogspot.com/2011/09/philip-klass-and-socorro-ufo-landing.html*.

4. For more details, see Chapter 3.

5. Project Blue Book files, roll no. 50, case no. 8766.

6. Klass, *UFOs Explained,* pp. 111–12.

7. Ibid., p. 112.

8. Ibid., p. 113.

9. Harden, *www.caminorealheritage.org/PH/ph.htm*, originally accessed September 12, 2011.

10. Project Blue Book files, roll no. 50, case no. 8766.

11. Ibid.

12. Ibid.

13. Tony Bragalia, emails to Kevin Randle, January 20, 2015; January 21, 2015; January 25, 2015; and February 9, 2015; Tom Printy, January 21, 2017; Robert Sheaffer, January 20, 2015; and Vincente-Juan Ballester Olmos, January 25, 2015.

14. Tony Bragalia, email to Kevin Randle, December 2, 2009. See *http://kevinrandle.blogspot.com/2009/10/lonnie-zamora-socorro-ufo-and-new.html*.

15. Project Blue Book files, roll no. 50, case no. 8766.

16. Ibid.

17. Tony Bragalia, emails to Kevin Randle, January 20, 2015; January 21, 2015; January 25, 2015; and February 9, 2015.

18. Project Blue Book files, roll no. 50, case no. 8766.

19. Ibid.

20. Ibid.

21. Thomas, "A Different Angle," pp. 5–6, see also Thomas, "The Socorro."

22. Ibid.

23. Quintanilla, *UFOs*, pp. 29–33.

24. Ibid.

Chapter 11

1. Robert Shaw, personal interview with Kevin Randle, August 2, 1973; Howard Groves, personal interview with Kevin Randle, August 2, 1973; Randle, "Mysterious Clues," pp. 20–23, 76–78; Randle, "A Closer Look," pp. 44–49.

2. Howard Groves, personal interview with Kevin Randle, August 2, 1973.

3. Ibid.

4. Johnson, "Birthday Landing," p. 1.

5. Randle, "A Closer Look," pp. 44–49; Robert Shaw, personal interview with Kevin Randle, August 2, 1973.

6. Howard Groves, personal interview with Kevin Randle, August 2, 1973; Randle, "Mysterious Clues," p. 22.

7. Randle, "A Closer Look," pp. 44–49; Robert Shaw, personal interview with Kevin Randle, August 2, 1973.

8. Randle, "A Closer Look," pp. 4–49; "Those Iowa Craters," pp. 1, 4–5.

9. Ibid.

10. Randle, "A Closer Look," pp. 44–49.

11. Steiger, *Mysteries,* pp. 100–103; Pat Barr and Warren Barr, personal interviews with Kevin Randle, September 1972.

12. Steiger, *Mysteries,* p. 102.

13. Ibid.

14. Ibid., pp. 103–105.

15. Project Blue Book files, roll no. 41, case no. 7203; "Object Lands," pp. 1–2; Hall, *The UFO Evidence,* p. 43.

16. Hall, *The UFO Evidence,* p. 43.

17. "Object Lands, Takes Off in Texas." The A.P.R.O. Bulletin, March 1961, pp. 1–2.

18. Project Blue Book files, roll no. 41, case no. 7203.

19. Ibid.

20. Ibid.

21. Project Blue Book files, roll no. 65, case no. 10944; "Landing in North Dakota," pp. 1, 3.

22. Project Blue Book files, roll no. 65, case no. 10944.

23. Ibid.

24. Ibid.

25. Ibid.

26. Hynek, *The Hynek UFO Report,* pp. 160–162; Project Blue Book files, roll no. 57, case no. 9808.

27. "The Cherry Creek," p. 7.

28. Project Blue Book files, roll no. 65, case no. 10944.

29. "Landing Probed," p. 7.

30. Project Blue Book files, roll no. 65, case no. 10944.

31. Ibid.

32. Ibid.

33. Clark, *UFO Encyclopedia,* pp. 324–326; Faruk, "The Delphos Landing," pp. 21–25; Faruk, "Further Comment," pp. 134–137; "Landing Case in Kansas," pp. 1, 3; "More on the Kansas," pp. 8–9; Vallee, *Dimensions,* pp. 164–166; Klass, *UFOs Explained,* pp. 312–332; "UFO Knocks Down," pp. 3–4.

34. Clark, *UFO Encyclopedia,* p. 324; Klass, *UFOs Explained,* pp. 318–319.

35. Ibid.

36. Clark, *UFO Encyclopedia,* p. 324.

37. Ibid., p. 325.

38. Clark, *UFO Encyclopedia,* p. 325; Klass, *UFOs Explained,* pp. 321–322.

39. *www.isaackoi.com/best-ufo-cases/10-consensus-lists-national-enquirer-panel.html,* accessed April 9, 2017.

40. Klass, *UFOs Explained,* p. 323.

41. Ibid.

42. Gillmor, *Final Report.*

43. Klass, *UFOs Explained,* pp. 328–330.

44. "Alleged UFO."

45. *oxalicacidinfo.com,* accessed March 1, 2017.

46. Klass, *UFOs Explained,* pp. 312–332.

47. Ibid.

48. Swords, "Soil Analysis," pp. 120–122.

49. Ibid., pp. 313–314, 326–328.

50. Ibid., p. 327.

Chapter 12

1. Project Blue Book files, roll numbers 86 and 87, designated as "Administrative Files." As an example, on April 1, 1960, Francis Archer, a scientific advisor to Blue Book, in a letter to Major General Dougher, commenting on a memo written by Colonel Evans, wrote, "[I] had tried to get

bluebook out of ATIC for 10 years...and do not agree that the loos of prestige to the UFO project is a disadvantage." See also, Randle and Cornett, "How the Air Force," pp. 18–21, 53–54, 56–57.

2. Review of the Blue Book files including the multiple witness and radar case from Minot, North Dakota, October 24, 1968. Interview with Carmon Marano, former Project Blue Book officer, November 2, 2016. Memos for the record confirm the telephonic investigation. Project Blue Book files, roll no. 81, case no. 12548.

3. The information in this section came primarily from the Project Blue Book files. See also, Randle, *Project Blue Book,* pp. 151–163.

4. In discussions with Carmon Marano, both during the radio interview and in the prep prior to that interview, he confirmed that neither he nor Lt. Col. Hector Quintanilla, the chief of Project Blue Book, had visited Minot Air Force Base.

5. Project Blue Book files, Project Card, roll no. 81, case no. 12548.

6. Clark, *UFO Encyclopedia,* p. 564.

7. Information developed by Wendy Connors and Michael Hall. For additional information see Randle, *The Government,* pp. 47–63.

8. Swords and Powell, *UFOs and Government,* pp. 30–71; Project Blue Book files, rolls no. 86 and 87; Ruppelt, *The Report,* pp. 26–44.

9. *www.project1947.com/fig/projsauc.htm,* accessed April 10, 2017; Swords and Powell, *UFOs and Government,* p. 210.

10. Ruppelt, *The Report,* pp. 58–59; Swords and Powell, *UFOs and Government,* p. 42–43.

11. Hall and Connors, *Captain Edward,* pp. 1–35.

12. Ruppelt, *The Report,* pp. 275–296.

13. Based on an analysis of the investigative conclusions in the Project Blue Book files.

14. "AF Intimidates," pp. 1–3, 4.

15. "AF Secretly," pp. 5–6.

16. Ibid.

17. "AF Intimidates," pp. 1–3, 4.

18. Gillmor, *Scientific Study,* pp 529–533; Project Blue Book, Administrative Files, roll nos. 85–86.

19. Project Blue Book files, roll no. 45, case nos. 7868, 7869.

20. In discussions with Carmon Marano, both during the radio interview and in the prep prior to that interview, he described the final months at Project Blue Book and what happened to the material collected by the project.

21. Carmon Marano, telephone interview with Kevin Randle October 27, 2016; radio interview November 2, 2016.

22. Ibid.

23. Ibid.

24. Ibid.

25. Unofficial Socorro file scanned and sent to Randle, courtesy of Rob Mercer.

Chapter 13

1. Stanford, *Socorro "Saucer,"* p. 31.

2. Lorenzen, "UAO Landing," p. 3.

3. Project Blue Book files, roll no. 50, case no. 8766.

4. Lorenzen, "UAO Landing," p. 3.

5. Stanford, *Socorro "Saucer,"* p. 36.

6. Holden signed report, Project Blue Book files, roll no. 50, case no. 8766.

7. Project Blue Book files, roll no. 50, case no. 8766.

8. Lorenzen, "UAO Landing," p. 3.

9. Project Blue Book files, roll no. 50, case no. 8766.

10. Ibid.

11. Ibid. This information, though in the Blue Book files, is uncorroborated hearsay from the residents of Socorro. Hynek also took samples of the sap.

12. Ibid.

13. Stanford, *Socorro "Saucer,"* p. 55.

14. "Unidentified Flying Object Report," Socorro, New Mexico, 24 April 1964, Project Blue Book files, roll no. 50, case no. 8766.

15. Project Blue Book files, roll no. 50, case no. 8766.

16. Ibid.

17. James E. McDonald letter to Richard Hall, September 5, 1968; Clark, *UFO Encyclopedia,* p. 864; Stanford, *Socorro "Saucer,"* p. 73–74.

18. Stanford, *Socorro "Saucer,"* pp. 74–75.

19. Clark, *UFO Encyclopedia,* pp. 862–863; Stanford, *Socorro "Saucer,"* pp. 78–84; Hall, "Pentagon Pantry," pp. 15–18; Stanford, "The Pentagon Pantry Is Not Bare! (Part 1)," pp. 13–15, 20; Stanford, "The Pentagon Pantry Is Not Bare! (Part 2)," pp. 10–13.

20. Stanford, *Socorro "Saucer,"* p. 130.

21. Ibid., pp. 133–134.

22. Ibid., p. 134.

23. Clark, *UFO Encyclopedia,* pp. 862–863.

24. For another look at this, see Brener, *Walking Through Walls,* pp. 20–21; Dolan, *UFOs,* p. 275.

25. "Socorro Analysis," p. 4.

26. Hall, "Pentagon Pantry," p. 15.

27. Ibid, p. 16.

Conclusions

1. Project Blue Book files, roll no. 50, case no. 8766.

2. Quintanilla, *UFOs,* p. 32.

3. Ibid., p. 33.

4. Ibid., p. 32.

Bibliography

"AF Intimidates Witnesses," *The U.F.O. Investigator,* March–April 1965.

"AF Secretly Warns Pilot of Danger," *The U.F.O. Investigator,* March–April 1965

Akers, Doyle. "Landing Region Checked," *Santa Fe New Mexican,* April 28, 1964.

"Alleged UFO Landing in Delphos, Kansas," *www.openminds.tv/ufo-landing-in-delphos-kansas/37970,* accessed March 1, 2017.

Baca, Rick. Telephone interview with Kevin Randle, March 6, 2017.

Badufos, *blogspot.com/2016/08/Kenneth-arnold-and-pelicans.html,* accessed March 26, 2017.

Barker, Gray. *They Knew Too Much about Flying Saucers* (New York: Tower Books, 1967).

Bloecher, Ted. "Herr Linke and the Flying Warming Pan," *MUFON UFO Journal*, no. 153, November 1980.

Bragalia, Tony. Emails to Kevin Randle, January 20, 2015; January 21, 2015; January 25, 2015; and February 9, 2015.

Brener, Milton F. *Walking Through Walls and Other Impossibilities* (Xlibris Corporation, 2011).

Bullard, Thomas E. *UFO Abductions: The Measure of a Mystery. Volume 1: Comparative Study of Abduction Reports* (Mount Rainier, Md.: Fund for UFO Research, 1987).

Butt, Walter. Telephone interview by Kevin Randle, November 19, 1988.

"The Cherry Creek Incident," *The A.P.R.O. Bulletin*, November–December, 1965.

Chop, Albert. Telephone interview with Kevin Randle, August 20, 1995.

Clark, Jerome. *UFO Encyclopedia, Second Edition, Volume 1 & 2* (Detroit, Mich.: Omnigraphics, 1998).

"Couple reports Sighting Objects," *Albuquerque Journal*, April 29, 1964.

Crawford, Hal, Hayden Hewes, and Kietha Hewes. *The Intruders* (Oklahoma City, Okla.: International UFO Bureau, 1971).

Davis, Isabel and Ted Bloecher. Close Encounter at Kelly and Others of 1955. Chicago: J. Allen Hynek Center for UFO Studies, 1978.

DeGraw, Ralph. "Socorro Witness Interviews." MUFON UFO Journal, No. 131 (October 1978).

Dolan, Richard M. UFOs and the National Security State. Charlottesville, VA: Hampton Roads Publishing Company, 2002.

"Edgewood Man Says He Shot at and Hit Flying Object," *Albuquerque Tribune*, April 28, 1964.

Edwards, Frank. *Flying Saucers—Serious Business* (New York: Bantam Books, 1966).

Emenegger, Robert. *UFOs Past, Present & Future* (New York: Ballantine Books, 1974).

"Evidence of UFO Landing Observed," *El Defensor-Chieftain* [Socorro, New Mexico], April 28, 1964.

Faruk, Erol A. "The Delphos Landing: New Evidence from the Laboratory," *International UFO Reporter 12,1*, January/February 1987.

———. "Further Comment on the Delphos Data," *Journal of UFO Studies 1* (new series), 1989.

"'Flying Bathtub' Seen by Motorist," *Albuquerque Tribune,* April 27, 1964.

"Flying Object Expert Check Socorro Scene," *Albuquerque Tribune,* April 29, 1964.

"Flying Saucer Puts La Madera on Map," *Las Vegas* [Nevada] *Review-Journal,* January 27, 1970.

"'Flying Saucer' Reports Spread in New Mexico," *Albuquerque Journal,* April 28, 1964.

Fournet, Dewey. Telephone interview with Kevin Randle, July 17, 1995.

Gillmor, Daniel S., ed. *Scientific Study of Unidentified Flying Objects* (New York: Bantam Books, 1969).

Good, Timothy. *Alien Contact: Top Secret UFO Files Revealed* (New York: William Morrow and Company, Inc., 1991, 1993).

Gordon, Stan. "Kecksburg Crash Update," *MUFON UFO Journal, 258,* October 1989.

———. "The Military UFO Retrieval at Kecksburg, Pennsylvania," *Pursuit 20,4,* Fourth Quarter 1987.

Groves, Howard. Interview with Kevin Randle, August 2, 1973.

Hall, Michael David, and Wendy Ann Connors. *Captain Edward J. Ruppelt: Summer of the Saucers - 1952* (Albuquerque, N.M.: Rose Press International, 2000).

Hall, Richard. "Pentagon Pantry: Is the Cupboard Bare?" *MUFON UFO Journal no. 108,* November 1976.

Hall, Richard, ed. *The UFO Evidence* (Washington, D.C.: NICAP, 1964).

Harden, Paul. *www.caminorealheritage.org/PH/ph.htm,* originally accessed September 12, 2011.

———. Emails to Kevin Randle, September 17, 2011; December 2, 2016; December 3, 2016; March 1, 2017; and March 2, 2017.

Hewes, Hayden. "The Oklahoma Humanoid," *True Flying Saucers and UFOs Quarterly,* Spring 1976.

Holden, Richard T. Signed report, Project Blue Book files, roll no. 50, case no. 8766.

Holloway, Scott. "The Nevada Fireball," *www.paranormalnews.com. aspx?id=1425.*

Hynek, J. Allen. *The Hynek UFO Report* (New York: Barnes & Noble Books, 1997).

———. "Socorro Revisited." Statement in the Project Blue Book files.

———. *The UFO Experience: A Scientific Enquiry* (Chicago, Ill.: Henry Regency Company, 1972).

Johnson, Stephen. "Birthday Landing for UFO?" *Des Moines Register,* July 20, 1973.

Kean, Leslie. "Forty Years of Secrecy: NASA, the Military, and the 1965 Kecksburg Crash," *International UFO Reporter 30,1,* October 2005.

Keyhoe, Donald. *Flying Saucers from Outer Space* (New York: Henry Holt and Company, 1975).

Klass, Philip. *UFOs Explained* (New York: Random House).

Kottmeyer, Martin. "Missing Linke," *Magonia Supplement* 48, October 2003.

"Landing Case in Kansas," *The A.P.R.O. Bulletin,* November–December 1971.

"Landing in North Dakota," *The A.P.R.O. Bulletin,* July–August 1966.

"Landing Probed by NICAP, AF," *The U.F.O. Investigator,* August–September 1965.

"The Levelland Case," *The A.P.R.O. Bulletin,* November 1957.

Long, Greg. "Kenneth Arnold Revisited," *MUFON UFO Journal 230,* June 1987: 3–7.

Lorenzen, Coral. *Flying Saucers: The Startling Evidence of the Invasion from Outer Space* (New York: New American Library, 1966).

———. "Incident at La Madera," *The A.P.R.O. Bulletin,* July 1964.

———. "Little, Little Men in Minn," *The A.P.R.O. Bulletin,* November–December 1965.

———. "The Stull Case," *The A.P.R.O. Bulletin,* May 1964.

Lorenzen, Coral, and Jim Lorenzen. *Encounters With UFO Occupants* (New York: Berkley Medallion Book, 1967).

———. *Flying Saucer Occupants* (New York: Signet Books, 1967).

Maccabee, Bruce. "The Arnold Phenomenon," *International UFO Reporter Pt. I 20,1,* January/February 1995: 14–17.

———. "The Arnold Phenomenon," *International UFO Reporter Pt. II 20,2,* March/April 1995: 10–13, 24.

———. "The Arnold Phenomenon," *International UFO Reporter Pt. III 20,3*, May/June 1995:6–7.

Marano, Carmon. Telephone interview with Kevin Randle on X-Zone Broadcast Network, November 2, 2016.

Marcel, Jesse Jr. Interviews with Kevin Randle and Donald Schmitt, August 2, 1989 and August 18, 1990.

Marcel, Jesse Jr., and Linda Marcel. *The Roswell Legacy* (Franklin Lakes, N.J.: New Page Books).

McDonald, James E. Letter to Richard Hall, September 5, 1968.

"More on the 'Green Monster,'" *www.project1947.com/shg/csi/csiv1-2.html*, accessed on January 2, 2017.

"More on the Kansas Case," *The A.P.R.O. Bulletin*, March–April 1972.

Murphy, John. "Object in the Woods." WHJR radio, December 1965. Transcript by Kevin Randle.

"Mystery Object Report Is Told," *Albuquerque Tribune*, April 27, 1964.

Nickell, Joe. "The Flatwoods UFO Monster," *Investigative Files, Volume 24.6*, November/December 2000.

"Object Lands, Takes Off in Texas," *The A.P.R.O. Bulletin*, March 1961.

Oxalicacidinfo.com, accessed March 1, 2017.

Painter, Deborah. "What Happened in Flatwoods, West Virginia, Is Still Very Much a Mystery," *Fate, No. 727*, 2015.

Paskind, Marty. "Man Here Claims He Saw Saucers 5 Times," *Albuquerque Journal*, April 30, 1964.

Peeples, Curtis. *Watch the Skies!* (New York: Berkley Books, 1994).

Pflock, Karl. *Roswell: Inconvenient Fact and the Will to Believe* (Amherst, N.Y.: Prometheus Books, 2001).

"Physical Evidence, Landing Report," *NICAP U.F.O. Investigator*, July/August 1964.

Printy, Tim. *SUNlite 3,6*, November–October 2011.

Project Blue Book files, roll no. 1, case no. 10.

Project Blue Book files, roll no. 1, case no. 34.

Project Blue Book file, roll no. 14, case no. 1972.

Project Blue Book files, roll 15, case no. 2078.

Project Blue Book files, roll no. 24.

Project Blue Book, files roll no. 29, case no. 5120.

Project Blue Book files, roll no. 41, case no. 7203.

Project Blue Book files roll no. 45, case no. 7868, 7869.

Project Blue Book files, roll no. 48, case 8398.

Project Blue Book files, roll 50, case no. 8755.

Project Blue Book files, roll no. 50, case no.8759.

Project Blue Book files roll no. 50, case no. 8766.

Project Blue Book Files, roll no. 54, case no. 9338.

Project Blue Book files, roll no. 60, case 10274.

Project Blue Book files, roll no. 65, case no. 10944.

Project Blue Book files, Project Card, roll no. 81, case no. 12548.

Project Blue Book Special Report #14.

Quintanilla, Hector. *UFOs, An Air Force Dilemma* (Self-published, 1974)

Randle, Kevin D. "A Closer Look at the Flying Saucer Evidence," *True Flying Saucers & UFOs Quarterly,* Summer 1977.

———. *Crash: When UFOs Fall From the Sky* (Franklin Lakes, N.J.: New Page Books, 2010).

———. *The Government UFO Files* (Detroit, Mich.: Visible Ink Press, 2014).

———. *Invasion: Washington* (New York: Avon Books, 2001).

———. "Mysterious Clues Left Behind by UFOs," *Saga's 1973 UFO Special,* 1973.

———. "The Nevada Fireball," *http://kevinrandle.bolgspot.com/2013/02/the-nevada-fireball-april-18-1962.html.*

———. *Project Blue Book—Exposed* (New York: Marlowe & Company, 1997).

———. *The UFO Dossier: 100 Years of Government Secrets, Conspiracies and Cover-Ups* (Detroit, Mich.: Visible Ink Press, 2016).

Randle, Kevin D., and Robert Charles Cornett. "How the Air Force Hid UFO Evidence from the Public," *UFO Report 2,5,* Fall 1975: 18–21, 53–54, 56–57.

Richards, Charles. "UFO Witness Sighs at Reports of What He Supposedly Said," *Albuquerque Journal,* April 27, 1964.

Ruppelt, Edward J. *The Report on Unidentified Flying Objects* (New York: Ace Books, 1956).

Sanderson, Ivan T. *Uninvited Visitors: A Biologist Looks at UFOs* (New York: Cowles, 1967).

Shaw Robert. Interview with Kevin Randle, August 2, 1973.

Sheaffer, Robert. "Discovery Canada Serves Up the Kecksburg Crash Yarn," *Badufos.blogspot.com/2014/01/discovery-canada-serves-up-kecksburg.html*, accessed April 4, 2017.

Smothers, Jerry. "Girl Says She Was Burned While Watching UFO Here," *Albuquerque Journal*, April 28, 1964.

Snitowski, George, as told to Paul Lieb. "The West Virginia Monster," *Male 5,7*, July 1955.

"Socorro Analysis." *The U.F.O Investigator*, NICAP, September/October 1964.

"Spacecraft Story Starts Other UFO Reports," *Long Prairie Leader*, October 28, 1965.

Stalnaker, Jim. "Brilliant Red Explosion Flares in Las Vegas Sky," *Las Vegas Sun*, April 19, 1962.

Stanford, Ray. "The Pentagon Pantry Is Not Bare! (Part 1)," *MUFON UFO Journal no. 116*, July 1977.

———. "The Pentagon Pantry Is Not Bare! (Part 2)," *MUFON UFO Journal no. 117*, August 1977.

———. *Socorro "Saucer" in a Pentagon Pantry* (Austin, Tex.: Blueapple Books, 1976).

———. Telephone interviews with Kevin Randle, November 22, 2016, and February 23, 2016.

Steiger, Brad. *Mysteries of Time & Space* (Englewood Cliffs, N.J.: Prentice-Hall, Inc. 1974).

———. *Project Blue Book* (New York: Ballantine Books, 1976).

———. *Strangers From the Skies* (New York: Award Books, 1966).

Story, Ronald. *The Encyclopedia of Extraterrestrial Encounters* (New York: New American Library, 2001).

"Story of Space-ship, 12 Little Men Probed Today," *Kentucky New Era* (newspaper), August 22, 1955.

Sutherly, Curt. "Ken Arnold—First American Pilot to Report UFOs," *UFO Report 3,6*, March 1977.

Swords, Michael D. "Soil Analysis Results," *Journal of UFO Studies, n.s. 3,* 1991.

Swords, Michael, and Robert Powell. *UFOs and Government* (San Antonio, Tex.: Anomalist Books, 2012).

Thomas, David E. "A Different Angle on the Socorro UFO of 1964," *Skeptical Inquirer 25,4,* July/August 2001.

———. "The Socorro, NM UFO—Explained," *www.nmsr.org/socorro. htm,* accessed February 23, 2017.

Thomas, Dick. "'Flying Saucers' in New Mexico," *Denver Post,* May 3, 1964.

"Those Iowa Craters." *The A.P.R.O. Bulletin,* July–August 1972.

Toy, Glenn H. Telephone interview with Kevin Randle, December 11, 2014.

———. Statement in Project Blue Book files, roll no. 50, case no. 5101.

"Two Dubuquers Spot Flying Saucer," *Dubuque (Iowa) Telegraph–Herald,* April 29, 1964.

"UAO Landing in New Mexico," *The A.P.R.O. Bulletin,* May 1964.

"UFO Cover-Up?" Live, prod. Michael Seligman, distributor, Lexington Broadcast Service (LBS), October 14, 1988.

"UFO Knocks Down Tree, Leaves Phosphorescent Circle on Kansas Farm," *Skylook No. 50,* January 1972.

"UFO Sighting Re-Enacted; No Help to Scientist," *Albuquerque Journal,* April 30, 1964.

Vallee, Jacques. *Dimensions: A Casebook of Alien Contact* (New York: Ballantine Books, 1998).

———. *Revelations* (New York: Ballantine Books, 1991).

Vigil, Martin E. Letter to Richard H. Hall, June 9, 1964.

Wilson, Patty A. "East of Roswell," *Fate,* July 1999.

Young, Robert R. *The Kecksburg UFO Crash "Columbus Connection": Recovery of a 36-Year-Old Flying Saucer Hoax?* (Self-published, 1993).

Index